SNIP1NG
AN ILLUSTRATED HISTORY

Pat Farey & Mark Spicer

ZENITH PRESS

First published in 2008 by Zenith Press, an imprint of
MBI Publishing Company, 400 First Avenue North,
Suite 300, Minneapolis, MN 55401 USA

Zenith Press titles are also available at discounts in
bulk quantity for industrial or sales-promotional use.
For details write to Special Sales Manager at MBI
Publishing Company, 400 First Avenue North, Suite
300, Minneapolis, MN 55401 USA.

To find out more about our books, join us online at
www.zenithpress.com.

ISBN-13: 978-0-7603-3717-2

Project manager: Ray Bonds
Design: Compendium Design
Layout: Mark Tennent
Digrams: Mark Franklin

Printed in China

PAGE 1: *"California Joe" (Truman Head) was one of the most colorful characters of the Union's Army of the Potomac, serving under Hiram Berdan.* (NA)

PAGES 2–3: *US snipers in Iraq.* (Mark Spicer)

RIGHT: *A sniper of D Company, 1st Battalion, 4th Marines, casually takes aim on movement during Operation Nanking, October 14, 1968.* (NA)

Contents

INTRODUCTION

It has been said that in World War II there were something like 25,000 rounds fired by Allied troops for every enemy killed. In the Vietnam War that figure had risen to around 200,000 shots fired by American troops for every North Vietnamese combatant killed. A modern sniper can expect to fire an average of about 1.3 rounds for each "kill." The sniper has always been—and will probably remain—one of the most effective and economic of all military resources.

There are various opinions as to what really constitutes the definition of a true "sniper." Any rifleman who can hit a target at long range has the potential to be a sniper, but good marksmanship—although obviously a vitally important factor—is only one of the many talents that a sniper must possess.

Perhaps the most basic perception of what a sniper is must come from those being shot at. If somebody is firing at you, and you can't see him, then as far as you are concerned the shooter is a sniper. He may actually be a trained marksman with a scoped rifle deliberately targeting you, or he may be just an ordinary infantryman with a standard issue rifle who has got lucky with a couple of close shots fired from cover. Even official records and war correspondents have tended to take this view. Going right back to the American Civil War, many photographs of dead Confederates were usually labeled "sharpshooters" by the Union press, and certainly during and since World War II newspapers have tended to report any incoming firearms rounds as "sniper fire," simply because the correspondents couldn't see the enemy.

The very fact that any dead rifleman was elevated to "sniper" by the press is a sure indicator of the perceived status of the sniper in the public psyche. The sniper could kill without being seen—and could choose you as

BELOW: *By the mid-Victorian era the British Army had issued rifled arms to all its troops and had also taken great steps forward in marksmanship training—it was a start, but it took more than accurate shooting to produce snipers.* (Richard Clark)

his or her next victim....The possibility of being deliberately targeted like this is one of the most terrifying prospects for soldiers and civilians alike.

This has brought various reactions to the sniper, from the extremes of hero worship (if the sniper was on your side and his exploits were being publicized) through to loathing (if he was an enemy); you will also find some troops who are not too keen on snipers even if they are on their own side....

In fact the modern military sniper is a multi-skilled specialist with the accuracy of a marksman, the fieldcraft of a scout, and the keen eye and expert judgment of the trained observer. He must be able to move into and maintain an advantageous position, possibly close to or behind enemy lines, while remaining unseen by the enemy, so a good knowledge of camouflage and other methods of concealment is vital. He must also be able to observe the enemy, and expertly report exactly what he sees—this is one of the crucial roles of the sniper/scout, and it has been since the time of Rogers' Rangers in the French Indian Wars of the 1700s right up to the modern conflicts in Iraq and Afghanistan. The sniper must be able to accurately assess targets and decide whether it is beneficial to engage them or not. He must then have the patience and stamina to wait for a window of opportunity in which to take his shots, then make every shot count. Last but not least, he has to be able to extricate himself

and his team safely from the danger zone once the mission is completed.

Throughout the early chapters of this book—covering the period from before the American War of Independence right up to the opening years of World War I—you will notice how, during times of military conflict, skilled hunters were enlisted into the various armies to employ their natural talents to engage the enemy at longer range, thereby giving a physical and psychological advantage to their own side. However, throughout the rest of the 20th Century and onwards, military snipers were rarely drawn from the ranks of hunters (or other civilian marksmen) simply because there were so few of them left. The society of many countries had radically changed from a rural to an urban base, and (particularly in Europe) laws had been passed to restrict civilian ownership of guns. Indeed, most European soldiers from the end of World War I onward had never handled a rifle before joining their army. This meant that the majority of snipers that were to "emerge" from the ranks were taught their skills from scratch.

Nevertheless, the hunters' skills are still important and have to be learned. Even now troops volunteering for sniper training would usually be expected to have taken a reconnaissance course (or at least have some knowledge of scouting techniques), which in effect are the modern equivalent of the hunter's fieldcraft.

ABOVE: *Even during the American Civil War, when both sides were issued with rifles that had far greater range and accuracy than smoothbore muskets, the majority of battles were still fought using Napoleonic tactics—volley fire into the massed ranks of the enemy, followed by bayonet charges until one or other side "broke."*
(Roy Daines)

OVERLEAF: *Today's sniper has the advantage of some incredible advances in weapons and equipment technology. Here we see a sniper instructor using a Leica laser range finder—which will accurately predict the distance to the target to within +/-1 yard—while to his left is a Leupold x40 spotting scope mounted on a tripod.*
(Mark Spicer)

Of course sniping is not just about marksmanship, nor is it only about the multitude of other abilities that a modern army sniper has to acquire: these skills can all be taught. Ultimately, the sniper has to kill or inflict damage, and he has to do it while closely observing his target. This differentiates him from many of his infantry and artillery colleagues. Captain Jim Land, who set up the US Marine Corps sniping school and worked with top American snipers in Vietnam, commented on this final defining factor: *"When you look through a scope the first thing you see is the eyes. There is a lot of difference between shooting at a shadow, at an outline and shooting at a pair of eyes. It is amazing to put that scope on somebody and the first thing that pops out at you is their eyes. Many men can't do it (pull the trigger) at that point."*

The same thing can happen with novice hunters; they can be taught how to locate, track, and stalk their quarry, and how to make the final calculations and adjustments for aim... but at the point of taking the shot it is their own mindset that will decide whether they can remain cool and calm enough—some would say "detached"—in order to pull the trigger and take the life. This very human frailty—the aversion to deliberately taking a life—is no small obstacle to overcome, and this is possibly the greatest challenge for both the sniper and the hunter.

In this book we are concentrating on the history of military sniping from the middle of the 18th Century up to the present day, following the close relationship between the development of the sniper and the evolution of rifles, advanced optical equipment, camouflage, and tactics—from the 18th Century backwoodsman who simply adapted his hunting skills and everyday tools for warfare,

to the fully trained modern sniper with his hi-tech equipment and extremely specialized weapons. We also look at the developing role of the sniper, from sharpshooter, scout, and skirmisher through to the hidden marksmen that dominated the trenches of World War I, the tactical and propaganda value of sniper and counter-sniper in World War II, to the expert, long-range riflemen performing their craft today.

We see how tactics have also changed. For example, the use of single sharpshooters eventually led to pairs with one spotter and one shooter, and now to the present idea of using larger four- and six-man teams in certain situations.

Although not regarded by some as "real snipers," the exploits of some terrorist, insurgent, and criminal snipers will also be taken into account, along with the methods used to counteract them.

One of the recurring themes is the way that, throughout history, long-range marksmanship training, and the teaching of other sniper skills, have often been dropped by armies every time a "current" war is over, only to be reinstated as soon as the next war begins. This also carries over to the development and supply of effective sniping equipment, which in many past conflicts has only been resolved once the need has become painfully obvious. This attitude by military authorities has really only begun to change in fairly recent times, and especially since the apparent resurgence of the sniper in the international policing and anti-terrorist operations that have marked the past decade or so.

Another notable theme is the way that first sharpshooters and then trained snipers chose their targets, first tackling immediate tactical threats and then

LEFT: *A sniper in a ghillie suit can become almost "invisible." Camouflage and concealment are among the many sniper skills required to be able to get close enough to identify the target. Then the sniper still has to remain concealed—often for many hours—while either stalking his prey or waiting in ambush, until an opportune moment arises in which to take the shot.* (Mark Spicer)

high value strategic targets. If the opportunity arose they would always shoot officers, NCOs, artillerymen, signalmen, transport, and so on, the idea being to disrupt the line of command, remove the threat of artillery, confuse and demoralize the enemy, and cut their lines of supply.

Modern snipers do exactly the same thing, but now they also have the ability to destroy vital equipment—such as communications and radar—with large-caliber, long-range rifles. They are also increasingly used as support units for infantry, laying down covering fire from fixed positions at long range, while also keeping an eye on enemy movements, gathering intelligence, and calling in mortar, artillery or air support if necessary.

Today's snipers also help to carry out "hearts and minds" missions, designed to make the local populations feel safer and bring them "on side." One such British sniper operation in the Middle East was the control of dangerous feral dogs that were causing serious problems for local villagers. Details of this operation were featured in the western press along with other "good news" stories about snipers that appear much more in the media now, their exploits being reported as never before—apart from the Soviet "super-soldiers" propaganda of World War II.

As more modern equipment is developed for the sniper, such as .50-caliber extreme-range rifles, laser rangefinders, and night vision equipment, so too does the invention of counter-sniper measures. Sniper detection equipment such as "air displacement tracking" and other devices are gradually being introduced but, like other arms developments, these tend to "leap-frog" each other, as arms manufacturers, tacticians, and the snipers themselves find new ways and means to counteract them.

Whatever one might think of this very special group of men, it is certain that the trained sniper, operating alone or in small teams, still remains a powerful tool and one of the most efficient resources for the modern military machine, and on present evidence will continue to do so for a long time to come.

Pat Farey

ACKNOWLEDGMENTS

The authors and publishers are grateful for the cooperation of individuals and organizations that have contributed to this book, in particular the following:

Steve Broadbent

Michael Butterfield (Queens Rangers): queensrangers.captain@talk21.com

Bob Chalk

Richard Clark: www.mayhemphotographics.co.uk

Andy Colborn/Graham Mitchell (Second Battle Group): sbg1@mistral.co.uk

Roy Daines (SoSkan): RDPixs@aol.com

Carsten Edler

Neil Hoddle (Berdan Sharpshooters UK): info@ussharpshooters.co.uk

Graham Lay

John Norris: john.norris3@btinternet.com

John C. Pearce (Infantry Regt. von Goeben, No. 28): lr28vongoeben@hotmail.com

Gareth Sprack/Steve Neville (Great War Society): gareth@glsprack.fsnet.co.uk

Michael Yardley

CHAPTER ONE:
FROM MUSKET TO RIFLE, SHOOTER TO SNIPER

CHAPTER ONE:
FROM MUSKET TO RIFLE, SHOOTER TO SNIPER

1 1111111111As will be made clear later in this book, the modern sniper has a multiple role to fill and embraces a whole range of expert skills, but in the early years of warfare with firearms, the forerunner of the sniper was primarily a marksman; basically a man who could be relied on to hit a given "mark" or target with a degree of accuracy that surpassed the skills of the average soldier. However, to achieve the objective he needed the right tools, and that didn't really come along until the rifled barrel was invented. Therefore, the history of the sniper is inevitably interlinked with the development of the rifle and to some degree its predecessor, the smoothbore musket.

RIGHT: *The forerunner of the sniper was primarily just a marksman—someone who could hit what he was aiming at.* (Roy Daines)

Volley fire, muskets, and the massed ranks

Ever since the power of gunpowder-fueled arms was discovered, men have striven to improve the performance of the weapons and the skills of those who use them. The search for the twin "holy grails" of accuracy and extended range have run parallel with the development of the sniper as a specialist soldier.

From the middle of the 17th Century up to the early 19th Century European infantry tactics were largely based on the massed use of smoothbore muskets. These weapons had restricted range and even more limited accuracy, yet their widespread use was assured because they were still effective weapons when combined with the correct tactics of the time. For riflemen to achieve substantial damage to the enemy their targets had to be within the working range of their weapons and their ranks would have to be relatively closely packed—almost literally shoulder to shoulder—to ensure a dense volume of fire. Unfortunately, they also presented a sizable target.

PREVIOUS PAGE: *A rifleman of the 95th Rifles, the first British Army unit to be completely issued with the Baker rifle instead of smoothbore muskets, and to adopt a green uniform in place of scarlet tunics. Most importantly, these men were accurate with their weapons and were encouraged to use their own initiative in battle.* (Richard Clark)

Opposing lines of infantryman would stand and wait, often being "softened up" by the pounding of enemy artillery, before being marched up towards each other until they were little more than a hundred yards or so apart. Only then would they be allowed to discharge their muskets in ordered volleys so as to inflict as much damage on the opposition as possible. Volley firing in three ranks—one rank firing, one loading, one preparing to fire—enabled six or seven volleys a minute to be discharged at the enemy.

This was eventually followed by a bayonet charge by one side or the other, with the attacking lines trying to cross the "field of fire" as fast as possible to minimize casualties before engaging the defenders in close combat and hopefully breaking their line and forcing them to turn and run. Alternatively, the opposing fire would halt the advance and force the attackers to retreat. Loss of life and wounding could be horrific but, aside from the numbers involved, it was the crucial balance between fear and discipline that would generally decide the outcome.

The reason that sane men would seemingly stand and face death or mutilation willingly—or even run toward it— was that they were drilled and disciplined to do so. The consequences of disobedience or dereliction of duty overcame their trepidation in facing the enemy. No doubt many of them believed in a cause, country, or even a career, and in some cases this may have been a greater spur to heroic action, but the vast majority probably faced the enemy with a combination of adrenalin-fueled anticipation, and apprehension verging on dread. Yet still they "held the line," programmed by their training to obey orders and do their duty, no matter what.

While this style of face-to-face fighting with massed ranks of muskets was generally accepted—certainly in Europe—there were some armies that began to see the advantages in other weapons and tactics.

Scouts and skirmishers

The two main 18th Century conflicts in north-east America—the French-Indian Wars (1754–1763) and the American War of Independence (1775–1783)—started to sow small seeds of change in infantry tactics, certainly in the use of scouts and skirmishers, although the vast majority of battles would still continue to be fought in the traditional manner for at least another hundred years.

BROWN BESS

The Brown Bess smoothbore musket was the standard firearm of the British Army for over a hundred years. This is a Short Land Pattern flintlock musket (Brown Bess) made c1785. The lock is marked Tower with "crown" over GR. It has a swan neck cock and the number 55 stamped behind the escutcheon plate on the stock wrist. Barrel marked WH. (Australian War Memorial REL24670)

The most widely used infantry weapon of the 18th and early 19th Centuries was the smoothbore flintlock musket. A good example of this is the British Land Pattern musket and its derivatives, universally known as the Brown Bess.

In its various versions this firearm was in service with the British Army from 1722 to 1838. Rifles were standardized at .75 caliber, while carbines were .65 caliber. The Long Land Pattern had an overall length of sixty-two inches with a forty-six-inch barrel, while the Short Land Pattern had a forty-two-inch barrel. While still long, the latter was not an unwieldy weapon. In 1797 the India Pattern was adopted, since it proved easier and cheaper to manufacture, and this was later superseded by the New Land Pattern. Like most military muskets of the time, the Brown Bess had a smooth and oversized bore for quicker, easier loading, especially after a few shots when the barrel would be fouled. Therefore, as the ball was not a good fit, it would rattle up the barrel before exiting the muzzle at minutely inconsistent angles—not ideal for accuracy—so in modern terms this could be regarded only as a short-range weapon. Tests in the 19th Century showed that even the later, more standardized, models

had a usable range of only around a hundred yards, being inaccurate and losing velocity fairly quickly. In the environment of an 18th Century battle, with smoke, noise, movement, adrenalin (and a general lack of practice), an ordinary soldier would have to be extremely skillful (or lucky) to hit an enemy soldier that he was specifically aiming at from that distance.

Despite these results, it may be said that, when being used at its optimum, the Brown Bess could still be accurate for a smoothbore. Under controlled conditions (using precisely measured charges and tight-fitting patched balls), modern muzzle-loading specialists can achieve amazing accuracy with replica smoothbore Brown Bess muskets, hitting man-sized targets in excess of 150 yards.

The strengths of the Brown Bess lay in its simple, robust design, relatively low cost, and its ease of use in the battlefield. Disciplined troops could fire two to three rounds per minute. Despite its lack of accuracy as an individual weapon, when fired en masse at closely packed ranks of enemy troops, it proved highly effective, and as a result it remained in service with the British Army for over a hundred years.

ABOVE: Close up of a recently fired Brown Bess lock—note the fouling of the cock, frizzen., and barrel caused by the "flash" of ignition.

During the French-Indian Wars tactics were to some extent dictated by the vast size of the territory involved and the scattered locations of some of the frontier settlements. This resulted in a lot of smaller engagements taking place between locally raised militia as well as the larger pitched battles between the armies of the main antagonists—France and Britain. Both sides employed native Indians to bolster their numbers; the Iroquois Confederacy were allied to the British, while the French had support from the Algonquin, Ottawa, Ojibwa, Shawnee, and other tribes.

Both the British and French adopted raiding as a main strategy, learning from their Indian allies, as well as from the colonist hunters and trappers of European origin who lived in much the same way. The French encouraged—and sometimes led—Indian raids, attacking the more remote British townships and outposts, in order to force the settlers away from the interior. The British retaliated by sacking the villages of France's Indian allies, destroying their homes and food supplies. These raids often involved relatively small forces of up to a few hundred men. Some of these were made up of sixty-man ranger companies, which were specifically recruited from backwoodsmen who already had skills in wilderness survival and marksmanship.

Probably the most famous of these were Rogers' Rangers, formed in 1756 by Major Robert Rogers. Dressed in distinctive green uniforms, they based their unconventional (for the time) yet highly practical fighting methods on "Rogers' Rules of Ranging." Rogers hired men solely on merit and shocked regular commanders with his use of Indians and freed slaves. Armed with muskets, tomahawks and knives, they were famed for their marksmanship, yet Rogers' Rules seem to suggest firing at close range when being attacked, although they also advised the Rangers to make themselves smaller targets by laying down or kneeling, and firing from cover.

The methods used by both sides were what we would loosely call "guerrilla tactics" today: moving great distances, staying concealed from larger enemy forces, then employing shock hit-and-run tactics to destroy settlements, kill or drive the settlers from their homes, and generally spread terror and chaos among the civilian populations.

This introduced two major ingredients of modern skirmisher and scouting tactics to warfare, and laid the grounds for the even more specialist role of the modern sniper. Camouflage and fieldcraft were vital to these small groups of raiders, in order to avoid engagement with the enemy until it was advantageous for their purposes. Of

OVERLEAF: Right up to the early 19th Century, European infantry tactics were based on the massed use of smoothbore muskets. (Richard Clark)

these skills would die of starvation or exposure while in the midst of everything that they needed to survive.

Although most of the raiders would be armed with muskets of various kinds, some of them would have rifles. The difference between muskets and rifles was simply that the latter had spiraled grooves cut into the bore (rifling) and it was used in conjunction with a "patched ball." This was a ball that was sitting in a greased patch of cloth that would fit tightly into the bore, and would need to be "rammed home" quite forcefully in order to get it down the full length of the barrel. This took more time and effort (and a touch more skill) than was required to load an ordinary smoothbore musket. Also, the rifling would get fouled with spent powder residue and lead much more quickly than a smoothbore, and would therefore need more frequent cleaning. Nevertheless, the rewards were worth it, since the tight-fitting ball would engage the spiral rifling as it traveled up the barrel, thereby taking on a spin and leaving the muzzle at the same point at each shot. This greatly increased both range and accuracy, but even so, the user of the weapon had a lot of input into the success of the shot.

Militia from the towns, who generally had no weapons of their own, were usually issued smoothbore muskets, and sometimes these would have been inferior—through age or wear—to those carried by regular soldiers. Frontiersmen and other volunteers armed with their own rifles would have a very real advantage over those armed only with muskets. A rifle would have been a significantly more expensive purchase than a smoothbore, so the fact

ABOVE: *British ranger groups were taught to dress and fight like their main foes—the Indian tribes and trappers loyal to the French. These are reenactors portraying typical rangers of the French-Indian wars.*

ABOVE: *Major Rogers' "Rules of Rangering."*

RIGHT: *Most fighters in the French-Indian wars would be armed with muskets—but some would have the far more accurate rifles. (Culpepper Minutemen UK)*

course, these methods had always been used by North American Indians for their very survival—hunting and trapping depended on them. Therefore, instead of the bright, often garish uniforms worn by the regular British and French troops, designed to attract attention, the colonist militias and their Indian allies would wear simple camouflage in the form of predominantly green and brown clothing, either of dyed wool or cotton, or animal skins. The edges and sleeves of their jackets would often be fringed in order to break up their outline even further.

Fieldcraft included the skill of being aware of your surroundings, and taking advantage of them to give cover, protect your movement from prying eyes, and most importantly, predicting where your enemy might be located, and therefore avoid ambush, while being able to use that same ground for your own benefit to engage them. Another very important part of fieldcraft in these particular wars was the ability to live off the land. Although the North American environment of the time was bountiful with fish, game, and vegetable food matter, it took skill to harvest it. The native peoples were well practiced in fieldcraft, as were many of the established colonists, but quite a few newly arrived Europeans that hadn't learned

that a man carried a rifle would almost certainly mean that he owned it, and would also indicate that he would probably know how to use it.

Even some men who owned their own smoothbore guns could prove to be particularly good shots, taking into account the limitations of their weapons. Ordinary muskets could be made to fire a lot more accurately by using the patched ball method of loading, despite there being no rifling in the barrel to impart spin. Many of the colonists in this period would have used patched balls in muskets for their greater accuracy when hunting, where speed of reloading was not a great factor, whereas for military purposes, volume of fire—and therefore rapid loading—was absolutely vital.

When engaged with the main armies in major campaigns, the various ranger companies and their like became scouts, tracking, observing, and reporting on the whereabouts of the enemy. They also served as effective skirmishers, adopting small-scale ambushing and harassing tactics, and using aimed shots with accurate weapons to take a deadly toll while staying hidden or out of range of the volley-fired muskets of the enemy. These men were just as willing to fight as their scarlet comrades in arms, but they chose to wear drab, inconspicuous clothing and use methods that would give them the greatest chance of staying alive.

The chosen target and the well-aimed shot

It was probably at the time of the American War of Independence that the tactic we regard as sniping actually emerged: the deliberate choosing of an important enemy target by a marksman, and then the accurate placement of the shot, while remaining concealed or at a distance that would make it difficult for the opponent to retaliate. The term "sniping" would probably not have been in use at the time, although it is claimed to have been invented around 1770 by British soldiers in India who hunted the snipe, a particularly difficult bird to shoot. However, some East Anglians insist that it is a term from their area of the British Isles, simply meaning shooting from cover, and it has been in use almost since fowling pieces were invented.

Whether they called it sniping or not, the militia of the French-Indian Wars had introduced several of the skills of the modern sniper, and the American War of Independence brought acknowledgment of these qualities along with the will to organize them into official units of the army.

In the early days of the war, the Second Congress authorized the formation of several companies of riflemen, nearly 1,000-strong in total, as part of the Continental army. Their main task would be to use

ABOVE: *The death of General Montgomery at Quebec. (Engraving by W. Ketterlinus, 1808, from the painting by John Trumbull.) This is interesting as it shows the scouts and skirmishers (bottom left) who appear to be wearing fringed buckskin yet are carrying muskets with fixed bayonets.* (NA)

LOADING A FLINTLOCK "MUZZLELOADER" AND THE IMPORTANCE OF "FOLLOW THROUGH"

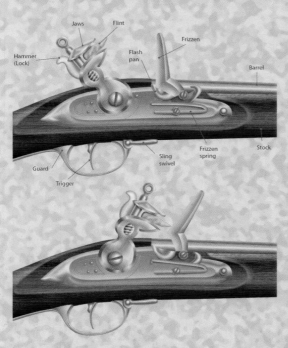

Apart from some rare exceptions like the Ferguson rifle, military firearms of the 18th Century were all muzzleloaders–this applies to both smoothbores and rifled weapons–which means that they had to be loaded from the muzzle end of the barrel. Ordinary infantry companies were issued with smoothbore muskets.

Generally, these used "paper cartridges," which contained a lead ball and black powder (gunpowder). To load a smoothbore, the flintlock action (hammer) had to be pulled back to "half-cock," which would ensure that accidentally touching the trigger while loading would not detonate the charge. The end of the paper cartridge was then bitten off, a touch of powder was poured into the flashpan, and the frizzen was pulled down to keep this powder in place. The rest of the powder was then poured down the muzzle, then the loose-fitting lead ball was dropped on top of it. The empty paper cartridge was then put into the muzzle and a ramrod was used to push ball and powder down to the bottom (breech end) of the barrel. The paper would act as a wadding, holding the ball and its powder charge in place. The ramrod would then be replaced back beneath the barrel. When the user was ready to fire the musket, the hammer would be pulled back to full cock, and the trigger was pulled.

With a flintlock there were several distinct stages between the trigger being pulled until the ball left the barrel. Pulling the trigger released the sprung hammer that held a small piece of flint in its "jaws" The hammer fell, allowing the flint it carried to strike the steel frizzen, creating a shower of sparks and simultaneously pushing the frizzen up and forward. This exposed the flash pan, allowing the sparks to ignite the small measure of gunpowder that it contained and causing the resultant "flash" to pass through a small "touch hole" in the barrel, thereby igniting

ABOVE LEFT: *Flintlock mechanism in the loaded and cocked position (top) and the position during firing – when the frizzen is knocked off the flash pan and the flint runs down the frizzen's cross-hatched surface, sending sparks into the flash pan to ignite the priming powder sending a flash through the touch hole and thereby the main charge in musket's barrel.*

ABOVE: *British Grenadiers priming the flash pans on their Brown Bess muskets with powder. (Richard Clark)*

the main charge of powder and sending the ball up the barrel. This sounds like a long-winded process and it did have real consequences when taking a shot, since the time between pulling the trigger and the ball leaving the barrel was quite substantial when compared to the speed of modern firearms. For this reason "follow through" was used; this was the technique of keeping the weapon directed at the point of aim for a second or so after pulling the trigger, to ensure that the ball had definitely exited the barrel and was on its way. When infantry fired volleys from smoothbore muskets at each other this was not so important, but when an individual took aim with a rifle at a specific target, it was vital for any kind of accuracy. Follow through is such an important consideration that is it is still taught as one of the key components of marksmanship, even with today's high-velocity weapons.

CENTER LEFT: *To load a military musket, the end of the paper cartridge had to be bitten off, then the powder poured into the barrel followed by the ball. (Richard Clark)*

LEFT: *Typical paper cartridge with powder and ball for loading a smoothbore musket.*

ABOVE: *A reproduction of a "Kentucky" long rifle, as used by American sharpshooters in the War of Independence.* (Courtesy of Davide Pedersoli)

accurate long-range rifle fire to harass and hopefully demoralize the enemy infantry. Apart from the physical damage that these riflemen could do to the enemy, the Americans realized that the effect of long-range fire could prove very confidence-draining to the average British soldier. They were also aware that the British military authorities themselves, despite their continued reliance on the musket, were conscious of the potentially devastating firepower of the rifle.

The Rifle Battalion, under the command of Colonel William Thompson consisted of twelve companies of men. These men were already hunters and sharpshooters, well practiced frontiersmen drawn from the rural heartlands of Pennsylvania, Maryland, and Virginia. The icing on the cake was that they were all armed with Pennsylvania rifles (now sometimes referred to as Kentucky rifles), undoubtedly one of the finest firearms of its day.

The secret of accuracy with any rifle is to get the load right, and then stick with it—and that's as true today as it was with the Pennsylvania rifle. The best sharpshooters would work out the most effective powder load for their particular rifle, and then make a measure so that every shot received the same charge. Fine powder could be sifted from the main batch and would be used to prime the flash pan, so as to get a better ignition and cause less fouling of the flash hole. A ball mold would be supplied with the rifle, so actual caliber and ball weight would be constant.

Once the sharpshooter had decided on the distance that he wanted his "zero" to be set at, he would set the rear sight for windage on a calm day to achieve dead center horizontally. This was achieved by tapping (or drifting) the rear sight, which was set in a dovetail slot on the barrel. Then elevation to the required zero distance was set by filing down the front sight blade. By practicing at various other distances the shooter could predict how far to elevate his rifle for any given range.

For the first time, the British Army would be outgunned by a whole regiment armed with much superior long-range firearms. In the hands of a reasonable shooter the Pennsylvania long rifle could easily hit most man-sized targets at 200 yards, and some marksmen could push that out even further. Provided that

ABOVE: *The word "sniping" is said to come from the sport of shooting snipe—a small, fast-flying bird.* (LoC)

the shooter could gauge the distance correctly, and get the elevation right, he could engage a large target at even greater distances—like a group of officers or a row of infantry at 300 yards.

Long-range rifle fire was also used to counter the potentially devastating use of artillery. The sharpshooters would pick off the opposing artillerymen, which would inevitably silence the batteries or make them pull back to a less effective range. In one engagement alone, American riflemen killed or wounded thirty-six out of the forty-eight British artillerymen on just one battery. (The duel between light artillery and snipers was a recurring theme throughout over a century and a half, from the American War of Independence right up to World War II.)

The intentional targeting of officers became a common ploy of rebel sharpshooters, although the idea of "aiming at an officer" was frowned upon by the British. So when officers in particular began to fall from long-range shots, there would have been little doubt that they were chosen targets, which must have been a new and very uncomfortable concept for anybody with rank. In

THE PENNSYLVANIA LONG RIFLE

ABOVE: *The Pennsylvania rifle was the most accurate and far reaching firearm of its day.* (Courtesy of Davide Pedersoli)

This lightweight, long, slender, and very elegant-looking flintlock rifle originated in the early 18th Century in Lancaster County, Pennsylvania, probably having been developed by Martin Meylin, a Swiss gunsmith, and then being produced in the workshops of many local gunmakers.

Although each gunsmith added his own design elements and characteristics to the design, a typical Pennsylvania rifle weighed anywhere between seven and nine pounds, and had an overall length of around fifty-eight to sixty-two inches—hence "long" rifle. The rifled barrel could be forty-six inches or more long and usually had a twist of one full turn for the barrel's length.

The long barrel allowed the sights to be set further apart than on other firearms—another aid to accuracy.

Whether in civilian or military use, this rifle would have been carried all day, so it was made specifically to be lightweight. Calibers averaged .45 inches but could be anything between .40 and .50 inches, and the ammunition was always a patched ball for greater accuracy. A small patchbox with either a hinged or sliding brass lid was inset into the side of the butt stock to carry the greased cloth patches. Sometimes the Pennsylvania Rifle is called the Kentucky Rifle. This is nothing to do with its origins, but rather the

fact that it was used to great effect by a Kentucky regiment during the Battle of New Orleans in the War of 1812—once again against the British.

Early examples of these rifles at the time of the War of Independence were entirely handmade, from their maple stocks right down to the lock screws, so each rifle would be slightly different to the next. These rifles would have been the pinnacle of technology of their time, therefore they would have been a relatively expensive purchase for a settler to make. But what better investment than a firearm that could protect him and supply his family with food too? It's no wonder that owners treated their rifles with great respect.

RIGHT: *British infantrymen of the late 18th Century were armed with a smoothbore musket (Brown Bess), which was inferior to the rifle in both range and accuracy. However, they also had a bayonet and often a short sword too, which could be very effective at close range.*

1781, at the battle of Cowpens, when British troops were advancing on his position, General Morgan ordered his defending riflemen: "Aim for the epaulets"—an obvious order to shoot the officers first… a strategy that is favored by snipers to this day. At the end of the battle the British had about a hundred dead; fully thirty-nine of them were officers, which is a hugely unbalanced figure. An army that operated on a system of drill, discipline, and precise maneuver could not afford to take fatalities like this among its officers and NCOs.

Major George Hanger, a British officer and renowned firearms and ballistics expert, was shocked when he and a fellow officer came under attack from an American sharpshooter that he judged to be over 400 yards away. A rifle ball passed between the two officers and killed their bugler's horse, which was directly behind them; they wisely chose to withdraw before the marksman could get his eye in….

Unfortunately for General Simon Fraser, he did not follow the same course of action, and ended up paying the ultimate price. Fraser was commander of the British forces at the second battle of Saratoga in 1777, when he was specifically chosen as a target by the American high command. Fraser was well respected by both sides in the conflict, and was easily recognized on the day of the battle (October 7) as he was mounted on a fine gray horse and was being conspicuously cheered by his men as he passed by them. The effect of his appearance was obviously rallying the British troops, so the order to shoot him if possible was given to Daniel Morgan's company of riflemen. The task was delegated to a young Pennsylvanian by the name of Timothy Murphy, one of the best shots in

LEFT: *Ordinary American infantrymen were usually armed in the same manner as their British counterparts —with musket and bayonet.*

BELOW: *Battle of Lexington, April 19, 1775. In this contemporary image American "sharpshooters" in the trees can be seen taking a toll of the British Grenadiers—albeit at fairly close range. Note the wounded British officer in the foreground. (LoC)*

DANIEL MORGAN AND HIS SHARPSHOOTERS

When Congress created the Continental army in 1775, there was a call for volunteers to form ten companies of one hundred riflemen from the various colonies. Daniel Morgan was chosen to head one of two companies of sharpshooters from Virginia, most of them armed with very accurate Pennsylvania rifles. In their first engagement—at the siege of Boston—they caused so much havoc sniping at the British and loyalist defenders that they earned the name "Morgan's Sharpshooters."

Legend has it that the test for becoming one of Morgan's Sharpshooters was to hit a life-sized silhouette of King George's head at one hundred paces with your first shot. That may be debatable but, whenever possible, Morgan's men were certainly encouraged to choose officers, NCOs, and other important "strategic" targets, like artillerymen, before turning their attention to "other ranks." Morgan's Sharpshooters also served in the abortive invasion of Canada. At the Battle of Quebec, after General Montgomery—the leader of the American forces—was killed, the British surrounded the remains of the invading army and Morgan was captured along with some of his men. This may have been the end of the original Morgan's Sharpshooters, but their leader was soon back in action after the British exchanged him. In early 1777 he rejoined the Continental forces and became commander of a corps of

500 riflemen, mainly from his native Virginia. Used as light infantry and skirmishers, they participated in many more actions throughout the war, notably the Battle of Freeman's Farm, where Morgan's men shot every officer of the advancing British light infantry, forcing them to retreat, while at the second battle of Saratoga, Morgan famously ordered sharpshooter Timothy Murphy to kill General Fraser. This latter incident contributed to the retreat and eventual surrender of General Burgoyne's forces—a huge loss for the British, and a great morale-boosting gain for the Americans. In 1779, after being overlooked for promotion, Morgan resigned his commission, but a year later he was persuaded to rejoin the army as a brigadier general, once again in command of light infantry. At Cowpens, South Carolina, in 1781—ignoring his orders—he achieved a remarkable victory by directly confronting a British Army led by Colonel Banastre Tarleton, a notable British commander who was hated by the rebels for his "no quarter" treatment of beaten foes (although this accusation has been disputed). Morgan adopted the brilliantly simple tactics of using his riflemen to fire and then run, leading the British into a much larger force of militia at the front while turning the flank with an onslaught by further troops from the side. Almost all of Tarleton's command—over 1,000 men—were either killed or captured.

ABOVE: *Surrender of General Burgoyne at Saratoga. Painting by John Trumbull. Note the presence of Daniel Morgan, dressed in light-colored frontier clothing, in the right foreground.* (NA)

ABOVE TOP RIGHT: *An engraving of Daniel Morgan from a painting by Alonzo Chappel. Note the light color of his fringed clothing.* (NA)

ABOVE: *Colonel Banastre Tarleton; painting by Sir Joshua Reynolds, c1782. Tarleton's British Army was roundly defeated at Cowpens, South Carolina, in 1781 by Daniel Morgan's combined force of regulars and irregulars.* (NA)

the company. Although sharpshooters would naturally choose to target officers over other ranks, certainly since the French-Indian Wars, this may have been the first time that senior command had ordered the shooting of a known high ranking officer of the opposing force.

Murphy is said to have climbed up to the fork in a tree to get a better view of his target, or possibly better elevation for a long shot. His first shot hit the general's

saddle; his second shot passed across the neck of the horse in front of Fraser. It was obvious to the British that Fraser was being deliberately targeted, but he stubbornly refused to withdraw, on the grounds of duty. By this time Murphy had obviously got his mark, and his third shot mortally wounded Fraser, while his fourth shot struck down the general's aide-de-camp, Sir Frances Clerke.

Murphy was armed with a double-barrel superposed Pennsylvania rifle (an over and under), which might explain how he could get his second and fourth shots off so accurately—his target was mounted and may have been moving. Loading a rifle took time, so the advantages of having two shots available were that the sharpshooter could place the first, and if he missed he could immediately adjust his aim for the second. One thing is for sure, with a claimed distance in excess of 300 yards, this was a remarkable feat of marksmanship.

It wasn't only officers who suffered at the hands of American marksmen. At the siege of Boston, many ordinary British soldiers and sailors succumbed to pot-shots from the surrounding hills. In a letter to King George, British General Lord Howe referred to the Pennsylvania rifles as "The terrible gun of the rebels."

It wasn't long before the British started recruiting their own riflemen. One company in ten from each regiment were trained and equipped as "light companies" or skirmishers, and these were once again supplemented by ranger units—such as the Queen's Rangers, recruited mainly from loyalists, or Fraser's Company of Select Marksmen from regular British troops.

These ranger units were also intended to act as skirmishers and sharpshooters, but only a few of them carried rifles. Another source of riflemen fighting for the British cause were mercenary Hessian (German) soldiers, some of whom were specialist *Jägers*, or hunters. They carried relatively short rifles that had been developed from the hunting weapons used in the heavy woodlands of Central Europe. While these weapons were generally reckoned to be accurate, compared with the Pennsylvania rifles they had limited range due to their larger caliber and shorter barrel and sight base (the distance between front and rear sights). It certainly seems that Jägers usually came off worse whenever they came up against American sharpshooters armed with Pennsylvania rifles.

Despite the shortcomings of the Jäger rifles, a thousand weapons based on this hunting piece were ordered by the British to arm their new marksman units. Known as the Pattern 1776 rifle, it had a 30.5-inch barrel in .62 caliber and was designed by gunsmith William Grice. Eight hundred were produced by Grice and three other Birmingham (England) makers: Mathias Barker, Galton & Sons, and Benjamin Willets. A further two hundred Jäger rifles were obtained from Hanover, Germany.

Possibly the best British rifleman in the War of Independence was Captain Patrick Ferguson, a first class shot and the inventor of the innovative breechloading Ferguson rifle, based on the French Chaumette screw breech system, which was capable of four to six accurate shots per minute.

After seeing a demonstration of this fast-firing weapon, King George III commissioned Ferguson to recruit a corps of skirmishers, a hundred strong, all armed with the revolutionary breechloading rifle. Ferguson probably paid for these rifles out of his own funds. He certainly chose his men carefully from some of the best shots available to him and, like specialist riflemen to follow, they wore green uniforms.

Ferguson had personally demonstrated that his rifle was capable of repeatedly hitting a mark at 200 yards, and the adjustable back leaf sight was marked from 100 to 500 yards. Nevertheless, he missed his greatest opportunity to alter the course of the war and change history by choosing not to fire at all. This was the famous incident before the Battle of Brandywine, the first engagement that Ferguson's riflemen took part in. While skirmishing ahead of the main British advance, Ferguson and three of his men saw two officers on horseback, whom they later described as an American in the blue and buff of the Continental army and a French hussar. Ferguson refused to let his men fire on them, and he wouldn't take an unsporting shot himself, although he claimed he could have easily put six bullets into the backs of the officers before they galloped out of range.

Unfortunately, Ferguson was wounded in the battle some days later and while in hospital with a shattered

BELOW: *A rifleman from Morgan's Rifle Corps, c1775; note the long Pennsylvania-style rifle, native-style clothing, and even the warpaint.* (Military & Historical Image Bank. Don Troiani)

ABOVE: *A Hesse Cassel jäger, c1776, specialist forest fighter and rifleman from the Germanic states of Europe, employed by the British Army.* (Military & Historical Image Bank. Don Troiani)

FRASER'S COMPANY OF SELECT MARKSMEN

Some attempts were made by the British to counter the "hit-and-run" attacks by American raiders, especially at the start of the War of Independence. Captain Alexander Fraser, a veteran of the French-Indian Wars and the nephew of General Simon Fraser (who was shot by Timothy Murphy at the Battle of Saratoga) was himself an expert in the use of riflemen as light infantry, having formed a specialist company of skirmishers in 1776 from the best shots that he could find in the regiments stationed in Canada. Known as Fraser's Company of Select Marksmen, or the British Rangers, these men were hand picked and were armed with either rifles or muskets. The rifles were probably captured from the armory at Quebec, or may have been some of the first British rifles to arrive in the Americas.

Working closely with Britain's native Iroquois allies, Fraser's company combined the woodcraft and skirmishing skills of these warriors, but added a long-range firing capability with the controlled discipline to trade close-range volleys against "regular" enemy troops. Serving gallantly and with great success throughout the war, they suffered losses during General Burgoyne's disastrous Saratoga campaign, and some time after 1778 the remainder of Fraser's Company of Select Marksmen were absorbed into other light infantry units.

right elbow he learned that the American officer he allowed to ride away was almost certainly George Washington, commander of the Continental army. The identity of the "French" hussar remains a mystery, since there were no French cavalry at Brandywine, but it may have been Washington's aide-de-camp, the Polish cavalry officer, Count Pulaski.

Ferguson's rifle corps was disbanded after his wounding, but he was to continue playing his part in the war by commanding light troops and loyalist militia, until he was killed at King's Mountain in 1780.

Ferguson's refusal to take a shot at the retreating Washington is an example of one of the last vestiges of chivalry among the professional warrior class. In the War of Independence this also filtered down to the rank and file. Things were changing. The traditional military belief in "honorably" standing to directly face your foe, and slugging it out with ordered volleys of musketry fired in the general direction of the enemy, goes in some way to explain why many ordinary soldiers—even now—have an ambivalent attitude toward snipers. When firing in massed ranks at an enemy that was doing exactly the same thing to you there was always an element of luck in the equation, whether you got hit or not was largely

ABOVE: *The Jäger rifle was notably shorter and usually of a larger caliber than the Pennsylvania rifles of the Americans, yet they both had their origins in Germany and Switzerland.* (Courtesy of Davide Pedersoli)

"fortune of war." Now men could be shot at by riflemen who were concealed or who were at such a distance as to make it impossible to retaliate. This could be both frightening and frustrating for ordinary soldiers, and goes some way toward explaining the poor treatment meted out to some riflemen when they caught them.

In some circumstances riflemen could be at a disadvantage, especially against well-drilled infantry in numbers. If oncoming regular troops could withstand the initial fire from riflemen, they may have had enough time to make up the ground and deliver a volley with their own muskets at closer range, or even make a bayonet charge

THE QUEEN'S RANGERS

During the American War of Independence the British Army authorized the raising of a number of regiments from the colonial population still loyal to the Crown. The Queen's Rangers were named in honor of Queen Charlotte, the wife of King George III. This was the first regiment in the British Army to wear green uniforms and to have a rifle-armed section. Green was adopted initially to draw distinction between redcoat regulars and Provincial regulars; it was only later in the war that changing over to red became the mark of special light troops and other Provincials.

The Queen's Rangers was originally formed in New York, August 1776, by Colonel Robert Rogers, famed as the commander of Rogers' Rangers in the French-Indian War. The Queen's

Rangers wore a green jacket, plumed leather cap, and black accouterments. The Light Company (portrayed in the accompanying illustration) carried a Short Land Pattern musket. A half company (who wore a different plume on their caps) carried rifles, probably the British 1776 pattern. Rogers was replaced by a succession of British commanders, until in 1777 the command passed to Major John Graves Simcoe. These men fought and served throughout the war in many successful engagements, in various colonies, including New York, South Carolina, and Virginia, before finally being disbanded in Canada at the end of the war in 1781.

Simcoe later wrote, *"...green is without comparison the best colour for light troops with*

dark accouterments, and if put on in the spring, by autumn it nearly fades with the leaves, preserving it's characteristics of being scarcely discernable at a distance." (M. G. Butterfield, Group Historian for SKG3.)

ABOVE LEFT: *Most of the Queen's Rangers carried the Brown Bess musket, but a half company was armed with rifles, which were very scarce in the British Army of the period.* (Culpepper Minutemen UK)

ABOVE: *The Queen's Rangers wore green tunics, leather cap, and black accouterments.* (Culpepper Minutemen UK)

before the riflemen had a chance to reload. Adopting the fire-and-charge tactic, organized professional infantry were quite capable of withstanding one or two volleys of fire from the enemy, and still keep advancing. In such cases the riflemen would have had little defense—the Pennsylvania rifle was a civilian weapon, and not equipped to accept a bayonet. The riflemen could either try to defend themselves with their tomahawks and knives, or they could turn and run. In battles where close order bayonet charges succeeded in reaching the riflemen's lines, the result could be slaughter.

Another weakness of riflemen as snipers was that, when shooting from cover, their position would be given away immediately by the noise of discharge, flash of exploding powder, and of course a plume of smoke. This could result in a whole volley of shots being fired back in the general direction of the "smoke." Even when fired from

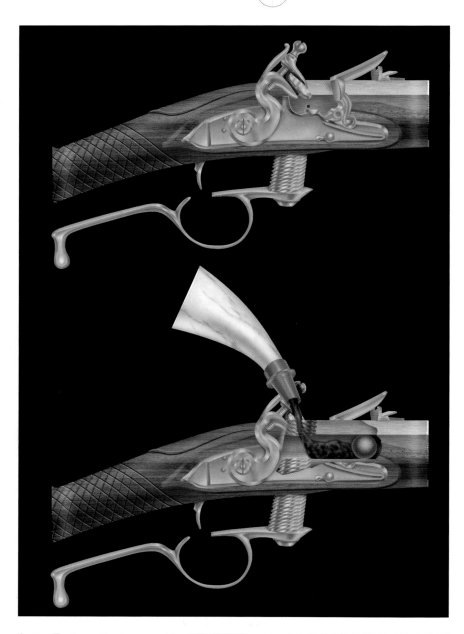

ABOVE: *Washington was said to be accompanied by a French hussar when he was spotted by Ferguson, but it was probably his aide-de-camp, Polish Count Casimir Pulaski—this engraving is by H. B. Hall.* (NA)

inaccurate military smoothbores, the shotgun effect of many musket balls crashing into a narrow area of foliage could be devastating for the concealed sniper. If a ball hit him, it didn't matter whether it was accurately aimed or not!

Despite the great contribution that the American sharpshooters and skirmishers made to the American War of Independence, they actually made up less than 5 percent of the rebel forces. It was the regular Continental army and their organized militia using mainly muskets and bayonets, and fighting conventional pitched battles, that eventually won the war against the British.

Immediately after the war the governments in both Britain and America seemed to forget how well rifleman could perform in certain situations, especially when used in the role of light infantry. Neither of them organized large-scale rifle units until virtually the turn of the century.

ABOVE: *The breechloading Ferguson rifle with a screw breech system. Top: with one complete turn of the guard, the top of the breech was exposed. Bottom: cutaway showing the open breech—a ball was dropped in, then a measure of powder was poured in behind, then the breech would be closed with a turn of the guard. The Ferguson would then be fired like an ordinary flintlock.*

RIGHT: *George Washington at Dorchester Heights. (Painting by Gilbert Stuart) Washington had a lucky escape when British marksman, Captain Patrick Ferguson, refused to take a shot, and let him ride away.* (LoC)

Still shoulder to shoulder

Towards the end of the 18th and opening of the 19th Centuries, major battle tactics and the equipment used remained largely the same as they had been for the previous hundred years—massed infantry units, standing shoulder to shoulder, still mainly armed with smoothbore muskets and bayonets, and supported by artillery and cavalry. However, there were stirrings of change—at least on a moderate scale—within the military thinking of the British. The importance of light troops had been noted, and in 1797 it was decided to include a battalion of riflemen into the 60th Regiment (formerly the 62nd Royal American Regiment and later to become King's Royal Rifles). At this time Britain was still at war with the French, being the sole partner still under arms after the collapse of the First Coalition of European nations that had combined against France in 1792. The threat of the French would hang heavily over Britain until Napoleon's final defeat at Waterloo in 1815, and "necessity being the mother of invention" is never truer than during times of war.

Approval was also given for an Experimental Corps of Riflemen, who would primarily be recruited within Britain, to be armed with a new rifle. After experiments at the Woolwich Arsenal, the Baker rifle was chosen as the most suitable weapon.

The Experimental Corps was formed as the 95th (Rifle) Regiment of Foot in 1800 under General Coot-

Manningham. Unlike the scarlet tunics of the line regiments, the 95th would wear green—which was to become the distinguishing uniform color of British riflemen.

Once again their role was to be as skirmishers, but now they were much more like the riflemen that the British had faced in the American wars; the men of the 95th were expected to fight in open order, think for themselves when necessary, and make use of cover. Above all, they had to practice their rifle skills to become the equal of any marksmen in the world. Although this may seem self evident for a specialist rifle corps, until then there had not been great emphasis put on individual marksmanship in the British Army; in the 95th Rifles men were expected to be competent with their rifles and were actively encouraged to compete against each other in target shooting contests.

From 1800 to 1850, the 95th fought in many engagements around the world—including acting as marine snipers in Nelson's fleet at Copenhagen—but they are probably most notably associated with the Peninsula War (1808 to 1814) in Portugal and Spain, and their part in the Battle of Waterloo (1815).

General Arthur Wellesley (later Lord Wellington) and his army were sent by Britain to aid her Portuguese and Spanish allies after their countries had been overrun by the French in 1807/8. As the confrontation took place on the Iberian Peninsula, it became known as the Peninsula War. Fought on the move, often in inhospitable

ABOVE: *Battle of Camden (1780); death of de Kalb. (Engraving from painting by Alonzo Chappel.) During the time it took American riflemen to reload they were susceptible to a bayonet charge or cavalry attack.* (NA)

OVERLEAF: *If a sharpshooter was spotted he could expect a whole volley of shots to be fired back at him.* (Richard Clark)

terrain, this was the ideal battlefield for light infantry tactics and guerrilla warfare—in fact this is where the term was invented, with Spanish and Portuguese irregular "guerrilleros" harassing the French supply columns, disrupting communications, and generally making it difficult to keep the country under control.

At the start of this campaign, the 95th and the 5/60th were brought together to form a brigade of riflemen. Being light troops they formed the vanguard of the army and were the first to go ashore in Portugal in 1808. The rifle-armed battalions fought together during the first battles of the campaign, actually firing the first shots of the war at Obidos, but later they were reorganized and the 60th provided light companies to scout and skirmish for each of the other brigades.

The 95th were reinforced with companies from England, but overall events weren't going in favor of the British who were running out of supplies, so they were forced to withdraw, with the French in pursuit. The 95th acted as rearguard and it was during this last action that Rifleman Thomas Plunkett made his legendary 300-yard shot, from a prone position, to bring down one of Napoleon's favorite young commanders—General Auguste Colbert. The 95th took part in the battle of Corunna under the leadership of Sir John Moore—who died in the action—and successfully helped to keep an

army of 20,000 French at bay while their comrades embarked on ships for England.

By the summer of 1809 the 95th were once more fighting the French, in Portugal, Spain, and Holland. In February 1810, four companies of the 95th—approximately 200 men—were guarding a bridge over the River Agueda, at Barba Del Puerco. Several minor skirmishes had already taken place, and one company of riflemen under the command of Captain Peter O'Hare was picketing the bridge. A French brigade of over 3,000 men was in the area, and their commander, General Ferey, decided that a night attack should be launched against the bridge. A force of around 600 voltigeurs and grenadiers were sent in as assault troops across the bridge, with around 1,500 men in reserve.

The weather was foul, and under cover of darkness the French were able to overrun and kill two riflemen acting as advance pickets, but one of them managed to fire off a shot, alerting thirteen more riflemen who were between the bridge and the rest of the company stationed in a hilltop church. The thirteen riflemen retreated up the hill, fighting as they went, and were supported by their comrades who now joined the action, firing down on the French.

On such a stormy black night the riflemen made difficult targets in their dark green uniforms, but the white

THE 60TH REGIMENT OF FOOT (RENAMED KING'S ROYAL RIFLE CORPS AFTER 1830)

In 1755, during the French-Indian Wars, a combined army of General Braddock's British redcoats and Virginian militia (incidentally commanded by Colonel George Washington) had been ambushed and routed by a much smaller force of French troops and Indians using guerrilla tactics more suited to the dense forests of north-east America. In 1756 the British responded by raising the 62nd (Royal American) Regiment to help defend the thirteen colonies against such attacks. This consisted of four battalions of 1,000 men, mainly American colonists and British volunteers, but also including experienced forest- and mountain-based fighters from Austria, Germany, and Switzerland. In 1757 the regiment's title was renumbered, becoming the 60th (Royal American) Regiment.

One of the regiment's officers, Henri Bouquet, a professional Swiss soldier, set about shaping his command (the 1st Battalion) into a force that could hold its own fighting against Native Americans on their own territory. This he succeeded in doing, making his battalion's name as light infantry and skirmishers throughout the French-Indian Wars, but also still capable of taking part as line troops in formal battles. Battalions of the regiment served at Quebec in 1759, Pontiac's War in 1763, the War of Independence, and also outside America.

In 1797 a fifth battalion consisting solely of riflemen was raised for the regiment under Baron Francis de Rottenburg. Many of these were jägers from various central European countries, and Germans who had formerly been loyal American colonists already in service with the British. After 1800 the 5th Battalion riflemen were armed with Baker rifles and were distinctively dressed in green jackets with red facings. These riflemen first saw action in the Napoleonic Wars and proved to be so successful in the role of light infantry that eventually all the other musket-armed light companies in the regiments were made into rifle companies.

A second rifle battalion (the 6th) was soon added to the regiment, serving in the Peninsula War with Wellington's army, while a 7th rifle battalion was raised for the American War of 1812. After the Napoleonic Wars the regiment's name was changed to The Duke of York's Own Rifle Corps, and then in 1830 it became the King's Royal Rifle Corps.

ABOVE: *Rifleman of the 5th Battalion, 60th Regt. (Napoleonic period) distinguishable by the red facings on his green uniform—and the unit markings on his water canteen.*
(Richard Clark)

RIGHT: *Men of the 95th (Rifle Brigade) became famous for their marksmanship, skirmishing tactics, and green uniforms.*
(Richard Clark)

crossbelts of the French stood out, even in the gloom—in fact these were often used as aiming marks by riflemen.

It was during this firefight that a genuine incident of a ramrod being "fired" from a rifle occurred. In an account by Rifleman William Green, it appears that he and his partner were charged by "three of these big ugly fellows who came within 10 yards." Green claims that, while loading his rifle, he was forced to fire both ball and ramrod, killing one of the French, while his partner killed a second. Green then continued to fight, having picked up a rifle from a wounded comrade.

Although hard pressed, the riflemen held on and were eventually joined by two more companies of rifles, led by Lieutenant Colonel Beckwith. Their timely intervention stopped the assault and caused the French to retreat down the hill and across the bridge, back to the protection of their main force. With three out of four companies engaged in the action (the fourth being held in reserve) the 95th had repelled 600 "elite" French troops with just 150 riflemen. The French suffered losses of over 100 killed and wounded, while the 95th had just seven riflemen killed and fifteen wounded.

This battle helped further establish the reputation of the 95th as a fighting unit, and certainly served as an example of what riflemen could achieve, even in close quarter combat. This was mainly due to the fact that the Baker rifle was designed for the military from the outset, and therefore it had a bayonet socket, unlike many of the civilian rifles used by sharpshooters in the past. In fact, the Baker rifle's "sword" bayonet was quite a formidable weapon in its own right. The bayonet had to be long because the Baker rifle was fairly short when compared to a military musket, so the deficit in reach—an important consideration in bayonet fighting—had to be made up. With its 24-inch-long blade, hand grip, and bow guard, the bayonet could also be used as a short sword, when not attached to the rifle. Of course for a specialist long-range shooter, "close combat" with an edged weapon would generally be regarded as "too close"!

Throughout the Peninsula War the riflemen of the Light Division proved their worth, both in general fighting and their more specialized duties: skirmishing, scouting and harassing the enemy with accurate long range rifle

BELOW: *The French also had specialist light infantry and assault troops, but few of them were armed with rifles.* (Richard Clark)

fire. Taught by their own officers to choose important targets, the riflemen picked off officers, drummers and buglers (communications), and of course artillerymen. At the Battle of Vimeiro (August 20, 1808) the long-range accuracy of the riflemen's fire cut down the French artillerymen and their horses, allowing their guns to be captured, while at other battles and sieges the French artillery barely got a shot off because of the incessant sniping of their positions.

Perhaps no finer tribute can be made to the early riflemen of the British Army than the words of one of the French commanders, Marshal Soult:

"There is an English battalion of the 60th, it is armed with a short rifle; the men are selected for their marksmanship; they perform the duties of scouts and in action are expressly ordered to pick off officers, especially field or general officers. This mode of making war and of injuring the enemy is very detrimental to us. Our casualties in officers are so great that after a couple of actions the whole number are usually disabled. I saw, yesterday, battalions whose officers had been disabled in the ratio of one officer to eight men! I also saw battalions which were reduced to two

ABOVE: *Riflemen were encouraged to learn marksmanship, firing their rifles from many different positions, including kneeling, sitting, and prone.* (Richard Clark)

OVERLEAF: *Rifleman using his shako to rest his rifle while firing from the prone position.* (Richard Clark)

THE BAKER RIFLE (THE INFANTRY RIFLE)

FAR LEFT: *When Napoleonic armies marched into battle, their close-packed ranks made easy targets, and their white cross belts made excellent aiming marks.* (Richard Clark)

At the end of the 18th Century, the British Army was looking for a suitable weapon with which to equip a corps of riflemen (eventually to become the Rifle Brigade). To this end an international competition was organized at Woolwich Arsenal on February 4, 1800. The winning design was a muzzleloading rifled musket from Ezekial Baker, a gunsmith based in Whitechapel Road in the East End of London. The barrel had just a quarter of a turn on the seven-groove rifling, compared with the more common three-quarter twist of many contemporary designs. The idea of this was to cut down on friction, yet still put enough spin on the projectile for stability.

The resulting rifle had an overall length of 45.25 inches and weight was around 9 lb. It had a .625-caliber barrel of 30 inches, with fixed sights. It used lead ball ammunition with a greased patch of cloth, so a "patch box" was incorporated into the right side of the stock's butt. The powder horn issued with the rifle had a cut-off to deliver the correct measure of powder (almost one third the weight of the ball).

Accuracy was good for at least 200 yards against a man-sized target—the sights were aimed at the enemy's cross-belts at this range—which was a vast improvement on the 60 yards or so accuracy range of the Brown Bess smoothbore musket.

The Baker was shorter and less cumbersome than a standard musket, and its only real disadvantage was that the loading process took longer, although in an emergency standard made-up powder cartridges could be used with an un-patched ball for faster loading, but some subsequent loss in accuracy. The Baker Rifle was in use in the British Army for nearly 40 years before it was replaced by the percussion-lock Brunswick rifle. During its long history it was used by many different nations—apparently even by some of the Mexican army at the Alamo. Many variations were produced for English volunteer units and there were even some sporting models made.

ABOVE: *The Baker Rifle was in use by specialist rifle units of the British Army for 40 years; this particular model is post 1823. Lock marked Tower with crown over GR but no service issue proof marks. Barrel made by E BAKER with fixed post sights and has a bayonet bar at the muzzle. Stock is the split type with a brass patch box.* (Australian War Memorial REL/04959.001)

or three officers, although less than one sixth of their men had been disabled."

The War of 1812 in America was a sideshow in scale when compared to the Napoleonic conflicts, but in terms of development of rifle tactics this often forgotten confrontation was just as important, perhaps more so.

The invading British forces—including at least one battalion of riflemen—came up against not only American militia and sharpshooters armed with their own hunting rifles, but also organized regular infantry with the new military Model 1803 rifle.

The campaign was a resounding defeat for the British, and one of the main lessons learned was that exposing

BELOW: *Groups of officers and artillerymen were prime targets for sharpshooters.*

THE 95TH RIFLES (RENAMED THE RIFLE BRIGADE AFTER 1816)

Raised as the Experimental Corps of Riflemen in 1800, this unit was the first to be equipped with the Baker Rifle. It was brought into the line as the 95th Rifles in 1802. The 95th joined the 43rd and 52nd Light Infantry Regiments in 1803. Under General Coote-Manningham and Sir John Moore, they followed the training manual for Riflemen and Light Troops that had been written by Colonel Baron de Rottenburg, commander of the 5th (Rifle) Battalion of the 60th Regiment.

Although not marines, some of the 95th saw early service at sea, as marksmen during the Battle of Copenhagen in 1801, when Nelson's ships destroyed the Danish fleet. Throughout the early 1800s the 95th was one of the busiest units of the army, seeing action in Spain and Germany, and even an initially successful but eventually abortive expedition against the Spanish in South America.

The 95th was involved in most major battles of the Peninsula War in Spain and Portugal, famously acting as the rearguard for the British Army's retreat to Corunna.

Probably the most famous story of individual marksmanship by a soldier of the 95th concerns Rifleman Thomas Plunkett during the Peninsula campaign. The 95th was acting as a rearguard while the army retreated to Corunna. Rifleman Plunkett spotted a mounted French officer urging his men into faster pursuit of the retreating British. Lying on his back, his Baker Rifle supported on his thigh and its sling pulled tight by his foot for extra stability, Plunkett took his shot... and the officer fell dead from his saddle. A bugler rode up to help the general, but Plunkett had reloaded, and took the opportunity to shoot him too. The

second shot proved that the first was no fluke, and later it was discovered that the officer was General Auguste Colbert. The shots were taken in access of 300 yards, and both Plunkett's victims had been shot in the head.

At the Battle of Waterloo, the first and second battalions of the 95th plus two companies from the 3rd Battalion—some 1,300 officers and men—were once more under the command of Lord Wellington. Taking part in the fighting around Quatre Bras, La Haye Sainte, and other actions, the riflemen of the 95th gave a good account of themselves, but were not used to their best effect. At the end of the battle they had suffered casualties of 35 officers and 482 men.

After 1816 the 95th Rifles was renamed The Rifle Brigade. Probably more than any other British Army unit, the 95th Rifles heralded a very different, modern form of soldiering and certainly introduced the basic skills of the sniper—choosing strategically important targets—as a regular army tactic.

TOP: *Although specialists in skirmishing and scouting, sometimes the Riflemen were used as regular infantry.* (John Norris)

ABOVE: *This is the position used by Rifleman Plunkett for his famous 300-yards shot which killed the French General Auguste Colbert.*

JÄGERS, CHASSEURS, CAÇADORES, TIRAILLEURS, AND VOLTIGEURS

ABOVE: *Although some of the European "hunter" troops were recruited for their shooting and fieldcraft skills, many were just armed with smoothbore muskets, not rifles, and some were used as line troops rather than light infantry.* (Richard Clark)

Many of the early riflemen of the main European powers were hunters who regarded the rifle as the main tool of their trade. Their marksmanship and stalking skills were ideally suited to a specialist military role, especially when the vast majority of infantry units were armed with the simple smoothbore musket. Employed as mercenaries, *jägers* came from many European countries, including Germany, Switzerland, Austria, Holland, Poland, and the Baltic states, some fighting for Britain, while others were in the pay of France. During the Peninsula Wars, Portugese *caçadores* fought closely with British light infantry and the Portuguese/Spanish *guerrilleros*, putting pressure on the French forces. *Chasseurs à pied* (foot hunters) were elite French troops generally recruited for their shooting skills, although, like their British light infantry equivalents, many were armed with smoothbore muskets, not rifles. *Tirailleurs* were specialist sharpshooters drawn from various areas in France and Italy; they also took on the light infantry scouting role. *Voltigeurs* (meaning leapers or vaulters) were also chosen sharpshooters in the French army, one company in each regiment taking the role of light infantry. Although classified as elite troops, many of these "hunters" and "sharpshooters," seemingly ideally suited to the role of light infantry, were used simply as ordinary infantrymen in major battles.

THE SHARPSHOOTER AT SEA

The exploits of marksmen weren't always carried out on land. The importance of having sharpshooters in the rigging in the days of sail should not be underestimated. While most "long" distance fighting on ships was done with cannon, until the vessels could get close enough for the crews to engage in close quarters combat, there was also quite a bit of "sniping" with muskets or rifles. In the late 18th and early 19th Centuries, the British navy mainly used marines armed with the Brown Bess musket, but they also employed riflemen of the 95th at the battle of Copenhagen in 1801.

In the War of Independence the American navy used riflemen and marines on shore and at sea to defend port towns from the British navy. Sailors were very exposed on vessels, especially when they were in the rigging. By the time of the War of 1812, both the American and British navies would get their marksmen to deliberately target officers.

Perhaps the most famous victim of naval sniping was Admiral Lord Horatio Nelson, at the Battle of Trafalgar (1805). While on the quarterdeck of HMS *Victory* the admiral was shot by a French marine–Robert Guillemard–from the rigging of the French ship *Redoutable*.

Shot from close range–it is suggested just fifty feet–the musket ball passed down through Nelson's shoulder, lung and spine. One of Britain's greatest heroes, he was taken below, but never recovered, dying in agony some hours later.

A small victory this obviously was, but the French nevertheless lost the battle, their fleet, and eventually their emperor and the war.

LEFT: *Admiral Lord Nelson, one of history's most famous victims of a sniper's shot.* (Courtesy Wallis & Wallis)

ABOVE: The Death of Pakenham at the Battle of New Orleans, *by F. O. C. Darley, c1860. Skilled American riflemen took an awful toll on the British at the Battle of New Orleans, clinically picking off the easily identifiable officers–including the British commander-in-chief, Lieutenant General Sir Edward Pakenham, brother-in-law of the Duke of Wellington–before turning their accurate fire on the lower ranks.* (LoC)

commanding officers within rifle range was inviting them to be shot. Among the British casualties in this comparatively short war were many high-ranking officers, including General Sir Isaac Brock and Major General Robert Ross, both extremely capable soldiers, but unfortunately still following the tradition of leading from the front. At the Battle of New Orleans (January 8, 1815), when 7,000 redcoats faced 4,000 Americans (half of them skilled riflemen), the British casualties included the commander-in-chief, Lieutenant General Sir Edward Pakenham, plus Major Generals Sir Samuel Gibbs and John Keane, Colonels Patterson and Dale, and Lieutenant Colonels Rennie, Debbieg, Jones, Faunce, and Brooke. Even lower ranking officers were specifically targeted: Major John Whittaker was felled by the first aimed rifle shot. He had been designated as a target by

Colonel Adair, the commanding officer of the Kentucky riflemen contingent of the American forces. In this instance, the advice to "aim for the epaulettes and gorgets"–gaudy marks of rank which easily distinguished British officers–had served the American sharpshooters well.

The deliberate targeting of officers was obviously a very effective strategy, and was eventually accepted as a "legitimate" tactic even by those that had suffered the most–British and French officers. It was becoming impossible to ignore the advantages of rifled weapons with adjustable sights–weapons that could be accurately aimed–over the literally "hit or miss" smoothbore muskets. Just as important was the realization that men needed to be trained to use their weapons accurately–and with discrimination–in order to achieve the maximum tactical potential. If a rifleman could shoot accurately he could choose his target to his best advantage and, as the British found out at the Battle of New Orleans, this could lead to the loss of important officers, the loss of co-ordination and cohesion in the army, and the subsequent loss of the battle.

Following the Napoleonic Wars and the War of 1812, there should have been little doubt about the changing nature of war, the obsolescence of the smoothbore musket, and the advantages of equipping all troops with rifles–and training them to use them to a good level of marksmanship.

RIGHT: *Officer's accouterments: throat gorget (not seen here), gold epaulettes, and distinctive headgear helped American sharpshooters pick out their targets in the War of 1812.* (John Norris)

CHAPTER TWO:
NEW SKILLS AND FORGOTTEN LESSONS

CHAPTER TWO:
NEW SKILLS AND FORGOTTEN LESSONS

PREVIOUS PAGE: *The P53 Enfield had range-adjustable sights as standard.*

BELOW: *Percussion lock (on a reproduction Enfield rifle), with percussion cap in place on nipple.*

The end of the Napoleonic Wars brought over thirty years of comparative peace in Europe. Nevertheless, advances in small arms technology accelerated. In fact, between 1830 and 1890, the standard arms for most European soldiers developed from the flintlock smoothbore musket right through to bolt-operated, magazine-fed cartridge rifles—and in Britain versions of the latter remained the main personal issue weapon right through to the Korean War and into the mid-1950s.

These major changes didn't follow a set pattern of development; instead, they occurred mainly by way of advances brought about by unconnected individuals putting their minds to solving particular problems with the firearms of their time. Quite often these improvements would come as a result of sporting shooters looking to gain an advantage over their quarry. This was the case with the introduction of the percussion cap, which was initially developed by a wildfowler because the sparks and flash of the flintlock ignition would give birds enough

warning to fly away before the shot could hit them. The percussion system solved this problem—and others—by using a simple metal cap to replace the notoriously unreliable and complex flintlock system consisting of flint, frizzen (striker), flash pan, and exposed ignition powder.

The percussion cap was a tiny metal cylinder capped at one end, with the interior base coated in a compound containing fulminate of mercury with chlorate of potash. This cap was put over a small hollow metal nipple connected to the barrel's breech, and when struck by the gun's hammer the cap's chemical coating would ignite, sending a flash through to the powder in the breech. This system was much more weather-proof, and therefore reliable; it had no shower of sparks or flash, and it also aided accuracy by reducing the time between pulling the trigger and the projectile leaving the muzzle.

The advantages of the system were obvious as far back as 1818, when rival private patents were taken out in Britain and France. Even the obstinate British military

THE PERCUSSION LOCK

No matter how good a flintlock mechanism was, it would always need a lot of care to keep it working in good order. Flints would have to be changed regularly, the powder in the flash pan had to be kept dry, and the touch hole in the breech had to be kept clear—otherwise there might be a "flash in the pan," meaning the initial ignition occurred but the resultant flame didn't reach the main charge in the breech.

In contrast, percussion firearms had fewer components to worry about, were much more weatherproof, and were far easier to use and maintain. The system consisted of a hammer, a small disposable copper cap with a volatile chemical coating inside, and a hollow metal "nipple" for the cap to sit on. When the trigger was pulled the hammer would strike the cap, crushing it and causing the chemical coating inside to explode, sending a flash of flame down the hollow nipple and onto the gunpowder in the breech, thereby discharging the firearm. The nipple was removable so that it exposed the touch hole into the breech for easier cleaning. Each time the gun was loaded, the rifleman would place a new percussion cap on the nipple prior to firing.

The percussion lock principle was invented around 1805 by a clergyman, Reverend Alexander Forsyth, who was also a keen wildfowler and skilled scientist. Working with an explosive but unstable compound of potassium chlorate and fulminate of mercury originally invented by Berthollet, a French chemist, Forsyth succeeded in making a usable detonation or "priming" powder that would ignite when struck. Originally developed to hide the flash and smoke of the flintlock ignition on sporting guns from ducks and geese, Forsyth's invention was seen as a great idea for military firearms and he was commissioned to develop it for the army. Unfortunately, the British government's Master of Ordnance changed, and the incoming Lord Chatham saw no future in percussion locks. So Forsyth was sent on his way.

The French on the other hand still thought highly of the system, and Napoleon offered Forsyth £20,000 for his invention—a small fortune at the time. Luckily for the British Army, Forsyth turned down the French offer and continued his work privately, being granted a patent in 1807 for a "scent-bottle" lock—named after the small container that carried the priming powder. This idea was good, and proved popular on sporting guns, but was still not without problems.

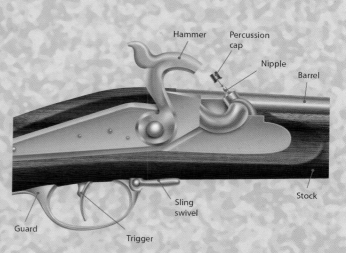

ABOVE: *The percussion lock was a great advance over the flintlock. When the hammer struck the cap, it caused the chemical coating inside to explode, sending a flame down the hollow nipple and into the breech, igniting the main powder charge.*

The percussion system only became viable for military use once the metal percussion cap had been invented in 1814 by Joshua Shaw, an Englishman living in America. Within six years the percussion cap was being used on sporting and other civilian arms by several British gunmakers, notably Joseph Manton and Joseph Egg. Even so, the British Army didn't start changing from flintlocks to percussion locks until 1838.

authorities accepted it after prolonged trials from 1834—especially since the French military had started their experiments in 1830. The percussion lock musket (P42) was adopted by the British in 1842 and by mid-century the percussion cap system was in general use by most modern armies of the time.

It had already been established that rifles had significant advantages over smoothbore weapons, but they were certainly more difficult to load and maintain—in other words, they required a greater input from the user. Certainly in the higher ranks of the British Army the opinion was that the standard infantry weapon required improvement in performance.

At roughly the same time that percussion locks were gaining in popularity, several gunsmiths and inventors were separately working on ways to increase the range of rifles, and simplify or improve the speed of reloading. The problem was that a tight-fitting projectile was required to engage the rifling in the barrel in order to achieve spin and therefore the best range and accuracy, whereas a loose-fitting projectile was faster and easier to load. The patched ball achieved extended accuracy, but was slow to load and required a certain amount of skill to be used effectively.

Various methods were experimented with, including ribbed bullets and belted balls—the latter being used in the Brunswick rifle, which had matching two-groove rifling in the barrel for the "belt" to engage with. Although the Brunswick was used in relatively small numbers by both the British Army and Navy, it was heavy and unreliable in the field, since the "belt" on the ball had to be perfectly formed and undamaged to fit properly. It was almost universally disliked by British servicemen and is generally regarded as one of the worst weapons ever issued.

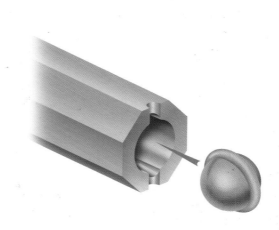

LEFT: *The Brunswick Rifle had a "belted ball" that exactly fitted the twin bands of rifling—but it could still be awkward to load, especially when the barrel was fouled with powder residue.*

The solution was to find a way to put a loose-fitting projectile into the barrel when loading, then expand it at the breech so that it would fit tightly as it traveled back up the barrel when fired. The ringed and pillared breech systems were two ideas that had their supporters. The first was where a fairly loose ball was dropped into the barrel then rammed hard against either a ring or a shoulder at the breech end of the barrel in order to expand the soft lead. The pillar system worked in a similar way, but used a central projection to expand the ball. Both these breech systems required a mallet or heavy ramrod to be used, and the projectiles were often deformed by the process—hardly conducive to good accuracy. That being said, there is a famous story regarding the Delvigne rifle—a weapon using a sub-caliber powder chamber at the breech end of the barrel, leaving a "shoulder" against which the ball would rest and then be rammed hard in order to expand into the rifling. Such rifles were being carried by French chasseurs commanded by the Duke of Orleans during the Algerian War (1830–48). Apparently an Arab (some accounts claim it was a sheik) was mocking and gesticulating at the French from afar. This offended the duke and spurred him to offer a reward for any of his sharpshooters who could hit the Arab. The challenge was taken up by one of the chasseurs, who cleanly shot the unfortunate Arab dead… at a distance claimed to be over 600 yards. This was some shot by any standards, especially for a rifle that supposedly fired deformed bullets.

Although several of these ideas made it into production, none of them was really satisfactory, and they were all made obsolete when the answer finally came in the shape of the self-expanding bullet. Although similar ideas came from gunsmiths on both sides of the English Channel, it was the self-expanding bullet invented by a French army officer, Captain Claude-Etienne Minié, in 1847 that was internationally adopted, and came to bear his name as the Minié ball. The original lead projectile was a hollow, one-piece cylindrical body with three exterior grease-filled grooves, a conical head, and a base fitted with an iron cup. It was slightly under bore size to make it easy to load—with minimum use of the ramrod— and when the gun was fired the iron cup would push up into the hollow body, expanding the lead bullet to fit snugly into the rifling. In some later versions the iron cup was replaced with a small wooden plug, which achieved the same effect. The Minié ball was used by both the British and French armies in the Crimean War (1853–56), by which time the British were using the simpler Metford-Pritchard bullet that had no separate metal cup or wooden plug, but expanded purely because of the design of the hollow concave base. The grease-filled grooves gave the bullet lubrication when loading, helped act as gas seals, and securely engaged the rifling but with minimal friction when fired.

THE MINIÉ BALL—EXTENDING RANGE AND ACCURACY

The importance of the Minié ball or bullet (sometimes known as the "Minny") cannot be overestimated in the development of long-range shooting. Arguably developed from an original idea by a British infantry officer, Captain Norton, the conical-cylindrical, self-expanding bullet was certainly perfected by Captain Claude-Etienne Minié, an instructor at the French army's school at Vincennes. He also developed the Minié rifle, which was adopted by the French and, for a short period, the British.

Being slightly sub-caliber (smaller than the bore) the Minié ball or bullet could be easily loaded, but when the weapon was fired the force of the gasses pushing the ball down the barrel would expand the hollow soft lead base, causing the outer ribs to engage the rifling. This made the bullet spin, which gave it stability through the air, helping it to travel farther and with more penetrative power. Crucially, when correctly loaded from its paper cartridge with its set charge, and teamed with a percussion lock for faster and more reliable ignition of the powder, the Minié bullet became a very consistent and predictable projectile. Accuracy is all about repeatability—being able to predict the point of impact for any given distance, time after time. This is especially true of long-range or precision shooting.

Under tests, the P51, a British version of the Minié rifle firing a .702 Minié bullet, had quite good accuracy up to 500 yards and even

achieved a hit on a 6ft x 3ft target at 900 yards in seven attempts. This was quite amazing accuracy for the time, and during the Kaffir War of 1846–52, when volley-fired by trained riflemen, their shots fell close enough at a claimed 1,200 yards to cause native warriors to withdraw.

With the later P53, a much better rifle using a smaller .577 Minié bullet, it was reckoned that a good marksman could hit an 8ft square target at

1,000 yards at least once in every two attempts, thus theoretically extending the range of accurate infantry fire by up to a factor of ten when compared with a smoothbore musket firing an unpatched ball.

ABOVE: *Lead Minié "ball" (on left), with grooves lubricated with tallow-based grease, compared to a Brown Bess musket ball (on right).*

THE ENFIELD PATTERN 1853 RIFLED MUSKET (P53)

ABOVE: *Pattern 1853 Enfield Rifle, 2nd Model. Lock marked Crown over V+R and 1856, with service proofs. Barrel has French and English proof marks, including a manufacturer's stamp F*P within an oval. The rear sight bed is graduated in 100-yard steps to 400, and the leaf sight to 1,000 yards. This particular model was made under contract by the St. Etienne Arsenal, France. (AWM. REL_04837)*

The P53 was a percussion lock .577-caliber muzzleloading rifled weapon first used in the Crimean War, and then throughout the British Empire from 1853 to 1867, as well as being one of the rifles used by both sides during the American Civil War. The rifle weighed around 8.8lb and measured 55 inches overall, while the barrel was 39 inches long with three shallow grooves giving a 1:78 rifling twist (a full turn in 78 inches). The P53 was fastened to its walnut stock with three metal bands. This gave rise to the common term "three band" model, whereas the shorter 33-inch barreled carbine version (49 inches overall) was often called the "two band" model. The carbine had an improved lock, and the barrel was given five-groove rifling with a 1:48 twist. This rifling was an improvement over the original, and was used for all later Enfield rifles, with progressive rifling (0.13 inches at the breech tapering to 0.005 inches at the muzzle) being adopted in 1858. All models were equipped with one of four types of adjustable rear sight graduated from 100 to up to 900 yards or more (depending on the model). The actual range that an ordinary soldier would be capable of hitting a single man-size target was around 150 yards from a standing position, possibly double that from a supported firing point. A skilled marksman could add at least one hundred yards to each of these distance figures.

ABOVE: *Enfield cartridge packet and paper cartridges for the Pattern 1853 Enfield Rifle. (Graham Lay)*

The rifle used greased paper cartridges containing 2.5 drams (68 grains) of black powder and a modified Minié-type bullet weighing 535-grain. This load would give a muzzle velocity of around 850–900 feet per second (fps). A competent soldier could load and fire around two to three rounds per minute.

Advances in machinery meant that mass production techniques could be used for the P53.

Therefore, many of the parts were easily interchangeable, lessening the reliance on specialist gunsmiths for repairs and replacements.

The Enfield P53 and its variants proved to be exceptional examples of their type. They were the last muzzleloading rifles in service with the British Army, not being replaced by the Snider—a breechloading derivative of the P53—until 1865.

The P53 was one of the major causes of the Indian Mutiny 1857–58 (also known as the Sepoy Rebellion). Word spread amongst native Indian troops (sepoys) in the service of the East India Company that the paper cartridges issued with their new Enfield rifles were greased with fat from a pig (an animal regarded as unclean to the Muslims) or beef tallow (the cow being sacred to Hindus). These paper cartridges had to be bitten in order to release the powder inside, and the thought of their mouths coming into contact with pig or cow fat was abhorrent to the sepoys. This, along with other social and political issues, was a factor in inciting the native troops to rebel. The mutiny and its ruthless suppression are now regarded as one of the bloodiest chapters in the history of the British Empire.

The Minié ball was carried in a paper cartridge with powder, and was loaded in much the same way as the old musket ball cartridges. The difference was that now the soldier was loading a rifle, not a smoothbore musket. The rifle was a much more accurate, longer-range firearm, and the addition of the percussion lock meant that it was easier and safer to prime, and generally much quicker and more efficient to use.

Captain Minié also developed the Minié rifle to take advantage of his ammunition. It proved highly successful, having good accuracy to at least 500 yards, and was adopted by the French army in 1846 for its zouave and chasseur sharpshooters. These Minié-armed units were used with some success in France's colonial campaigns in North Africa to counter the long-range shooting carried out by local tribesmen with their handmade long-barreled rifles.

Britain also adopted the Minié rifle in the form of the P51, which began to be issued in 1852, just in time for the start of the Crimean War a year later (although many units continued to use the P42 percussion lock smoothbore muskets). Despite their weight of nearly ten pounds, and the large .703-inch bore, it became obvious that the new rifles with their Minié ball ammunition far outperformed the muskets, and by the end of the war the future of rifles as the main weapon of the infantry was assured.

The P51 was soon to be replaced by the Enfield P53 percussion lock rifled musket, which weighed nearly a pound less, and used a smaller standardized caliber of .577 with the Metford-Pritchard bullet. This combination, once teething troubles were overcome, must be regarded as one of the best of its type. The P53 was easy to load, accurate, reliable, and straightforward to

ABOVE: *(Left to Right) Cross-sections of; original lead Minié ball with iron cup expander in base; early British style Minié ball with wooden plug expander in base; later Minié ball with larger expansion space in base and thinner walls.*

BELOW: *Packs of paper cartridge ammunition for the Enfield rifle. (Graham Lay)*

RIGHT: *Typical paper cartridge with powder and Minié ball for loading a rifled musket.*

RIGHT AND OVERLEAF: *Despite the much-extended range of the new rifles, Civil War battles were still being fought in massed ranks. (Roy Daines)*

maintain. It was virtually "soldier-proof" and was soon being used throughout the British Empire, and would be issued by both sides during the American Civil War. Similar cap-lock rifled arms were adopted by all the major military powers by the mid-1850s.

This meant that the ordinary soldier was now armed with a weapon that would enable him to be a marksman, provided that he put in the practice. The P53 had adjustable sights, so that estimating and adjusting the position of the weapon for the target distance and drift (now often referred to as "hold over" and "Kentucky windage") could now be accomplished by simply adjusting the sights and aiming "dead-on." Never before had the ordinary serviceman been better equipped. With their old smoothbore muskets they would have been lucky to hit a man at 100 yards. But now, with weapon familiarization and practice, it would have been possible for any ordinary soldier with a rifle to hit a man-sized target at 250 yards, while a skilled marksman could probably do the same at twice that distance.

The strange thing was that; despite the doubling of the effective range of the weapons, and likewise increasing each soldier's capability, infantry tactics remained largely the same as they had in the Napoleonic era and before.

Still fighting by Napoleonic drill

During the Crimean War and most of the American Civil War, armies faced each other in the open, still shoulder to shoulder and in massed ranks, yet their standard weapons were capable of hitting the enemy at 500 yards and beyond. Of course, the infantrymen had to be totally retrained, since previously they had merely leveled their smoothbore muskets in the general direction of the enemy, then discharged them en masse in the hope of causing a significant amount of casualties—and thereby reducing the return fire. Now they could aim their rifle and have a good chance of hitting the target if they had received the correct training. Even so, they would still do most of their firing in steps, by command.

Using a reasonably consistent powder charge and Minié ball in conjunction with a faster percussion lock and adjustable sights, it was possible for riflemen firing in unison to cause enormous damage to an advancing line of enemy infantry—provided that they had got their range right. To this end it became important to teach soldiers how to judge range, instead of relying on shouted instructions from NCOs or other senior experienced men as to where to set the distance on their rifle sights. As an aid, when conditions allowed, wooden stakes or stones would sometimes be set out at 100-yard intervals as range marks in front of the line before the battle.

The introduction of the rifle as the standard service weapon in Britain helped bring about a greater interest in volunteer rifle units, an increase in competitive shooting, and, most important of all, better instruction on marksmanship to the common soldier. The British Army School of Musketry at Hythe, Kent, in southern England,

THE JACOB'S RIFLE

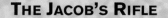

John Jacob, a British brigadier-general serving in India, invented a very unusual rifle, designed specifically for long-range shooting, with ammunition that exploded on impact. This was the first "anti-materiel" round for a rifle, as his intention was to use it to ignite the enemy artillery caissons (black powder storage), thereby possibly destroying a whole artillery position with one bullet.

The Jacob's Rifle was a double-barreled percussion weapon in .53-caliber and had sights calibrated out to a rather optimistic 2,000 yards. The bullets were also unusual, having four stabilizing "fins" that fitted the rifling, and an explosive charge in the tip. Misses on the target could be seen by the small explosions of these charges, allowing adjustment to be made until the bullet hit its mark—with potentially devastating effect. A further odd feature was that it came with probably the longest bayonet ever attached to a rifle.

The use of this rifle was demonstrated in the Crimea when Malcolm Green, a British officer returning from India, stopped off at Sebastopol to visit his brother. He had a Jacob's Rifle with him and used it to engage a Russian artillery position that was causing problems for the French allies of the British. No record is made of any severe damage done, but he did force the Russians to withdraw their guns.

The rather eccentric design of the Jacob's Rifle—and the undoubtedly brutal and horrific effects of exploding bullets on human bodies—were enough to see this weapon consigned to the side notes of military history.

ABOVE: *The unusual Jacob's long-range double rifle.*

was founded in 1853 by Lord Hardinge, the British Army commander-in-chief, for the purpose of teaching instructors for the various regiments of the army (the Rifle units already had their own training facilities). Hythe's extensive beaches were ideal for marksmanship training. Range estimation, various shooting positions (not just standing and kneeling), long-distance shooting (to 900 yards) were just some of the important new skills that were taught. By this time the army in general—not just the specialist sharpshooting units—had also accepted the idea of selective aiming, so now there was specific instruction on choosing targets of the greatest strategic value, i.e. officers and artillery. Could this have been the first "formal" sniper training?

These skills were passed on by the Hythe-trained instructors to the ordinary soldiers of Britain, and they were soon put to test against the Imperial Russian Army in the Crimean War (1854–56). Now that every man in the British Army was armed with a rifle, and had been trained in its use, the ability to engage the enemy with small arms fire at longer range was greater than ever before; an ordinary rifleman should have been able to hit a man-sized target at 400 yards, giving a potentially huge advantage over the Russians, who were mainly still armed with smoothbore muskets. Furthermore, the opportunity for specialist sharpshooters to emerge from the ranks had dramatically increased, simply because there was a far larger pool of skilled marksmen to choose from. To this end, the ten best shots in each battalion were chosen to become small sharpshooting units, deliberately targeting the Russian artillery. Taking into consideration that many artillery pieces were still smoothbores, often with less range than a rifle, the

ABOVE: *The School of Musketry at Hythe in Kent, England.*

potential for small arms to "silence the guns" had never been better. At Sebastopol an awful toll of artillerymen was taken by British riflemen, causing Russian officer Count Franz Totleben to comment, "It was more the fire of rifled small arms than that of the artillery which reached our artillerymen, the greater part of which were killed or wounded." The last part of this statement draws attention to the devastating effect of being struck by a Minié ball. These large, spinning projectiles caused horrific high-impact wounds. If hit in a limb, badly broken and splintered bones would be common, sometimes causing even further damage from fragments. This would often result in field amputation—this still being preferable to dying from hemorrhage or infection.

Exploits of long-range shooting were well recorded during the Crimean War, mainly due to the advances in communication, and therefore the presence of the press. One of the most noted British marksmen of the day was Captain G. L. Goodlake of the Coldstream Guards, who was also one of the first recipients of the Victoria Cross after his group of thirty sharpshooters repelled an attack by 500 Russian marines at Sebastopol. Also at the siege of this city, British sharpshooters were placed in forward positions to protect the sappers and keep the enemy heads down; it was one of these unknown marksmen who took an opportunist shot and killed the Russian commander, Admiral Pavel Nakhimov, while he was inspecting the city's defenses.

Lieutenant Henry Tryon of the 1st Rifle Brigade was probably the most prolific marksmen in the Crimea, having been credited with shooting over a hundred Russians during the war—thirty in one day at Inkerman—before succumbing to a bullet himself while storming

THE TWO-MAN TEAM

Conventional skirmishing tactics of the British light infantry at the time of the Napoleonic through to the Crimean Wars involved men in pairs about twelve paces apart in an extended line from right to left. When engaging the enemy, one of each pair would fire then step aside to reload while the second man in the pair stepped forward and fired. This system would be repeated, with each man taking his turn to fire and load as the skirmishers advanced. If the line of skirmishers were retiring, basically the same tactic was used while moving back—each man covering his partner, reloading while the group moved back. Some French skirmisher units used similar tactics, but in groups of four.

In the Crimea, this pairing of men was apparently extended for static sharpshooting, but with one man spotting targets for his partner to fire at. Experienced rifle expert Lieutenant Colonel D. Davidson mentioned seeing two soldiers practicing this tactic outside Sebastopol. One was lying prone, ready to fire his rifle, while the other used a telescope to locate the movement of enemy artillerymen and draw his shooting partner's attention to them. This was certainly the shape of things to come since, although it was not a method taught at Hythe at that time, it was to become standard sniping practice in the next century. Inspired by what he saw, Davidson went on to make a telescopic sight designed to be fitted to rifles.

Russian rifle pits (which were successfully taken) at Sebastopol on November 20, 1854. Marksmen of the 1st Rifles were awarded eight Victoria Cross medals during the Crimean War, more than any other regiment.

In open battle the Russian infantry, mainly armed with muskets, found that they were hopelessly outgunned by the British and French riflemen. When advancing in close order they found themselves taking massive casualties at ranges that had never before been reached by small arms fire.

While some engagements in the Crimea were still fought on traditional "Napoleonic" lines, men soon learned to avoid becoming a target. Now ordinary soldiers—rather than just skirmishers—became more adept at taking shelter, keeping low, and firing from cover whenever possible. Although the fixed trench lines of World War I were not present yet, the use of rifle pits, redoubts, artillery embrasures, and other quickly erected fortified positions became commonplace.

The Russians did have a few specialist rifle units of their own. Most of these riflemen acted in the traditional rifleman role as skirmishers and sharpshooters. These men achieved some success, but their heavy, large-caliber weapons were already outdated and outranged

ABOVE: *In the American Civil War some units—like the zouaves—were still turned out in brightly colored uniforms, making them easier targets.* (Roy Daines)

by the more modern weapons of their opponents, and the Russians were outgunned by the sheer volume of long-range rifle fire that the British and French Armies could now generate.

The Crimean War effectively ended the reign of the sharpshooters of the American Civil War. Lessons in military tactics and the advances in small arms technology were there for all to see in the Crimea. Newspaper coverage had reported the events worldwide, and many European soldiers who had fought in the war made their way over to the Americas, looking for a new life. Yet, less than ten years later, at the opening of the American Civil War, it seemed like all lessons had been forgotten. Now both sides were armed with percussion rifles, yet still they followed Napoleonic drill and marched out against one another in close ranks—some units even wearing the colorful and exceedingly impractical uniforms of exotic European colonial troops, such as the zouaves.

It was reported that at the first Battle of Bull Run (Manassas) the first great battle of the war, some congressmen and other leading dignitaries and ordinary citizens turned out in their finery to observe the spectacle…they were undoubtedly shocked by what they saw, as some 3,500 men were killed or wounded in the battle. Bearing in mind that the armies of both sides were relatively inexperienced, these losses were high, and this was just a foretaste of the carnage that was to follow.

Even though some smoothbore muskets were in use throughout the war, the majority of soldiers on both sides were armed with rifles. In some units, on both sides, these were the same models that had been used by the

British in the Crimea—the Enfield 1853 Rifled Muskets. These were either imported legally or illegally from Britain, and were estimated at numbering close on 900,000 by the end of the war. The only rifle used in the war that surpassed this total was the Springfield Model 1861 Rifled Musket, which was the main firearm of the Federal armies, but was also used in some numbers by the Confederacy.

Now that almost every man had a rifle, the difference between the ordinary soldier and the dedicated sharpshooter became more delineated by factors other than the weapon they carried. It is true that many expert marksmen would end up using very specialized arms and equipment, but the main distinction would be their advanced skills in shooting.

ABOVE: *The Enfield percussion rifle was the British standard issue weapon and was also used in large numbers by both sides in the American Civil War.* (Roy Daines)

LEFT: *The percussion lock on a reproduction Springfield rifle.*

THE SPRINGFIELD MODELS 1861 AND 1863 RIFLED MUSKETS

ABOVE: *The Springfield 1861 rifled musket was the Union Army's most widely used firearm.* (Courtesy of Davide Pedersoli)

Commonly referred to simply as the "Springfield," as its name suggests, the Model 1861 rifled musket was made in the Springfield Armory, Massachusetts, but orders were also subcontracted out to private companies to meet the Civil War demand. Over 750,000 Model 1861s were eventually made throughout the course of the war (nearly 500,000 being made under contract), but production of its derivative, the Model 1863 musket (270,000), pushed the total number of Springfields produced to over a million. The Springfield was

the most widely issued rifled musket in the Union Army, and was also one of the most popular with the Confederate forces, who took them from captured men and arsenals, or simply picked them up off the battlefield.

The rifle used a percussion cap lock, and fired a .58-caliber Minié bullet from its 40-inch barrel, which had three-groove 1:72 rifling. Overall length was 56 inches and weight was around nine pounds. Maximum effective range was reckoned to be 500 yards, although most ordinary soldiers would only be expected to hit

a man-sized target out to 300 yards. This was reflected in the graduations of the two flip-up leaf sights, while the battle sight was 100 yards.

The Model 1863 was basically an improved version of the Model 1861 with several modifications. Based on the "Special Contract" Model 1861 rifles made under contract by Colt, the changes included a case-hardened lock, redesigned hammer, shorter nipple bolster, and new barrel bands and ramrod.

OVERLEAF: *A dead Rebel sharpshooter in Devil's Den at Gettysburg in July 1863.* (NA)

ABOVE: *Even though everybody was armed with rifles, not much marksmanship training was actually given on either side during the Civil War.* (Roy Daines)

ABOVE RIGHT: *Both North and South had "natural" sharpshooters in their ranks from the very start.* (Roy Daines)

RIGHT: *With rifled arms, the potential was there for any good shot to become a "sharpshooter."* (Roy Daines)

OVERLEAF: *Berdan Sharpshooters wore green uniforms and usually carried Sharps rifles.* (1st US Sharpshooters UK)

At the beginning of the war, as men rushed to enlist in the opposing armies, they would usually join units that bore the name of their home state or town, but some would be attracted to many of the independent companies that bore more adventurous titles, quite a few of them incorporating the word "Sharpshooters." There's no doubt that many of these were sharpshooter units in name only. It is equally certain that some sharpshooter units actually did field a fair percentage of good marksmen, especially those recruited from areas where men were naturally at home with a rifle; but this didn't always mean that they would be used as such, because either way most army commanders would have just regarded them all as ordinary infantry.

Later, there would be specialist units formed and trained for precision shooting, but in the meantime sharpshooters would be chosen from the ranks—just as they had been in the Crimea and previous wars—because they exhibited a natural expertise.

Some of these men would not only be good shots, but would also feel at home in the field and take advantage of their surroundings—in short, they would have the skills of the hunter, just like the professional jägers, chasseurs, caçadores, and cacciatori from the various armies of Europe. The big difference was that, in

a land that still had a hostile frontier and lots of wild country—even in the settled areas—there would be more expert marksmen than in any other previous war.

The war had barely started before the first high-ranking staff officer—Confederate General Robert S. Garnett—fell to a Federal sharpshooter's bullet, on July 13, 1861. This went somewhat against the grain, since the Southern states were reckoned to have more natural sharpshooters at the start of the war, but Union officers would also come under conspicuously accurate fire soon enough.

In the meantime moves were already afoot to provide the Union forces with a whole regiment of skilled marksmen. Hiram Berdan, a competitive target shooter and a man of some wealth and political influence, had approached President Lincoln and the secretary of war in June 1861 with his idea of recruiting men that were already of a high standard of marksmanship. He was given permission to form the 1st U.S. Sharpshooter Regiment (unofficially known as Berdan's Sharpshooters) of ten companies and was commissioned as commander with the rank of colonel.

Hunters, competitive target shooters, and other experienced riflemen of the Northern States flocked to Berdan's well-publicized enlistment drives, and for the first time each man had to achieve a minimum standard

ABOVE: *The sharpshooters sometimes used heavy-barreled scoped rifles for extra-long-range shots.* (1st US Sharpshooters UK)

of accuracy before he was accepted into the ranks. Berdan's expectations of his men were high: "…no man will be received into the Corps, who does not come fully up to my requirements: every man must be good for a 50-inch string. Such a Corps would, I consider it safe to say, be relied upon, firing from a rest, to hit a man of ordinary size: every time at ·¼ of a mile, and three out of five times at ½ a mile. Many of them would do as well, if not better than this off-hand." These were high standards indeed for the time.

The actual test Berdan set was that a potential recruit had to aggregate fifty inches from dead center with ten shots at 200 yards—which, in simple terms, meant putting ten shots into a ten-inch ring—using his own or the company's rifle (fitted with aperture or telescopic sights) from a rested position. The original intention was that each man would bring his own rifle and carry it into battle, but some of the firearms were elaborate target rifles that were far too heavy (up to thirty pounds) for practical soldiering.

The recruitment drive was very successful and had so many qualifying riflemen that the 2nd Sharpshooter Regiment was formed, being fully enrolled with eight companies by January 1862. There would have been ten companies, but two companies from Massachusetts, known as "Andrews Sharpshooters," who had passed

Berdan's tests and were due to join the 2nd U.S. Sharpshooters, changed their minds and instead became sharpshooters for their state's own regiments.

The sharpshooters received thorough training in marksmanship with the rifle—which would seem obvious, but was not the case with most Union soldiers. They were also taught to keep low when under fire, make use of cover, and choose their targets carefully. The idea was that they would not be used as line infantry, but rather act independently in groups, from four-man squads right up to company strength or more, doing the most damage they could wherever it seemed necessary. Although they would sometimes act as skirmishers in the sense that they were maneuverable, and could protect advances and withdrawals with accurate fire, they were not quite like the European model of light infantry. Instead, they would be far more concerned with dispatching long-range strategic targets such as officers, NCOs, artillerymen, scouts, pickets, and of course, enemy sharpshooters.

The sharpshooters dressed in green uniforms, this now becoming somewhat of a tradition with specialist riflemen, and, like jägers and the British rifle regiments, they took orders by bugle call rather than drum. They also wore high leather gaiters and carried distinctive knapsacks made of

HIRAM BERDAN, CASPER TREPP, AND CALIFORNIA JOE

At the beginning of the Civil War, the Confederate forces had the greater number of sharpshooters within their ranks. In order to redress this imbalance, Hiram Berdan (1824–1893), a wealthy inventor and a crack shot, used his political influence to persuade the government to allow him to establish a regiment of Union sharpshooters. Recruited from across the Northern states, and meeting specific marksmanship restrictions, these men became the U.S. Sharpshooters, with Berdan as their commander with the rank of colonel.

Although undoubtedly a great marksman—which he was always keen to demonstrate—and equally passionate about his sharpshooter regiments, Berdan was not a military man as such, spending much of his time fighting bureaucratic battles behind the lines, rather than on them. Regardless of this, he made sure his men were well equipped and well trained, and had officers worthy of their title, thereby ensuring the loyalty of his men and his lasting recognition as the creator of Berdan's Sharpshooters. He left the army in January 1864, and went on to experiment with weapons and ammunition. He filed several important patents, including one for a repeating rifle and another for metallic cartridge primers.

Another famous officer of the Sharpshooters was Casper Trepp (1829–63), a Swiss-born marksman who had served as an officer with the British in the Crimean War. It may have been Trepp who originally suggested the idea of a sharpshooting regiment to Hiram Berdan. He certainly took a role within the 1st U.S. Sharpshooters once formed, being the first captain of Company A, and eventually becoming a lieutenant colonel and taking command of the regiment.

Trepp was an experienced infantryman and had seen the out-of-date Napoleonic battle tactics of European armies, as well as the increased range and accuracy of the latest rifles. He understood what potential advantage could be gained if a whole army could be fielded with these weapons, and the skills to use them correctly. This was never going to happen with the vast armies of

the North, but even just a regiment or two of U.S. Sharpshooters would be a tremendous benefit. Having witnessed how British rifle regiments operated, he may also be credited with the methods adopted by the Union sharpshooters; harassing the enemy at distance with accurate rifle fire; operating in small groups, often under their own initiative; and using the terrain and its features to the maximum advantage.

Casper Trepp proved himself to be a competent officer as well as a visionary in his modern approach to infantry tactics. Unfortunately, his promising career was brought to an end when he was killed at the Battle of Mine Run, November 30, 1863. Ironically, it was said that he was hit by a shot from a Confederate sharpshooter.

The most famous enlisted man in the U.S. Sharpshooters—and possibly the most famous marksman in the whole army—was Truman Head (1809–88), also known as "California Joe," a colorful character by any standards. He signed up in 1861 claiming to be forty-two years of age—he was a mere ten years older, but then it was not unusual for men to lie about their age, either up or down, in order to qualify for service.

When enlisting, Head stated his profession as "hunter," and it was claimed that he hunted bear. He was certainly a crack shot with the Sharps rifle that he had privately purchased. The Union was looking for new "heroes" to distract from their poor start to the war and attract new recruits to the army, and Truman fitted the bill. Having been successful at gold panning in California, he was saddled with the sobriquet "California Joe" in Northern newspapers that recounted his exploits with relish.

The Sharps was not the only rifle that Head used: he was also a noted marksman with a scoped target rifle. This may have been his own, or more likely was one of the regiment's heavy muzzleloading target rifles, carried in the sharpshooters' baggage train and used only when they weren't on the move. It is not recorded what manufacture these were, but they were weighty at around thirty pounds, and had a hexagonal barrel mounted with a 7x magnification brass

scope. Head is said to have made a half-mile shot with this set-up, hitting a Confederate artillery officer—the sharpshooter's favorite prey—and effectively silencing that particular battery.

Although he enlisted for three years, Head was discharged in November 1862 for "senility and impaired vision," which may not have had the same serious connotations that they appear to have today. He certainly lived for another twenty-six years, after once again having served his country working for the Customs in San Francisco.

ABOVE LEFT: *Hiram Berdan recruited men of a high standard of marksmanship to form the 1st U.S. Sharpshooter Regiment—Berdan's Sharpshooters—with himself as commander, with the rank of colonel.* (NA)

ABOVE RIGHT: *"California Joe" was one of the most colorful characters of the Berdan Sharpshooters.* (NA)

BELOW: *U.S. Sharpshooters (reenactors) reloading their rifles in the considerable smoke of battle.* (Roy Daines)

ABOVE: *The Berdan Sharpshooters would usually operate on the fringes of the main army.* (1st US Sharpshooters UK)

unscraped calf skin. Perhaps their most distinguishing feature was that they were all armed with breechloading Sharps rifles (after trying other models), unlike the majority of the Union infantrymen, who carried muzzleloading rifles. There had been a struggle with the army to get the Sharps rifle issued, partly because of the cost—around $40 for the Sharps compared to $16 to $20 for a Springfield rifled musket, depending on grade (how well it was made), and partly because the Sharps factory was too busy making carbines for cavalry regiments. It is said that President Lincoln himself intervened, but whatever influence was brought to bear, Berdan finally equipped his men with one of the finest rifles of its day.

The M1859 Sharps .52-caliber was a reasonable extra-long-range rifle—though it couldn't match the precision of a target rifle. Where it did excel was as a fast-firing and exceptionally accurate mid-to-long-range rifle (certainly out to 500 yards). The breechloading Sharps could rattle off five shots or more in the time that it took to load and fire a muzzleloader once. When used in numbers, the fast and accurate fire of the Sharps could be devastatingly effective in breaking up all but the most determined of attacks.

The sharpshooters also had "artillery" in reserve—this was the name given to heavy-barreled, muzzleloading target rifles fitted with either aperture (globe) or

telescopic sights and used for particularly long-range work. Some of these telescopic-sighted models were Morgan James rifles, but there were others of various manufacture, privately owned by individual soldiers. Some of these rifles could weigh anything between twelve to thirty pounds or even more, the heavier models being too weighty to be carried as a standard firearm. So these would be kept in the regiment's supply wagons until needed, then returned once the job was done.

In terms of effectiveness it has been claimed that Berdan's sharpshooters killed more of the enemy than any other regiment in the Union army. Although this is difficult to quantify, it is probably correct, considering that the sharpshooters took part in sixty-five battles and other engagements, and all men in the regiment were tested marksmen. By contrast, most Union troops would have been lucky to have fired five rounds in target practice with their issued military rifle before being sent into battle.

Other independent Union sharpshooter units were also formed, mainly at company strength, although some states fielded larger units of sharpshooters, such as the Bucktails from Pennsylvania. This was a rifle battalion organized by Thomas Kane with the permission of the Pennsylvania governor. Their name came from the deer's tail that they wore on their forage caps, implying that

THE "BERDAN" SHARPS MODEL 1859 RIFLE

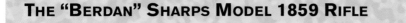

ABOVE: *The breechloading Berdan Sharps was very similar to the Model 1859 rifle.*

This single-shot, capping, breechloading rifle with falling block action was designed by Christian Sharps. It had a 30-inch barrel in .52-caliber, with six-groove 1:48 rifling, an overall length of 47 inches and a weight of around ten pounds. When the trigger guard under-lever was pulled down the block dropped, exposing the barrel's breech. A paper cartridge was loaded, and the lever pulled back up, raising the block, which sheared through the end of the paper cartridge, exposing the powder in the now-closed breech.

The special Sharps used by Berdan's Sharpshooters was a basic breechloading Model 1859 rifle but was fitted with a double-set trigger and finer graduated sights. It had no bayonet lug (but it accepted a socket bayonet). On the set trigger mechanism, the first trigger was used to set the second, which then became a "hair trigger," requiring very little pressure to release the external hammer, which would ignite the percussion cap and discharge the rifle. This helped accuracy, as did the fact that, the rifle being a breechloader, the bullet could be made to fit the bore perfectly. In close-range action, when speed was of the essence, the first trigger on the double-set mechanism could be ignored and the user could just pull the second trigger (though the let off weight would be substantially heavier).

During the Civil War more than 11,000 Sharps rifles were purchased by the Federal government. To put a fairly common misconception right, the term "sharpshooter" has nothing to do with the Sharps rifle; the term is a corruption of *Scharfschütze*, the German word for marksman, and was in use long before the Sharps rifle was even thought of.

ABOVE: *Detail of a set trigger (double-blade "hair" trigger) on a reproduction Sharps rifle.*

BELOW: *A combined force of Union marksmen; Berdan's Sharpshooters and Bucktails, mainly armed with Sharps rifles (reenactment).* (Roy Daines)

THE WHITWORTH RIFLE

This exceptionally accurate percussion rifle was invented by Sir Joseph Whitworth (1803–87), one of the leading British engineers of his time. He was commissioned by Lord Hardinge, commander-in-chief of the British Army, to design a rifle to replace the P53 Enfield. The famous gunsmith, Westley Richards, was appointed to assist Whitworth, who was a superb engineer but was not accustomed to designing guns.

The design was unique: a muzzleloading firearm with hexagonal rifling (rather than grooves), taking a matching hexagonal bullet. The 33-inch barrel had a fast rifling twist of 1:20 and a bore of just 0.451 inches. Overall length was 52½ inches, and weight was approximately nine pounds.

In tests at Hythe in 1857 the Whitworth proved to have far superior accuracy than the P53, especially at extended ranges. The test was the average in inches of ten shots measured from the center of the bull when fired from a rest. At that time the best performance of any military rifle at 500 yards was 27 inches. On the day, the Whitworth dramatically reduced that to just 4½ inches, with the Enfield making a respectable 28¾ inches. The Whitworth continued giving a superior performance to the P53 at 800, 1,000, 1,400 (where the P53 performed so badly it dropped out of the equation), and 1,800 yards (the P53 wasn't even tested at

this range). Despite this amazing performance, the Whitworth's hexagonal bore was prone to fouling in the recesses of the angles. For this reason it was rejected by the British Army, but went on to have great success as a competition target arm—and as a specialist sharpshooter's weapon with the Confederate army.

Some of the weapons that found their way to the Southern states were used with ordinary leaf sights, others with "globe" (aperture) target sights, and some with optical sights. The most common optical sight fitted to this rifle was the side-mounted "Davidson Telescopic Rifle Sight," which was a fairly short model (14½ inches) compared with many others of the time that extended almost the whole barrel length. Although it undoubtedly worked, the side mounting made it extremely difficult to get a correct head position while still maintaining a natural shooting position—all good rifles are designed to put the shooter's eye "naturally" behind the sights on top of the barrel. (Author's note: I am a right-handed shooter, and having tried aiming a rifle fitted with a side-mounted replica of a Malcolm barrel-length telescopic sight, I can say that, although the sight picture was surprisingly good for such a long tube, actually getting my head lined up was extremely difficult. However, the owner showed me how he

coped—he simply used his left eye instead of his right. Although we couldn't fire the rifle at the time, he said he had obtained good results with it.)

When the Whitworths were purchased by the Confederacy—at a claimed $1,000 apiece, including scope, they also came with 1,000 rounds of ammunition. It has been said that when the sharpshooters ran out of hexagonal Whitworth bullets, they substituted Minié balls and had no great loss in accuracy.

The Whitworth proved to be a highly effective long-range rifle, which claimed many Union lives, including those of General Lytle at Chickamauga and General Sedgwick at Spotsylvania.

ABOVE LEFT: *The Davidson Telescopic Rifle Sight fitted on the side of the rifle by detachable mounts, as can be seen from these views.*

ABOVE RIGHT: *The distinctive hexagonal rifling (and ramrod) of the Whitworth rifle.*

BELOW LEFT: *The Whitworth used a percussion lock action.*

BELOW: *Packs of Whitworth cartridges.* (Graham Lay)

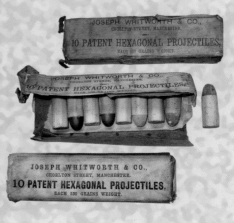

these men had the skills of the deer hunter—and many of them probably did. They followed the path of most state sharpshooting units of the Union, being used mainly as ordinary infantry, even though they were issued with Sharps rifles later in the war. Their fame came not so much from their sharpshooting skills—although this was recognized—but from their courageous involvement in many of the great battles of the war and their easily recognized "bucktail" adornment.

Confederate sharpshooters may not have been as organized as their Union counterparts, but they were certainly as skilled and in some cases better equipped for their long-range shooting duties. As mentioned previously, it was generally regarded that standards of marksmanship among the Southern regiments was higher than in the Northern states. The commanders would soon come to recognize which of their men "stood out" as exceptional shots, and these would be assigned the role of sharpshooters when a particularly difficult shot had to be taken. As always, many of these men were hunters, and therefore their fieldcraft skills would qualify them as good scouts and skirmishers too.

The general infantry long arms of the South included the Enfield P53, Springfield rifled muskets, 1841 Mississippi rifle, and virtually any other serviceable firearm that was available. Of these the Enfield was probably the most used sharpshooter weapon, partly because it was the most commonly available, but also

because it had an excellent sighting system for a military rifle of the time.

A few Southern sharpshooters carried target-style rifles fitted with either telescopic sights or precision aperture sights (known as globe sights). Although often mentioned, these must have been few and far between, and were probably privately owned rather than issued.

A number of British-made Whitworth rifles, and the similar Kerr target rifles, were actually issued by the Confederate army and effectively used by its sharpshooters, sometimes with standard sights,

ABOVE: *When used as ordinary infantry, the Sharpshooters lost their greatest advantages—long-range accuracy and their ability to stay out of the direct line of fire.* (Roy Daines)

BELOW: *A Confederate sharpshooter (reenactor) with a side-mounted scope on his rifle.* (Roy Daines)

ABOVE: *A "Bucktail" sharpshooter (reenactor) takes aim at advancing Confederates.* (Roy Daines)

RIGHT: *Exceptional marksmen in the Confederate ranks would soon be assigned the role of sharpshooters.* (Roy Daines)

FAR RIGHT: *A Confederate sharpshooter (reenactor) with reproduction scoped rifle.* (John Norris)

sometimes with enhanced target-sighting systems, including telescopic sights. Some of these were the side-mounted "Davidson Telescopic Rifle Sight" invented by a British Army officer. This sight was fairly unusual for its day, being only 14½ inches long, with a tube of just under one-inch diameter, whereas most other scopes were usually as long (or longer) than the barrels of the guns they were attached to.

Typical of these longer "barrel-length" optical sights was the scope manufactured by William Malcolm of Syracuse, New York. This was simply a ¾-inch diameter brass tube containing a magnifying lens system and cross-wire reticle (cross-hair) aiming mark. The front mount could be used for coarse windage during zero alignment, but elevation and all fine adjustment for zeroing or point-of-aim correction were done on the rear base unit.

Magnification of the target was the greatest advantage of the telescopic sight over the aperture target sight but, even so, most early scopes were fairly low-powered at between 3x and 7x. Even so, it helped the sharpshooter observe as well as aim. (Author's note: Having watched modern competitive shooters using both 19th Century aperture sights and telescopic sights on Sharps rifles at ranges up to 600 yards, I'd say there's little in it when it comes to placing the shot—but at longer

distances perhaps the scope would gain points for its magnification of the target.)

Some Confederate sharpshooters worked better singly, while others worked in pairs, much like their modern counterparts, especially when using heavy-barreled, target-type rifles. There would be one man spotting and offering covering fire if needed, while the other took the long-range shots. Other outfits would use a variation on the skirmishing tactics used by light infantrymen, operating in sections of four, alternately firing, loading, and covering each other.

As the Russians and British had done in the Crimea, when statically engaged in defense or siege, both sides in the Civil War used rifle-pits to get close enough to

AN EXPERIMENT IN MARKSMANSHIP–RECREATING THE LONG-RANGE SHOT AT PRESIDENT LINCOLN

In July 1864, forces from Confederate General Jubal A. Early's Army of Northern Virginia were on the outskirts of Washington, D.C., the Federal capital. President Lincoln visited Fort Stevens, one of the defensive positions, "to see what was going on." Despite several Union soldiers already having been hit by long-range sharpshooter fire, and ignoring warnings for his own safety, the president stood on a parapet in open view of the distant "Rebs" and immediately drew the attention of their sharpshooters, although it is highly unlikely that they recognized him—even if using a telescopic sight. Several shots whizzed past, one striking a cannon barrel and ricocheting into an unlucky army surgeon. Lincoln was unharmed and finally took the advice of his staff to remove himself from harm's way.

In a TV series on unique shooting incidents in history, including the assassinations of several American presidents, British shooting expert, writer, and broadcaster Michael Yardley attempted to recreate the Confederate attempt on President Lincoln's life at Fort Stevens, using the most accurate weapon of the Confederate sharpshooters—a Whitworth rifle. Yardley had this to say, "I made a documentary for the Discovery Channel some years ago concerning the attempted long-range shooting of Abraham Lincoln. It appears that a Confederate sniper may

have taken a pot shot at Lincoln when he was observing a battle (caused by Confederate General Jubal Anderson Early's raid on Washington, D.C., in 1864). Lincoln had to duck to avoid being shot while observing the ensuing battle from a parapet of Fort Stevens (becoming the first president of the United States to come under fire whilst in office).

"We recreated the incident using a Whitworth rifle (because it was known that the Confederacy had bought a small number of these for sniping purposes at great cost), although there was no direct evidence that one was actually used in the Fort Stevens incident. We conducted initial experiments on the ranges of the Blackwater training facility in North Carolina and, later, moved to Western Pennsylvania. Although, I am a trained rifle marksman, I had to familiarize myself with the black-powder, muzzleloading Whitworth and its unusual hexagonal rifling and bullet. We found that we could not get good accuracy by paper patching the bullets, but found that we obtained excellent results with simple beeswax and tallow.

"The rifle is inherently extremely accurate. Once suitable loads had been developed we considered the sighting system. Early in our experiments we tried a short (twelve inches or so) side-mounted telescopic sight of contemporary manufacture. It proved to be completely impractical because of the

required changes in elevation. Optically, it was just about adequate. Although optical sights were sometimes used by Civil War snipers, I could see no practical advantage in using them. We managed two-inch groups with open sights at 100 yards, achieving excellent results at 400 yards as well. On our first attempt using the raised ladder sight, we managed three out of four hits on a man-sized silhouette at 800 yards, and a first shot 'kill' at 1,000. What did strike me however was that no long-range shooting could be done with raised metallic sights with the head on the stock—the elevation was simply too great. This opens an interesting debate on how early snipers actually used their weapons. The same comments would also apply to big bore, low stocked, breechloaders."

TOP LEFT: *A scoped rifle was tried, but good results came just using the standard iron sights.*

TOP RIGHT: *Michael Yardley indicates the strikes achieved on a man-sized silhouette target.*

ABOVE LEFT: *A spent Whitworth bullet recovered from the target.*

ABOVE RIGHT: *Fort Stevens, a defensive position on the outskirts of Washington, where President Lincoln was almost hit by a sharpshooter's bullet. (NA)*

snipe effectively, but not close enough to attract the massed fire of the enemy. Sometimes these were properly excavated earthworks, but more often than not they were just fox-holes, dug at night, with the removed dirt being thrown in front as a low screen, enough to conceal a man, but not making enough difference to the terrain to attract the attention of a vigilant enemy.

In these cases the shooter with a breechloader would have a considerable advantage over one with a muzzleloader. The breechloading rifle could be reloaded easily from virtually any shooting position—including prone. The most effective stance for recharging a muzzleloader was standing up; in any other position it involved at best an awkward and lengthy procedure, and at worst it could expose the user to enemy fire. With a muzzleloader, even when trying to reload from a kneeling or prone position in light cover, the movement of the weapon and extended arm action required could easily attract the attention of an enemy sharpshooter.

Many contemporary prints and drawings show Civil War marksmen firing from the branches of trees, but the resultant smoke from their black powder weapons would surely have attracted the attention of opposing sharpshooters. One shot may have been safe enough if the surrounding battle was generating lots of smoke, but any more would have been inviting return fire. When fired

during a quiet period, even a single shot with its accompanying "give-away" smoke and flash could have proved disastrous for the sharpshooter if spotted. Of course, the trunk of the tree might have given some protection from enemy fire to the front, but the sniper would still have been open to flanking fire. Once again, the man armed with a breechloader would have had an advantage; the best precision shooting with a

ABOVE: *Snipers would often work in teams, sometimes spotting for one another or just covering the shooter's back.* (Roy Daines)

BELOW: *Civil War sniper with long barrel-mounted Malcolm-type optical sight.*

ABOVE: *Sharpshooters in a well-prepared earthwork.*

RIGHT: *Gun emplacements were the natural targets of sharpshooters.* (NA)

FAR RIGHT: *A Union soldier (reenactor) using a heavy target rifle with scope.* (Richard Clark)

OVERLEAF: *Massed artillery, with its attendant bombardiers and officers, was probably the prime target for sharpshooters.* (Roy Daines)

muzzleloader required correct loading procedure, which could be ponderous enough when standing at a firing bench let alone while trying to balance in a tree.

When engaging artillery, sharpshooters proved particularly successful. Distance provided less protection for the gunners, as the effective range of a standard infantry rifle matched that of some field batteries. With men and equipment exposed and concentrated in a relatively small area, artillery batteries made good targets. At distances of 500 yards or so, sharpshooters could down any man servicing unprotected artillery. This made life particularly difficult for light artillery units. In a traditional battle scenario they would gallop to wherever they were needed, rake the enemy lines with fire, then withdraw just as quickly. But in this new war there were times when they suffered so many casualties from rifle fire that they didn't get any effective shots off at all. Only artillery positions with embrasures or earthworks offered any real protection, and even then the gunners had to make best use of the cover, as exposure of any kind would almost certainly attract a shot. Horses and caissons were also prime targets, for without them no field battery could function.

When faced with bombardment at extreme range, a strategy borrowed from the British was to measure the range and angle required for a given long-distance target then "volley fire" with a whole group of marksmen to increase the chances of hits. This was not sharpshooting as such, since an individual wasn't targeted, but it achieved the same result of eliminating an objective at extended ranges.

CONTINUED ON PAGE 84

ABOVE: *Dead soldiers in a well-fortified dug-out.* (NA)

PREVIOUS PAGES: *Even by the time of the American Civil War, men would still advance against each other "shoulder to shoulder" in waves.* (Roy Daines)

BELOW: *Major General John Sedgwick was shot dead by a Confederate sharpshooter although he thought he was out of range.* (NA)

yards an American bison target just under life size, silhouetted in solid black, looks like a slightly irregular shaped "full stop"). Yet even with the looping trajectory of a heavy caliber Minié bullet, if a skilled marksman with his Enfield rifle could lob a round onto an eight-foot-square target at 900 yards, then a small group of men would make a very tempting target. Even at this extreme range it could result in a hit; for the sharpshooter it was certainly worth a bullet to find out.

If the target men were mounted on horses the overall target would be even bigger—and it would almost certainly have been an officer, or artillery, or cavalry with an officer. If the shot only struck a horse or if a low-ranked man was hit, it might at least make the group uncomfortable or force them to take cover. If an officer was hit then it would not only cause problems with the chain of command, but it would probably be believed that he was being personally and deliberately aimed for—making it even more unnerving, plus giving greater credence and kudos to the shooting abilities of the enemy snipers. Many times during the war—and many times before and since, a hit from "out of the blue" was claimed as the work of a sharpshooter, when in fact it could have been a chance shot from an ordinary infantryman or even a stray bullet.

This was certainly not the case when Union Major General John Sedgwick was shot dead by a Confederate sharpshooter at Spotsylvania on May 9, 1864, after uttering the immortal words, "Why, they couldn't hit an elephant at this dist…." This shot, estimated at 880 yards (approximately half a mile), was deliberately aimed by a sharpshooter who was using a Whitworth rifle. Amazing as it may seem, deliberately aimed shots at this distance—with a fair share of successful hits—were well documented for both Union and Confederate sharpshooters using scoped target rifles. With such accurate shooting, and with high ranking officers still taking to the field in virtually every engagement, it is not surprising that sharpshooters were directly and correctly attributed with the deaths of more than twenty generals, dozens of majors and colonels, and countless lower ranked officers.

The American Civil War was the testing ground for many advances in the technology of warfare. As far as sniping is concerned, the introduction of accurate, long-range, breechloading rifles and rifle-mounted optical sights were probably the most important developments at the time, but metallic cartridges, smokeless powder, and repeating rifles—all introduced in this period—would also make their mark later.

As well as this improvement in equipment, the period probably defines the point in time when at least some sharpshooters actually took on the complete role of the modern sniper—even though the term "sniper" itself was not in common usage yet. The main duty of the Civil War

A similar tactic could be used by single sharpshooters at extended ranges by aiming generally at groups, rather than at specific individuals, to increase the size of their target. If men had been at such a distance that they did not feel exposed or vulnerable, they would surely have been considerably shaken if one of their number had been hit.

Without a telescopic sight to magnify the target, or an aperture sight to "concentrate" the aim, it would have been very difficult to distinguish man-sized targets with the naked eye at ranges over 800 yards or so (at 1,000

sharpshooter was to cause as much damage and havoc among the enemy as he could, and it would prove to be a vitally important role in this conflict. When removing officers and NCOs the chain of command could be broken; shooting pickets, flag bearers, signalers, drummers, and buglers disrupted communications and lowered the enemy morale; putting a steady fire on artillery in the field could either eliminate or discourage the artillerymen; shooting wagon drivers, draft horses, and pack mules could disrupt supply lines and immobilize a whole army. At the same time, the accurate "countering" of enemy sharpshooters could stop them doing all of the above to your own side.

Despite their obvious successes, the sharpshooters still weren't being used to their maximum potential. While the U.S. sharpshooter regiments were a grand idea, and may have worked even better if they had been used as originally intended, eventually the army was always going to use a large body of men as just another infantry unit. The army certainly didn't value such regiments enough to keep them established after the war. Perhaps the more fluid Confederate model was better, either by choice or circumstance, with single sharpshooters or pairs or sometimes groups being attached to larger units and being allowed to take on any targets they thought would be worthwhile.

Despite all the lessons learned, the U.S. Army still didn't train sharpshooters in the broader role of snipers that we now have as a specific tool of infantry units. Apart from standard marksmanship training, there would not be an American sniper school until the next century.

Less than twenty years after the American Civil War and some 8,000 miles away, the British would once again be fighting a major conflict, and learning more lessons in rifle craft from an enemy who had virtually a whole army of crack shots.

Sharpshooters on horseback

The First Anglo-Boer War (1880–81) began when the Boers of the Transvaal (South Africa), who were mainly of Dutch and German descent, declared independence from Great Britain. They were later joined by some Boers from the Orange Free State. In a conflict of sieges, it was the successful Boer tactics in small engagements on open ground that brought the war to a rapid conclusion.

At this time, although general British Army tactics had evolved because of the many small colonial wars, the average soldier remained better trained for pitched battles than skirmishing, which was still regarded as the province of the light infantry. On the other hand, the Boers, who were mainly farmers, had formed into small groups of fast-moving, horse-mounted "commandos," and were adept at skirmishing tactics. On their vast farms the Boers virtually lived in the saddle, and most were expert hunters, and therefore had excellent stalking and shooting skills. Although they were good horsemen, they didn't take the role of cavalry; instead they operated as

ABOVE: *The sharpshooter was best used as an individual, or in pairs or small groups, taking on targets of opportunity.* (Roy Daines)

OVERLEAF: *Even toward the end of the 19th Century British troops were still wearing scarlet tunics.* (Richard Clark)

THE METALLIC CARTRIDGE AND SMOKELESS POWDER

The invention of the metallic cartridge (the rifle cartridge as we know it today) transformed rifle design, making breechloading much easier and paving the way for multiple-shot rifles in a number of different designs, the most important to us being the magazine-fed rifle.

Basically, the metal cartridge brought all the ammunition components required—the ball or bullet, powder charge, and primer—into one convenient package. By using an expanding metal (usually brass) cartridge case instead of paper or linen, the breech could be effectively sealed when the charge was detonated, since the metal cartridge expanded to fit the breech perfectly, permitting gasses from the detonation to go only one way, straight up the barrel behind the bullet.

The first design to see popular acceptance was the pin-fire cartridge system, invented in France in the middle of the 19th Century. The pin-fire was so called because it had a small pin at the bottom of the cartridge which was struck by the firearm's hammer in order to ignite the self-contained percussion cap. This system worked, but it was more suited to pistols than to rifles, and was soon superseded by metallic expanding cartridges with a recessed percussion cap in the base (center-fire) or the bottom rim (rimfire), which were struck by a striker or firing pin in the rifle's action. By the third quarter of the 19th Century, all major military powers were using metallic cartridges and breechloading rifles.

The basic design of center-fire cartridges has changed little over the intervening years, apart from some of the materials used, perhaps the most important being smokeless powder. This was a chemical propellant that could be substituted for gunpowder.

When "guncotton", a gunpowder substitute, was invented by Christian Friedrich Schönbein in 1846 it was far too powerful and unstable to be used in small arms. It was not until 1884 that Paul Marie

Eugène Vieille would invent a way of producing a smokeless powder (which he called Poudre B) that was very safe to handle and offered many advantages over gunpowder. It was far more powerful, allowing less powder to be used yet still giving higher power. This in turn influenced the design of rifles, with smaller, higher-velocity calibers proving as effective as the larger predecessors, thereby allowing more ammunition to be carried by the average soldier. It allowed rapid volley fire with breechloaders, as there was no dense cloud of smoke to obscure aim, and it would also still work if damp—unlike gunpowder, which had to be kept bone dry—so it was easier to store and transport.

It was first used by the French in the bolt-action, tubular-magazine Lebel rifle in 1886, although other countries soon developed their own smokeless powders with cartridges and rifles that could fully exploit this great advance in small arms technology.

The importance of smokeless powder to the sniper cannot be overestimated; it did not emit a cloud of smoke when fired, so it would not give the sniper's position away. It was cleaner burning than gunpowder, with far less fouling of the bore, so tolerances could be tighter and allowance didn't have to be made for a quick buildup of powder residue. This led to superior rifle designs. Most significantly, this more efficient smokeless powder—when combined with metallic cartridges and modern rifles—gave greater velocity, flatter trajectory, and subsequently, longer range and more predictable accuracy.

ABOVE: *Four stages in the evolution of metallic cartridges (from left to right): A .577-caliber Snider cartridge; a Zulu War-era rolled brass foil .577/450 Martini-Henry cartridge; a later drawn brass .577/450 Martini-Henry cartridge; and a .303-caliber British Mk VII SAA Ball cartridge. (Commander Zulu)*

mounted infantry, using their horses to quickly traverse the country, but dismounting and engaging the British with long-range rifle fire whenever possible.

For the most part, the British Army in Africa were still wearing bright scarlet tunics and white pith helmets, making them easy targets for modern riflemen. The Boers on the other hand wore clothing that, like their nature, was sober in color and workmanlike. In addition, riding a horse on the dusty veldt (plain) would soon give it an earthy appearance. Over the years the Boers had learned not to wear clothing that attracted the attention of man or beast, and from their hunting and occasional brushes with the local natives they knew how best to use available cover and terrain.

By this time the breechloading rifle and metallic cartridges were in common use, with the Martini-Henry rifle being the standard issue weapon for the British Army, while the Boers used similar falling block rifles and other breechloading designs of both military and sporting origins.

While the British were more used to using their Martini-Henrys from a standing or kneeling position in ranks—which could often prove to be devastating when used against charging Zulus or dervishes – the Boers took best advantage of their breechloaders and fired them from a prone position whenever possible. This not only gave them more chance of an accurate hit—prone being the most stable shooting position—but also made them a much smaller target for return fire.

In this war the Boers also perfected a standard military tactic of today—suppressive fire and movement. In Afrikaans this was called "vuur en bewug" and was used with great effect at Ingogo and Majuba Hill, to move one group of men forward or into advantageous positions while keeping the enemy's "heads down" with sustained accurate fire support.

To get some idea of the superiority of Boer rifle fire and fighting methods, take a look at the following casualty figures for four engagements in two months.

On December 20, 1880, at Bronkhorstspruit, a British Army supply column of 34 wagons with 260 men and 6 officers was engaged by Boers (some say ambushed, but this is not correct). Shooting from a distance of just 200 yards, the Boers took just fifteen minutes to force a surrender, having first killed the draft animals on the first and last wagons, thereby preventing escape, then pouring fire onto the trapped British, causing 157 casualties (77 dead and 80 wounded) with only 2 Boers killed and 5 wounded.

At the battle of Laing's Nek on January 18, 1881, 400 entrenched Boers repelled a British force of around 1,200 men. The British lost 84 killed and 113 wounded, while the Boers had

THE MARTINI-HENRY RIFLE

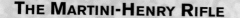

ABOVE: *The Martini-Henry breechloading rifle.*

This rifle used a lever-operated falling block, single-shot, self-cocking action refined by Friedrich von Martini of Switzerland, coupled with a 1:22 seven-groove rifling system designed by a Scotsman, Alexander Henry. It used a .577/450-caliber black powder cartridge, which fired a 480-grain bullet at 900fps. Four gradually altered versions of the Martini-Henry were made over the years, all approximately fifty inches long and weighing around nine pounds or less.

The Martini-Henry had a graduated, sliding-ramp rear sight sighted to 1,400 yards. The rifle had an effective range of 600 yards, and a good infantryman could get off ten rounds a minute with the falling block action, but there were problems with cartridge extraction in some cases. The Martini-Henry was adopted as the standard infantry rifle of the British Army in 1871 and gave good service until gradually being phased out after the introduction of the bolt-action Lee-Metford magazine rifle in 1888.

14 killed and 27 wounded. Both of the main assault commanders were shot, as was Lieutenant Baillie who was carrying the regimental colors; in fact this would be the last time that any British regiment would be allowed to carry its colors into battle.

At the Battle of Ingogo on February 7, 1881, the Boers took on skilled British riflemen, who should have been experts in skirmishing tactics. Here, riflemen of the 3/60th Rifles (King's Royal Rifles) and other troops (approximately 300 in all) with two nine-pound cannons were occupying a ridge on a long, sloping hill called Schuinshoogte, overlooking the Ingogo river. A similar-sized force of Boers attacked them with accurate rifle fire for around five hours until the weather got so bad that the engagement ended. The British were able to abandon their position and withdraw back across the Ingogo. Despite the fact that the 60th Rifles were expert riflemen who wore green uniforms rather than scarlet, and were in an elevated position supported by artillery, they came off far worse. The British casualties were 75 dead (including 9 drowned when washed away by the swollen river during the withdrawal) and 68 wounded. The Boers lost just 8 men killed on the day with another two (of 6 wounded) dying of their wounds later.

Finally, one of the most memorable victories of the Boers was the battle of Majuba Hill on February 27, 1881, when Major-General Sir George Colley led approximately 600 men to the top of the hill overlooking the Boer army's camp. The summit offered a wide perimeter that was thinly defended, and although the British

had been in position all night, no rifle pits had been dug. The Boers stormed the hill, using "vuur en bewug" tactics, with their own marksmen laying down a withering fire on the summit. Keeping to paths that protected them from rifle fire off the summit the Boers crested the hill virtually unscathed. The attacking Boers then started to pick off the defenders at range, causing them to retreat down the rear slope of the hill, where they were once again put under fire from Boers on the summit. The battle lasted for about one hour, during which time the British lost 93 killed (including Sir George Colley) and 133 wounded, with 58 taken prisoner, while the Boers had just one man killed and 5 wounded.

In this and the other engagements during the war all the British infantry were armed with rifles that took a metallic cartridge. However, the Boers had a few such rifles but also used many breechloaders with a paper cartridge and a separate percussion cap, so theoretically would produce a slower rate of fire. The main advantages that the Boers had were that they thoroughly knew their weapons, tactics, and terrain—and how to get the most from them all.

This First Anglo-Boer War was a disastrous campaign by the British Army, and Majuba Hill was one of its worst defeats. However, the public outcry "back home" did at least help increase the British interest in marksmanship. Many civilian rifle clubs and volunteer rifle units sprang up in the 1880s–90s with the slogan "Remember Majuba"—which would once more be heard as a rallying cry when Britain fought the Boer sharpshooters again in the Second Anglo-Boer War.

ABOVE: *Paper cartridge with exposed bullet for a percussion cap breech-loading rifle*

CHAPTER THREE:
A New Century

CHAPTER THREE:
A NEW CENTURY

By the time Britain faced the Boers again in 1899, in what is known as the Second Anglo-Boer War, arms technology had leaped forward once more, and both sides were armed with bolt-action repeating rifles—probably the pinnacle of manually operated, self-loading designs—with smokeless-powder-charged, metallic cartridge ammunition. The British were armed with modern Lee-Enfield rifles, while the Boers had a mixture of arms but crucially including over 30,000 new Mauser Mod.95 8mm rifles, purchased before the outbreak of war by General Joubert, the commander of the Boer army. Other rifles used by the Boers included some Krag-Jørgensens and many Martini-Henrys, the latter having been bought from Britain and Belgium then sold by the Boer government at cost price to its citizens.

The British force was modern and for the most part the soldiers were well trained (although there were some inexperienced volunteers), but they had never before

faced an enemy armed with similar modern weaponry. The Boer commandos on the other hand had generally received no formal military training at all; instead they had learned marksmanship and fieldcraft through hunting, almost from childhood.

After the First Anglo-Boer War, the British should not have been surprised by the tactics and marksmanship of these tough farmers. The British had at last abandoned their scarlet tunics and were now dressed in khaki, which helped make them look less conspicuous. However, early on there were still many casualties because the troops didn't take advantage of cover—something they should have already learned from their adversaries. The British soldiers had also mainly been trained to fight in close order—under a cascading command hierarchy of officers and NCOs—while the Boers could fight in small groups or large, either taking orders or thinking and acting independently to suit the situation. In addition, most British troops were mainly taught to fire in the standing or kneeling stance, but in the African veldt the prone position was the only way to shoot if there was no cover.

The resulting British casualties were just as horrific as in the first war, and this time many of the Boers had accurate Mauser magazine-fed rifles, so they could fire

BOX MAGAZINES AND BOLT ACTIONS

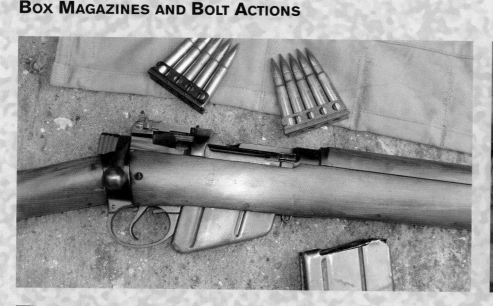

The developments in metallic cartridge ammunition made it possible for practical repeating rifles to be designed for military use. The bolt-action system was mainly used with a box magazine (either fixed or removable), although the first Mauser, the Mod.1871, used black powder cartridges and an eight-round tubular magazine. The bolt-action and box magazine, such as featured in the later Mauser Mod 93 and the British Lee-Metford, were more suited to military use than the alternatives, such as a revolving cylinder (as seen in Colt's 1855 model which was briefly issued to Berdan's Sharpshooters) or the various lever-actions and pump-actions that used tubular magazines. Bolt-actions were quicker to load, safer to use, and were usually easier to maintain and keep in service.

To load a box magazine, bolt-action rifle, required lifting of a handle on the right of the bolt, which would unlock the mechanism and allow the bolt to be pulled back to a rear position. This would expose the rifle's breech and the magazine's floor plate, which was held up under tension by a spring. Cartridges would be pushed down unto the magazine plate, compressing the spring below until the magazine was full to capacity. Removable box magazines could also be filled when removed from the rifle—so that a loaded spare magazine could be carried and quickly slotted into the base of the rifle if a quick reload was needed.

Some bolt-action rifles could be loaded from a "stripper-clip" or "charger," which was a grooved metal strip holding multiple cartridges (usually a full- or half-magazine capacity), which located onto a guide slot above the magazine. This gave a quick reload since the soldier could push all the cartridges on the charger into the magazine at once. When the bolt was returned (pushed forward) it would allow a cartridge to be pushed up from the magazine by spring pressure, and the bolt moving forward would chamber the cartridge. Pushing the bolt handle down would lock the mechanism. The action of withdrawing or returning the bolt—depending on the design of the rifle—would also lock back the firing pin and set the trigger, making the rifle ready to fire. After firing, the cycling of the bolt would extract and expel the spent cartridge case and load the next live round. Although this action is long winded to describe, in practice it allowed the ordinary soldier to fire off a magazine full of ammunition (usually between five and ten cartridges) as quickly as he could cycle the bolt, aim, and pull the trigger.

TOP LEFT: *The Lee-Enfield had a removable magazine and stripper-clip loading—it took two five-round clips to fully load the magazine through the top of the receiver. The magazine could be removed or attached to the rifle's receiver (from underneath) in a matter of seconds. This versatile system meant that in addition to the loaded magazine on the rifle, a spare magazine could be carried, ready-loaded with ten rounds, or stripper clips of five rounds could be used to "top up" the magazine after five rounds or more had been fired. Alternatively, single cartridges could be loaded and fired.*

TOP RIGHT: *The Lee-Enfield magazine could be loaded with a stripper-clip through the top of the receiver—this would be impossible with a scope mounted, so loading would be through single cartridges into the receiver, or changing the ten-shot magazine.*

ABOVE: *View from the top of the receiver of a Lee-Enfield—the stripper-clip was placed in a locating channel on the receiver; then the cartridges were pushed into the magazine with the thumb, leaving the stripper-clip empty. Some other rifles would retain the clip and cartridges together in the magazine, then eject the empty clip once it was empty.*

faster and even more effectively. During the sieges of British-held towns, soldiers would soon learn that just to show a part of their body above the defenses could invite a shot from Boer snipers. They also knew that the hours around dawn were an especially dangerous time, as Boer sharpshooters would take up advantageous positions during cover of night, often deliberately keeping the glaring African sun behind them, and would shoot at any incautious guards or pickets in the British lines, before slipping back out of range. Likewise, at dusk the British had to learn to avoid being lit up by a lantern or silhouetted against the fading light of the sun. Any target would be taken; it just had to be in rifle range, and a standard modern rifle in the hands of a marksman could strike a man-sized target at 600 yards or more.

After the initial phase of sieges and set battles, the Boers were reduced to guerrilla tactics, at which their small "commando" units of mounted infantry proved very

RIGHT: *Major Frederick Russell Burnham, a famous American adventurer, who became the British Army chief of scouts.*

adept, and which they kept up for nearly two years, even when opposed by superior numbers of better supplied Commonwealth troops. Each commando unit would operate in a district they knew well, relying on support and supplies from the local people. They hit the British whenever an opportunity presented itself, avoiding close confrontation, and often using long-distance rifle fire to cause damage and hold up columns, then disengaging as soon as they themselves came under fire. This "hit and run" strategy took its toll on British resources and morale. However, the British troops would eventually begin to adapt to the situation and conditions that they found themselves in.

The Commonwealth soldiers that fought alongside them—from Australia, Canada, and New Zealand, plus loyal South Africans—had more respect for the Boers from the onset, and in some cases fought like them. Many of these Commonwealth soldiers were straight out of their own countries' wilderness regions, and like the Boers they were natural hunters, being well used to rifles and horses. Some of them were also used to following trails and recognizing the telltale signs of an enemy's movements. For this reason the duties of scouting, tracking, and observing the elusive Boer commandos were often undertaken by Commonwealth mounted infantry, plus other specialist units such as Lord Lovat's Scouts, who were commanded by the famous American adventurer, Major Frederick Russell Burnham, the British Army chief of scouts.

Lovat's Scouts were initially raised from Scottish highlanders, many of them gamekeepers, stalkers, and even poachers, but all of them being well versed in marksmanship and concealment—they were later to

ABOVE: *A Canadian mounted scout during the Boer War. British Commonwealth troops often fought the Boer on his terms, using their own natural abilities with horses and rifles to get to grips with the commandos.*

develop the "ghillie" suit, a military version of the camouflage capes used by gamekeepers. Using telescopes and signaling equipment (like the heliograph and semaphore, which were innovations of the time), Lovat's men provided much needed intelligence on enemy movements. Observation was to become a key element in the modern sniper's role, and Lovat's Scouts eventually developed into scout-snipers—Lovat Scouts (Sharpshooters)—a dual role that they took right through to World War II.

SPANISH-AMERICAN WAR (APRIL–AUGUST 1898)

This brief war brought two of the main bolt-action rifles later used by the Boers into direct conflict—the Norwegian-designed Krag-Jørgensen (the first bolt-action rifle adopted by U.S. forces) and the Model 93 Mauser (often called the Spanish Mauser, because of its use by Spain and several Latin American nations).

The Mauser had a standard box magazine that held five 7x57mm smokeless rounds that could be loaded quickly by stripper-clip. Most American regular units had the new Krag-Jørgensen rifle. This featured a fixed magazine that was loaded from the side by lifting a hinged cover, and fired a .30-40 smokeless round. The old single-shot Trap-Door Springfield rifle—a design that basically converted the old muzzleloading Springfield rifle into a breechloader—firing a black powder cartridge, was also used by some American units.

During the war in Cuba, a few hundred Spanish riflemen harassed and delayed the

progress of some 15,000 U.S. soldiers, by sniping at them with their Mausers from trees and heavy undergrowth. The smokeless cartridge made it difficult to spot single sharpshooters in the denser vegetation, thereby making them much harder to deal with. When a direct assault was made by the Americans at the famous Battle of San Juan Hill, approximately 800 Spanish infantry in entrenched positions faced a combined force of 15,000 U.S. troops and 4,000 Cuban rebels. The Americans lost 124 dead and over 800 wounded, while the Spanish casualties were 58 dead and 170 wounded. This was a first taste of war with both sides armed with modern repeating rifles.

RIGHT: *U.S. troops using Krag-Jørgensen rifles in action during the Spanish-American War—on the defense in the Philippines on January 1, 1899.* (NA)

The Murderous Acre–Spion Kop

Above: *A typical bolt-action Mauser rifle of the Boer War. Dated 1896, this rifle was owned by F. W. Conradie, whose name is marked on the side of the stock's butt—this was normal practice (either by crude engraving or burning), so that each man could easily identify his own rifle. This particular Boer fought with Botha's Commando of the Orange Free State. (Canadian War Museum 19980093-010)*

On the January 24, 1900, during an attempt at relieving the Boer siege of Ladysmith, at the River Tugela in Northern Natal, South Africa, a British force of 20,000 men under the command of General Sir Redvers Buller encountered a Boer army of 8,000 led by General Botha. During this campaign, a British force under Lieutenant General Warren occupied Spion Kop (Spionkop or Look-out Hill), in order to cover the advance on Ladysmith. The hill was taken at night with little resistance, and Royal Engineers dug entrenchments along the crest. In the morning it was realized that the British force occupied little more than an acre of the summit, and even that was overlooked by the actual perimeter of the hill that was now occupied by Boer riflemen. In addition, the "trenches" were little more than shallow ditches.

A Boer artillery bombardment began, and riflemen on the lip of the summit and on other nearby hills fired into the shallow entrenched area. The British, concentrated into such a small space, and under heavy, accurate rifle fire, began to take casualties, including General Edward Woodgate and many other senior commanders. Boer sharpshooters were adept at picking off anybody who appeared to be giving orders.

Warren sent reinforcements up the hill, but that just exacerbated the situation, causing even more crowded conditions. The Boers took casualties too, as British volunteers climbed to the summit. More and more British troops were committed to the battle, and more of them fell victim to rifle fire and artillery. The 3rd King's Rifles finally moved the Boers off the nearby Twin Peaks, which caused the Boers on Spion Kop to withdraw. By this time it was nightfall, and some of the British defenders had been under fire all day in the searing heat. Not knowing the battle had been won, the British officer left in command on the summit, Lieutenant Colonel Thorneycroft, withdrew the weary defenders. By the next morning the Boers were back on top of Spion Kop and the British Army had abandoned the attempt to relieve Ladysmith.

By the end of this disastrous battle, the British had suffered 1,500 casualties, including 243 dead. Although some British troops had died by artillery fire, many more had been shot by Boer marksmen with their Mausers. Not that the Lee-Enfields had let the defenders down, since 68 Boers were killed and a further 277 wounded.

Above: *Three Boer snipers on an overlooking position at Spion Kop, a prominent feature dominating the terrain in the Tugela River area. (AWM. P02578-008)*

Left: *Dead British soldiers lying in their shallow trenches at Spion Kop.*

It was inevitable that the British would win the Second Anglo-Boer War by virtue of overwhelming force—some 250,000 troops were deployed against the Boers. They also had a ready supply of munitions and used some pretty ruthless strategies, including attrition and the first concentration camps. What they learned was that whole armies—no matter how well trained and equipped—can be held at bay by small groups of determined men who are armed with modern weapons, are mobile, and know the terrain.

The Boer War triggered a root and branch reorganization of the British Army, including improved marksmanship training. Programs were even started to encourage working class men to take up rifle shooting—previously a middle class pastime. Even the Boy Scout movement—based on Lord Baden-Powell's exploits in South Africa—encouraged young lads to learn basic fieldcraft, while the army began to recognize the importance of those same skills as well as the Boer tactic of "fire and movement."

Unfortunately, the world was heading towards a conflict that wouldn't be about movement—instead it would become a long-drawn-out struggle between men living in trenches, bogged down in mud, and risking death every time they ventured to look above their sandbagged parapets.

LEE-ENFIELD RIFLES, 1888–1957

The Magazine Rifle Mk I or Lee-Metford was a bolt-action, box magazine-fed rifle taking its name from James Paris Lee, the action designer, and William E. Metford, creator of the barrel and rifling system. It was originally designed for use with black powder cartridges and was adopted for service with the British Army in 1888. But the barrel's shallow rifling didn't work well with the army's change to new .303-caliber, smokeless metallic cartridges in 1895, so it was replaced with more suitable rifling and a new rear sight by the Royal Small Arms Factory at Enfield, and the rifle became the Lee-Enfield.

When used in the Second Anglo-Boer War it became obvious that the Mauser rifles of the Boers were superior to the Lee rifles, mainly because of accuracy and speed of loading. These problems were addressed in 1902 with the Short Magazine Lee-Enfield Rifle Mk I or SMLE (universally known as the "Smelly"), which had a removable magazine that could be loaded in situ with ten rounds (via two five-round stripper clips), an improved sighting system, and a handy length of 44.5 inches–hence Short–to be commonly issued to all infantry, cavalry, and artillery units

alike. By World War I it was in its SMLE Mk III* guise, with various small changes and improvements, and proved to be a sturdy and reliable weapon. The action was short and slick, with minimal bolt movement and less effort required on extraction. This was because the rifle cocked on closing, unlike most other service rifles, including the Mauser, which combined both operations on the rear stroke. With the standard Lee-Enfield a competent soldier could easily fire between ten and fifteen aimed rounds a minute. (A sniper variant–the T4– will be described later.)

By the time Britain entered World War II in 1939 the SMLE had been almost completely replaced by its derivative, the more modern Lee-Enfield No 4 Mk 1. This heavier-barreled rifle had various improvements, including an aperture sight mounted on a stronger receiver, and was notably easier to mass-produce. Adopted by all Commonwealth countries, this rifle proved itself throughout World War II and the

Korean War, only being replaced in 1957 by the semi-automatic FN FAL rifle, although Lee-Enfield-based sniper variants in 7.62 NATO continued in service even after that.

TOP: *The SMLE (Short Magazine Lee-Enfield) Mk III* Rifle.*

ABOVE: *Close up of the SMLE bolt action.*

World War I–sniping in the trenches

Germany invaded France and the Low Countries in 1914, and after an initial period of rapid movement westward, they were checked by the French and their British allies, and the conflict settled down to trench warfare, with both sides "dug in" and only a barren, crater-filled strip of ground called "No Man's Land" dividing the opposing lines of earthworks and barricades. Despite the increased power and range of modern rifles, they would seldom be required to shoot at targets more than 400 yards or so away.

By this time the term "sniper" was in common usage by the British, and had been since referring to Boer marksmen a dozen years earlier, but it wasn't until World War I that all the elements of the modern sniper came together: accurate long-range rifles, optical sights, two-man teams (one spotting, one shooting), camouflage and fieldcraft, observation and scouting skills. All of these had been seen before to one degree or another, certainly in the American Civil War, but now there was to be official (and unofficial) training to bring all these qualities together for the sole, specific purpose of producing "snipers."

RIGHT: *Not all snipers would be equipped with scoped rifles; this applied to the Germans as well as the British and French.* (LoC)

BELOW: *The Germans had quite a few rifles fitted with telescopic sights from the very beginning of the war. The scope pictured here is a Voigtländer 4x.* (John Pearce/Inf. Regt. von Goeben (2.Rhein.) Nr.28. 1900–1919)

At the beginning of the 20th Century, Germany and Austria were leaders in optical technology, and made the best riflescopes in the world—and arguably, they still do. Many of these telescopic sights were initially designed for hunting, but it should come as no surprise that they were soon adapted for military use, especially as rifles by Mauser and the Austrian Steyr Mannlicher company were also used by hunters and the armies of Germany and the Austro-Hungarian Empire. In fact, the first scoped rifles to be sent to "the front" for use by German snipers were hunting models.

In addition, much of German culture revolved around hunting and target shooting, as witnessed by the abundance of *Schützenfest*, or "marksman festivals,"

THE MAUSER MODEL 98 RIFLE, 1898–1945

Many military rifles were made by the Mauser company of Germany, possibly the most successful being the Model 98. Developed from the Model 1893 and the later Mod.1895 and Mod.1896, this bolt-action rifle used a fixed, staggered, five-cartridge box magazine that could be quickly loaded by stripper-clip, while the three-lug bolt was designed for strength and safety. This proved to be a superbly accurate rifle, and the Mauser is still regarded as one of the greatest bolt-actions today.

Adopted for service in 1898 as the Gew 98, it had replaced all other rifles in the German army by 1912. It fired a 7.92 x 57 (8mm) cartridge with a 154-grain pointed "*spitzer*"-type bullet–this gave greater long-range accuracy due to its high ballistic coefficient (a measurement of projectile performance). The Gew 98 was the main German service rifle throughout World War I. The Kar 98 (Karabiner) was a shorter, carbine-length version of the Gew 98, and this also saw service in the war. In 1935 Kar 98 was adopted as the German standard-issue infantry rifle, and was known as the K98k ("K" stands for *kurz* or short) or simply the K98.

When used with standard open sights the Mauser 98 had an effective range of about 750 yards, but this could be greatly increased, to 1,000 yards or more, by the addition of an optical scope. The Mod.98 was used by German snipers in both World Wars, usually with a telescopic sight, but not always.

ABOVE: *Mauser Model G98 Sniper Rifle as used by German snipers on the Western Front. This rifle is fitted with a 4x telescopic sight made by C. P. Goertz of Berlin, serial number 99 (18869 underside), and has a leather eye pad.* (AWM. RELAWM03709)

RIGHT: *German snipers observing Allied troop movements from behind hastily erected shelters. They would have been armed with the Mauser Model G98 rifle, standard-issue to all German troops in World War I.* (NA)

RIGHT: *Dead German soldier–claimed as a sniper–with his unscoped Mauser at his side.* (LoC)

celebrated in the hunting regions of the Germanic states. There were plenty of young men of military age who were already skilled riflemen, and there was an even greater reserve of older, more experienced marksmen–many of whom would have served in the army–to train them.

Sniping rifles were issued to every regiment, and these filtered down to six men in each company. Each battalion also had a sniper section of two dozen men. Unless detailed to a specific task, these specialist snipers operated independently within their battalion's area, choosing the best positions in which to engage targets of opportunity.

The military Gew 98 Mauser sniper rifles were standard factory produced models but "specially selected" for the best accuracy after test firing. They used a turned down bolt, instead of the standard straight item, in order to clear the telescopic sight and mount. Ammunition was the standard 7.92x57mm military cartridge, although a higher quality "SmK" target grade round was also available after 1915.

Scopes were made by several manufacturers, and even though they were usually low powered (at around 3x to 4x magnification) they were of high quality, and well capable of their task at the distances over they had to perform–very rarely over 600 yards between opposing trenches, and usually much closer. Crucially, the soldiers who received them would either be familiar with their operation, or there would be someone within their ranks who could teach them. This was not the case with their opposite numbers in the French and British forces.

The exact number of scoped sniping rifles deployed by the Germans on the Western Front is unknown but it is estimated that it could have been as many as twenty thousand or more. Whatever the number, the German snipers certainly had a devastating effect on the Allied troops opposing them. Records, letters, and memoirs of British troops are littered with stories of sniper victims–almost all of them shot in the head. The reason for this is that in the trenches the head was the only part of the

TOP: *Note that this sniper's Pickelhaube (helmet) has had the spike unscrewed and a drab gray cloth cover has also been fitted so as not to attract the attention of enemy counter-snipers.*
(John Pearce/Inf. Regt. von Goeben (2.Rhein.) Nr.28. 1900–1919)

ABOVE: *A two-man team, with one "spotting" targets with binoculars for the sniper.*
(Photo. John Pearce/Inf. Regt. von Goeben (2.Rhein.) Nr.28. 1900–1919)

RIGHT: *A reenactor portraying a German "Unteroffizier" in the role of sniper.*
(Photo. John Pearce/Inf. Regt. von Goeben (2.Rhein.) Nr.28. 1900–1919)

body likely to be exposed; a brief look out of an entrenchment, or looking through observation slots, or just a momentary loss of attention when passing a lower, damaged section of trenchworks—just a second was all that it took to become the victim of a sniper. Add to this the fact that the German *spitzer* bullet (and its equivalent rounds used by the Allies) would tumble after initial penetration, leaving a small hole at the entry point but often making a fist-sized exit wound, so that head shots would inevitably be fatal.

This type of sniping action worked on a number of levels; first it obviously caused casualties; second, if carried out frequently and effectively, it created an oppressive, morale-sapping atmosphere and tension among the men under fire; thirdly, it could restrict movement and distract men from performing their duties. Without a doubt there must have been many times that snipers took shots and missed, but even when the intended victims were aware of their "close call" they might prefer to think that it was just a "stray" shot; but the killing shots, especially when a soldier lost a close comrade, would be burned into the memory forever as the work of a sniper. Most important of all, the soldier knew that if a marksman deliberately chose him as his

SPITZERS AND DUM-DUMS

With the introduction of smokeless powder, military rounds started to become smaller, lighter, and faster, but didn't seem to do the same amount of damage as the large, heavy, and slow rounds that they replaced. This led to experiments in increasing the lethality of rifle bullets.

The British had created ammunition—both soft points and hollow points—that expanded and fragmented on impact causing, massive internal damage, and greatly increasing lethality. The most notable of these was a jacketed bullet but with an exposed lead tip that had been developed in the Dumdum arsenal in India, and hence any expanding round (especially when used by criminals or the military) is often colloquially referred to as a "dum-dum" bullet. Certain other nations did not look kindly on this innovation, and at The Hague Convention of 1899—where the future "rules" for "civilized" warfare were agreed—the military use of expanding ammunition was outlawed.

In 1905 the German army adopted the "spitzer" round as their standard rifle ammunition; the spitzer got its name from the German word Spitzgeschoss—which means pointed bullet. The German 8mm cartridge fired the lightweight 154-grain spitzer bullet at nearly 2,900fps—an amazing velocity at the time.

The spitzer was a bullet (the projectile part of the cartridge) that took advantage of many new technical developments towards the end of the 19th Century. It was a jacketed bullet (with a hard copper covering of the lead core) in a long, pointed shape and usually with a "boat-tail-shaped" base. This type of bullet stood up much better than plain lead bullets to the high velocity and heat generated by smokeless powders, and its shape and weight distribution made it much more aerodynamic—therefore increasing range and accuracy. Because of its design, the spitzer would become unstable on impact, and was capable of causing extensive tissue damage. Another description for it was the "latent dum-dum." This was such an effective design that the military of many other nations, including the USA and Russia, also adopted spitzer-type bullets within a few years.

The British continued to experiment with their own .303 round but within the rules set by the Hague Convention, and eventually introduced the Mark VII cartridge with a 174-grain bullet in 1910, in plenty of time for World War I. The new bullet head had a lead core beneath an aluminum tip and was fully jacketed in copper. Like the spitzer, it was aerodynamic (leaving the muzzle at 2,440fps) but the distribution of weight within its jacketed body caused it to tumble once it hit fleshy tissue.

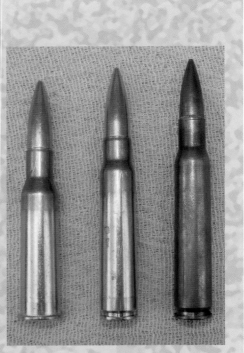

ABOVE: *By World War I the armies of all major nations were using "spitzer"-type ammunition; these three rounds are World War II vintage: from left to right— Russian 7.62x54r, German 7mm, and British .303.*

ABOVE: *A German* jäger *detachment in July 1917. In the early part of the war, jäger units kept their specialist scouting and "sharpshooting" role, but when the fighting stagnated into trench warfare they were incorporated into the general infantry units. This group of* jägers *seem to be equipped as stormtroopers (Sturmtruppen) or assault troops. (Military & Historical Image Bank)*

Major H. Hesketh-Pritchard, a British intelligence officer and keen big game hunter, recognized the domination of German snipers after a spell in the trenches in early 1915. After a short time back in Britain, he returned to France with several hunting rifles mounted with telescopic sights.

His work allowed him to visit various parts of the line to study the enemy sniping techniques, and he always took a scoped rifle with him. This was lent to various units suffering particularly bad sniper problems, and after a while a trickle of officially supplied scoped rifles started to arrive. Prior to 1915 these had been standard SMLE rifles fitted with assorted scopes from a number of different manufacturers, and an even more diverse selection of mounts. After 1915 there was a greater degree of standardization, with SMLE rifles being supplied with ready-zeroed scopes (set up for a minimum of 2MOA—a 2-inch group at 100 yards). Most of the scopes (over 8,000) were supplied by two main contractors—Aldis Brothers (of Birmingham) and the Periscopic Prism Company of London—with nearly a thousand more Winchester A5 scopes being bought from the USA. These official sniping rifles all suffered from the inconvenience of having the scope offset to the left, supposedly to allow charger loading of the magazine, even though the magazine was removable and could be loaded without a stripper-clip—in fact, early versions of the rifle had a magazine cut-out plate and were designed to be loaded one cartridge at a time unless a fast-fire facility was needed.

target, then the odds on his living were reduced considerably; in fact, the decision on whether he lived or not rested on the tip of the sniper's trigger finger.

Using zig-zag trenches, the German snipers could lay a flanking crossfire, covering each other, taking effective shots at the enemy but not being exposed directly themselves to fire from the front. They also used armor plate to good effect, making it difficult for the British and French to take countermeasures—and in truth, up to 1915, very little was officially done to neutralize the much more organized German snipers.

ABOVE: *With the sun shining directly at this bunker, the sniper can be easily spotted by counter-snipers. (John Pearce/Inf. Regt. von Goeben (2.Rhein.) Nr.28. 1900–1919)*

ABOVE RIGHT: *At twilight or in the shade, firing from the dark interior of the bunker, the sniper would be much more difficult to spot. (John Pearce/Inf. Regt. von Goeben (2.Rhein.) Nr.28. 1900–1919)*

BELOW: *German trenches were not laid out as formally as those of the Allies, allowing the German snipers to take advantage of the irregular, "disruptive" materials and outlines for camouflage. (John Pearce/Inf. Regt. von Goeben (2.Rhein.) Nr.28. 1900–1919)*

SNIPING AND 20TH CENTURY ARMOR

During World War I, and to a far lesser extent in World War II, some military experiments were made with plate armor for personal protection. This usually took the form of metal breast plates–like those used in medieval armor but made of much heavier and tougher steel. It is most usually seen as protection for machine gun crews, but it is also claimed that it was used by snipers, although it is difficult to see what advantage could be gained, as the sniper's chest area would normally be covered by the entrenchment he was shooting from. If out in the open he would almost certainly be shooting from the prone position, in which case only his head and upper shoulders would be exposed. Apart from anything else, the sniper would be severely hampered for movement if wearing armor plate.

The Germans also experimented with a half-inch-thick steel face mask that was curved to cover the face and neck, but had a cutout at the bottom right, in order that the user could shoulder his rifle. This mask had two tiny eye slits to see through and looked both impractical and ineffective. In any case, modern high velocity rounds could pierce most "light" armor plate (see the illustration of breast plates that have been tested against heavy machine gun rounds).

Fixed armor emplacements were used for both sniping and observation. In most cases these were heavy fixed positions, usually taking the shape of a giant post box (round or square) big enough for two men, and often made of cast iron over three inches thick, with an observation/sniping slot at the front.

A common use of armor was to affix a section of steel plate with an observation hole or firing slot in it on the trench wall, then disguise it by covering the front with sandbags. The Germans took great pains in this deception, even painting the plate in the same color as the bags surrounding it. There was good reason for this, as each side would scan the opposition's trench lines all the time; any slight change from day to day, any flicker of movement where there shouldn't be any, and any other clue that something wasn't quite what it seemed, would draw further observation, and inevitably sniper fire.

The biggest problem with steel plate was that it had to have a spy hole or loop hole to look through and shoot through. These usually had a cover of some kind. However, if an enemy sniper (with a scoped rifle) spotted one, it was a simple matter to keep it under observation until the cover was drawn back–indicating that somebody was looking through it–so the sniper simply had to put a round through the opening to hit the unfortunate victim "between the eyes"… quite literally in some instances. Many snipers and observers were shot dead while looking through the tiny slots in their "safe" armored positions.

One of the first counter-sniper measures that British sniping expert Hesketh-Pritchard introduced was to get men to stand to one side of the observation slot when opening it, and hold a cap (with cap badge) in front of it for seventeen seconds. If a shot didn't come from the enemy, it could be regarded as safe.

ABOVE: *Italian sniper with a movable steel armor plate.* (LoC)

BELOW: *A Canadian soldier inspects a captured armored German sniper's post (France, c1917) made from three-inch-thick Krupp steel. The post could be moved–but not easily!*

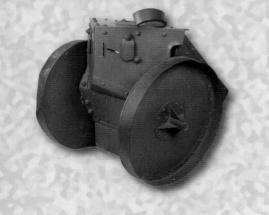

Hesketh-Pritchard managed to obtain some captured German plate steel used in the trenches, and in experiments he found that some high velocity hunting calibers were capable of piercing the steel plate. Britain's War Department actually issued a few large-caliber hunting rifles, and they certainly worked, but whether they were ever used to a great degree in the trenches is extremely doubtful. Nevertheless, when they were used it helped to prove to the British Tommies that German snipers were vulnerable, contrary to their previous reputation.

Movable armor was also used by the Germans. Fitted with wheels, it looked something like the steel shield found on artillery, but had observation and firing slots for a rifle. This was probably developed for wire obstruction clearance or forward observation, but it is doubtful whether it was successfully used for either of these tasks, let alone sniping, since it would have been very difficult to move on anything but good terrain, and it would undoubtedly have made an easy target for enemy artillery.

Although personal steel armor was not successful against modern weapons in World War I, it was still used to some degree by the Japanese army in World War II, when it proved equally ineffective.

FAR LEFT: *Gunner of a German machine gun crew wearing a breast plate (Sappenpanzer) and a brow plate (Stirnpanzer) on his helmet for extra protection. (Photo. John Pearce/Inf. Regt. von Goeben (2.Rhein.) Nr.28. 1900–1919)*

LEFT: *A mobile sniper post. Of riveted box construction with four observation slits and rifle slots that could be closed with swinging covers, it was moved on two steel wheels that had a diameter of about 24 inches. This mobile shield, or "one man tank," was of a type used on the Western Front by snipers and allied soldiers to creep forward to destroy barbed wire entanglements. It is believed to have been made from nickel steel. (AWM. REL-12494)*

TOP: *Result of Ordnance Department body armor test at Fort de la Peigney, Langres, France, showing the effect of pistol, rifle, and machine gun fire. Circa 1918. (NA)*

CENTER LEFT: *A German sniper carefully opening an observation slot in a steel shield. (Photo. John Pearce/Inf. Regt. von Goeben (2.Rhein.) Nr.28. 1900–1919)*

ABOVE: *Fixed armored sniping/observation posts were usually constructed of a steel plate set a little back from a camouflage covering of stacked sandbags; anything as obvious as an exposed observation slot—or a gap in sandbags—would always draw fire.*

ABOVE: *British snipers rarely had scoped rifles at the beginning of the war.* (Steve Neville/Gareth Sprack)

FAR RIGHT: *A British corporal showing his Lee-Enfield sniper rifle to his comrades.* (Cody)

Hesketh-Pritchard realized that these scoped rifles were next to useless if the person using them was not specifically trained to use an optical sight. Even worse, the men using them had not been trained in concealment and would be easy meat for German counter-snipers.

After convincing the army hierarchy of the necessity of sniper training, Hesketh-Pritchard was allowed to serve as the Third Army's sniping expert. Encouraged and aided by John Buchan, the brilliant author and *Times* correspondent, Hesketh-Pritchard set up a sniping school—to some extent privately funded—where he could train the right men for the job, set up scopes and rifle correctly, and generally experiment with anti-sniper countermeasures. He recognized that to be more effective each British sniper must be accompanied by a spotter with a powerful telescope in order to find targets and mark hits. This constant observation of the enemy lines was to prove invaluable, and the information gleaned by these sniper teams went far beyond just counter-sniper measures.

Hesketh-Pritchard taught observation by making men study a scene with a telescope out to 600 yards or so, and a selection of objects (including French, British, and

German "heads" made of papier-mâché) was raised into their line of sight for around fifteen seconds each. He would then get them to write down what they had seen. Another exercise was to place a number of objects on a landscape, including semi-concealed sniping points, and again get the observer to report on what he had seen. These methods proved extremely effective, and variations on these themes are still used today to teach snipers about observation.

Moving from battalion to battalion, Hesketh-Pritchard would spend a day or so with each group, teaching them how to adjust and use the telescopic sight, how to stay

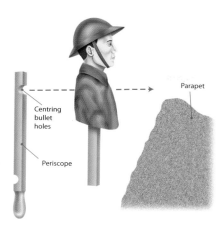

LEFT: *Dummy heads or models were sometimes used to "tempt" enemy snipers into taking a shot. The direction from which the bullet came from could then be roughly judged by either looking through the hole it made using a periscope (left) or by sliding a rod through the bullet hole in the model (far left). This would help to pin down the position of the enemy sniper.*

concealed and stay as safe as possible, how to find targets, and various other skills to counter the German snipers, and hopefully eliminate them. On the front line, some of the methods he used included the papier-mâché heads ruse to attract fire from enemy snipers in order to mark their positions, and the careful setting up of "loopholes"—offset and at angles—so as to be usable but make them difficult to penetrate by enemy fire. He also used the method of setting up a rifle on sandbags or another rest, so that the sights were adjusted and pointing just under the loophole or position of a known enemy sniper. This made it easy to get off a snap shot in seconds, as soon as the enemy showed himself. He used this very effectively against forward artillery observers—who had become one of the primary targets of snipers, now that most artillery was being fired from beyond rifle range, and often even beyond view of the trenches.

LEFT: *Article showing camouflage and "dummy heads"—the latter used by the Allies to train their own snipers and in some cases to draw German sniper fire.*

Other forward-thinking British commanders with knowledge of telescopic sights also started their own informal training "schools," some of them actually in the trenches, but it was not until 1916 that official Scouting, Observation and Sniping (SOS) schools were set up, first behind the lines in France, and later in England.

The Canadian armed forces certainly taught some of the finer points of combat marksmanship to their troops before they even left Canada. At Camp Borden in Ontario there were extensive sniping courses, and each Canadian infantry battalion was assigned its own specialist sniping and scouting sections.

Once again Commonwealth troops supplied some of the most notable snipers—men who seemed virtually born to the task, like Francis Pegahmagabow, an Ojibwa Indian who achieved 378 attributed kills, probably the highest sniper tally in World War I. The Canadian army had many other good snipers in its ranks, and they had an excellent weapon for the job—the Ross rifle. Although certainly not the best combat rifle of the time, it was a very accurate weapon, even when used with standard open sights, and it was even better with a target aperture sight, or better still, a Warner & Swasey 6x riflescope.

ABOVE: *Stamped US SPRINGFIELD ARMORY MODEL 1903, and the serial number. Barrel stamped 7-18. This rifle is fitted with a Warner & Swasey Model 1913 telescopic sight, serial number 3580. This type of rifle and telescopic sight were developed during World War I and were used on the Western Front by the U.S. Army.* (AWM. REL/19554)

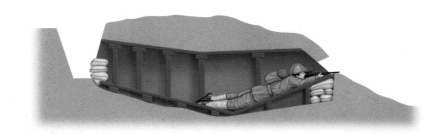

ABOVE: *Two examples of sniper positions, dug or built into the trench line and laid out in such a way that the sniper could safely enter and leave from the rear. Once inside, the physical stance that the sniper takes up–keeping the body lower than the rifle loop-hole– would offer the smallest possible target to an enemy counter-sniper.*

LEFT: *Canadian troops learning to use periscope-sighted rifles to counteract snipers in the trenches.*

BELOW LEFT: *American doughboys under sniper fire in France. (NA)*

RIGHT: *American sniper Pvt. Leo R Hahn in action with a Springfield M1903A3 Sniper Rifle and a Warner & Swasey scope. (AP)*

On their entry into the war in 1917 the U.S Army also used the Warner & Swasey scope on the sniper version of their standard service rifle, the Springfield M1903. They later switched to Winchester A5 scopes in 5x magnification.

The U.S. Model P17 rifle, a 30.06 chambered version of the Enfield P14 (itself based on a Mauser-type action), was also used in large numbers by American troops in

World War I, and this proved to be a very accurate and reliable weapon.

The Americans had an excellent marksmanship program in their training camps, notably Camp Perry, Ohio, and the U.S. Marine Corps facility at Quantico, Virginia. Indeed many of their recruits were already good hunters and target shooters. But being a good shot wasn't the same as facing skilled snipers in the trenches, so British officers and NCOs trained by Hesketh-Pritchard were seconded to help with the instruction of American snipers both in the USA and in SOS schools. The resulting snipers were some of the best in the war.

Good marksmen also came from South Africa and Rhodesia (a former British colony, now Zimbabwe). Notable among them were Sir Abe Bailey's Sharpshooters, who arrived in France in 1916. This group of twenty-four men was financed by Sir Abe Bailey, a South African millionaire who had stayed loyal to Britain during the Boer War. The most famous one of their number was Lieutenant Neville Methven, who personally made in excess of 100 killing shots. The Sharpshooters served with the British Army until the end of the war, taking part in many major battles including Passchendaele and the Somme. Six of them were killed in action, and more were wounded, but it is estimated that the original group of just two dozen men caused over 3,000 German casualties and fatalities.

FRANCIS "PEGGY" PEGAHMAGABOW (1891–1952)

Corporal Francis Pegahmagabow was a Canadian sniper, and possibly the most prolific of World War I. Although there are no exact figures recorded, accounts of his kills are estimated to be as high as 378, and he also captured another 300 men. He was of the Ojibwa people from Parry Island Indian Reserve, Ontario, and is the highest decorated native Canadian soldier in the nation's history, having been awarded the Military Medal and two bars. He was a deadly marksman and knew how to use the cratered landscape of "no-man's-land" to get into positions where he could be most effective.

Pegahmagabow enlisted with the 23rd Regiment (Northern Pioneers) in 1914 and served as a sniper, runner, and scout/observer on the Western Front in engagements including the Second Battle of Ypres, Amiens, Passchendaele, and Mount Sorrel—the latter being where he captured a large number of German soldiers. Pegahmagabow served and survived the full course of the war despite coming under gas attack and being wounded.

Other famous native Canadian snipers in the war include Henry Norwest (1884–1918), a Métis (Cree/French) who achieved 115 accredited kills and was awarded a Military Medal and bar; Lance Corporal Johnson Paudash, who was an Ojibwa native; and John Shiwak or Sikoak (1889–1917), an Inuit.

RIGHT: *Corporal Francis Pegahmagabow, a Canadian Indian, and one of the most successful snipers in World War I. (From a portrait by Irma Coucill, courtesy of The Indian Hall of Fame at the Woodland Cultural Center, Ontario)*

FAR RIGHT: *Warner & Swasey 6x riflescope on Ross rifle, viewed from above, showing offset mounting system. (Steve Broadbent Collection)*

ABOVE: *Ross Model 1910 Mk III (T) Sniper Rifle. The Canadian-made Ross rifle was very accurate, but disliked by some because of its "straight-pull" action, which was considered to be not as strong as a turn bolt. Withdrawn from general service in 1916, it remained the weapon of choice for Canadian snipers. This model is fitted with a Warner & Swasey 6x riflescope, but they were often used by snipers with just their open sights; this is probably the case with Francis Pegahmagabow.*

ABOVE: *Warner & Swasey 6x riflescope (left side). (Steve Broadbent Collection)*

BELOW: *Warner & Swasey 6x riflescope (right side) also showing the Ross' straight pull bolt action. (Steve Broadbent Collection)*

Turks and Aussies at Gallipoli

It wasn't just the soldiers on the Western Front that had to put up with the remorseless anxiety of avoiding sniper fire. In the Dardanelles Campaign in northwestern Turkey a sniper war was also being waged with the Turks (allied to Germany) against the French and British Commonwealth forces—many of the latter being "Anzacs," the Australian and New Zealand contingents. At Gallipoli, on the Turkish coast, neither side was able to gain the upper hand; a stalemate was reached, and trench warfare once more became the order of the day.

The Turks used Mauser rifles fitted with standard iron sights, but they had the advantage of higher ground,

firing down onto the sloping beachhead where the Allied attack had stalled. They did great damage both physically and mentally to the Anzac troops trapped on a broad strip of land between the front line and the sea. At first, anything that was looked down upon from the Turkish lines would be fired on, but once the Allied troops were dug in, it was only the naïve and the curious—those who chanced a look over the defenses—or the unwary who would present targets to Turkish snipers.

The Anzac forces had many soldiers in their ranks who were already good marksmen, coming from the ranches of the Australian outback and the great sheep farms of New Zealand. They just needed a chance to put their skills

to use, but this proved difficult because of the position of their lines in relation to that of the Turks. To overcome this they developed sniping methods of their own.

As on the Western Front, Australian observers would use trench periscopes to observe the enemy, who in turn would try to put a round through the periscope. This would not seriously wound anybody, but it once more enforced the dominance of the sniper and ensured that troops kept their heads down. The Australians refined this by having an observer working with a sniper; the observer initially pinpointed the target area where an enemy appeared, then relayed it to the sniper, who would get ready to shoot at that spot; then on the next appearance of the enemy, the observer would "call the shot" and the sniper would take a snap-shot at his previously ranged and sighted target. This proved to be a very efficient method of countering Turkish snipers—simply because they now had the fear of being fired back at, which in turn put them under pressure and made them more cautious.

The Australians used standard SMLE rifles for sniping, although some, like the famous Billy Sing, may have used aperture target sights brought from home.

The Australians certainly played their part in countering Turkish snipers; they also maintain that it was one of their number at Gallipoli who invented the periscope rifle. Other Allied forces also lay claim to this, but this is understandable since several different home-built patterns evolved as a case of "needs must." There was at least one design from the Germans.

The periscope rifle was basically a wooden frame with a rifle at the top, a stock and trigger pull at the bottom, a periscope for sighting purposes, and a remote trigger linkage in between. Even quite sophisticated remote mechanical linkages on modern bullpup rifles can leave a lot to be desired, so it can be imagined how awkward it must have been to use a home-made "string and pulley" contraption connected to a trigger on a military rifle (again not the most delicate of mechanisms) possibly

ABOVE: *American infantrymen tackling snipers during their advance.*

LEFT: *Back pack, helmet, and other equipment carried by a USMC sniper during World War I. (Carsten Edler)*

ABOVE: *Gallipoli, 1915–18. An Australian sniper team in a front line trench; the observer is looking for targets through a periscope, while the sniper waits, ready with a rifle equipped with a periscope sight. This is a typical sniping team developed by Australians at Gallipoli. Note the soft cloth cap on the soldier on the right, which helps camouflage his position. The periscope rifle was a homemade invention of mirrors, boxwood, and wire. It allowed the user to* *sight and fire a rifle over the parapet without exposing himself to enemy fire. Credit for the original invention of the periscope rifle at Gallipoli is usually given to Sergeant William Beech, although Private George Tostee, 10th Battalion, is also known to have demonstrated the device to his commanding officers. Versions of the periscope rifle were also used by the British and Germans on the Western Front. (AWM. A05767)*

some 18 to 24 inches away, while sighting down a periscope. But whether they hit the target or not, once more such systems gave the ordinary soldiers a chance to fire a few rounds back at the enemy, and in a war of nerves this is not to be discounted.

British sharpshooters were also present in Gallipoli, in the form of Lovat's Scouts (mentioned earlier), who went to the Turkish front in September 1915, and also served as scout/snipers in Egypt, Macedonia, and France between 1916 and the end of the war. These men were experts in concealment and observation, with intelligence and experience counting more than age, as witnessed by a recruitment poster stating, *"100 Stalkers and Glassmen between the ages of 41 and 45, for stalking – Bosches!"*

Possibly the greatest advantage that they gave British snipers was introducing the practice of using two-man teams, with a trained observer using a powerful 4-draw stalker's telescope often with a magnification of 20x or more, to spot targets for the second man—the shooter. These telescopes were far more powerful than the riflescopes of the time, which varied between 3x and 6x, and they gave much better definition of the target. In addition, the observer could change places with the shooter, or a second observer, to keep constant vigil

ALVIN C. YORK (1887–1964)

Possibly the most famous "sniper" of World War I, Sergeant Alvin Cullum York was much more a "sharpshooter" in the old sense of the word. Born in Tennessee, he handled a gun from childhood and by all accounts was a naturally gifted and experienced rifleman before he ever saw a military rifle range. In his younger days he was known as a "tearaway," but after his best friend was killed in a drunken brawl, Alvin changed his ways and became a committed Christian. He had a crisis of conscience after enlisting in the army, but nevertheless went on to become one of America's greatest heroes of the war.

When an American assault in the Argonne Forest was halted by German machine guns on a ridge, a platoon of seventeen men including York (at that time a corporal) were sent to flank the enemy positions. The group managed to get behind the machine guns, and in doing so captured the German command post. While they were rounding up a large group of prisoners, the men of one of the machine gun positions they had been circling had spotted the situation and had turned their gun around, firing on both the Americans and their own comrades. Six Americans were killed, with others wounded, leaving York in command. With the remaining Americans and their German prisoners taking cover, York stalked the machine gun crews who were now all trying to turn their guns around. Shooting and moving, York used a standard service rifle to pick off the machine gunners from their flank so that they couldn't all engage him at once. In his diary he wrote, *"At first I was shooting from a prone position; that is lying down; jes like we often shoot at the targets in the shooting*

matches in the mountains of Tennessee; and it was jes about the same distance. But the targets here were bigger. I jes couldn't miss a German's head or body at that distance. And I didn't. Besides, it weren't no time to miss nohow. I knowed that in order to shoot me the Germans would have to get their heads up to see where I was lying. And I knowed that my only chance was to keep their heads down. And I done it. I covered their positions and let fly every time I seed anything to shoot at. Every time a head come up I done knocked it down. Then they

would sorter stop for a moment and then another head would come up and I would knock it down, too. I was giving them the best I had."

He was then charged by five or six Germans whom he dispatched "last man first" with a Colt 1911 semi-auto pistol. *"In the middle of the fight,"* he wrote, *"a German officer and five men done jumped out of a trench and charged me with fixed bayonets. They had about twenty-five yards to come and they were coming right smart. I only had about half a clip left in my rifle; but I had my pistol ready. I done flipped it out fast and teched them off, too.*

"I teched off the sixth man first; then the fifth; then the fourth; then the third; and so on. That's the way we shoot wild turkeys at home. You see we don't want the front ones to know that we're getting the back ones, and then they keep on coming until we get them all. Of course, I hadn't time to think of that. I guess I jes naturally did it."

Finally, one of the captured German officers called for the rest of the machine gunners to surrender, which they did. Alvin York and the seven men ended up taking 132 German prisoners, and the next day some twenty-eight Germans were found dead (the same number or rounds that York fired), along with thirty-five abandoned machine guns.

For his actions York was awarded the Croix de Guerre from France, the Croce di Guerra from Italy, and from America the Distinguished Service Cross, which was later upgraded to the Medal of Honor.

ABOVE: *Sergeant Alvin Cullum York—more a sharpshooter than a sniper.*

without the team members suffering undue eyestrain or a loss of concentration, both being common occurrences with prolonged surveillance. The German sniper, on the other hand, while sometimes being part of a squad along a section of trench, would each inevitably be actually working alone, using his riflescope for observation as well as aiming.

ABOVE: *Lee-Enfield No. 4 MK. I(T) rifle with No. 32 sight, and spotting telescope with case. British snipers worked in two-man teams, with a spotter using a powerful stalker's telescope—as seen here—often with a magnification of 20x or more, to pick out targets for his partner, the shooter.*

BELOW: *German snipers were a constant threat throughout the war, but the influx of trained British and Commonwealth sniping teams, and later those from the United States, gradually began to turn the tide. (John Pearce/Inf. Regt. von Goeben (2.Rhein.) Nr.28. 1900–1919)*

WORLD WAR I CAMOUFLAGE

How the Elusive Sniper Hides Himself from Foes

ABOVE: *Two USMC snipers wearing their homemade "ghillie" suits. (AB)*

ABOVE RIGHT: *British snipers sometimes used loose clothing that disguised the human shape—such as hooded boiler suits or the loose-fitting Symien sniper suit, both of which are seen here. These could be plain canvas or sacking, or could be daubed with paint for an even more disruptive pattern.*

ABOVE: *The contemporary press had some strange ideas about camouflage—this is from* War Illustrated, *November 1916.*

BELOW: *USMC snipers wearing "ghillie" suits in Badenville, c1918. (AF)*

BELOW RIGHT: *World War I USMC reenactor making a "ghillie" suit. (Carsten Edler)*

By 1914 most modern armies had adopted drab colors for the uniforms of their men. Grays, browns, and other earthy tones were used to help the troops become as inconspicuous as possible—the exact opposite of the bright colors of the 18th Century, which were designed to make troops recognizable as their commanders maneuvered them on the battlefield like so many chess pieces.

Yet, even with these more subtle colors, the sniper needed more protection via concealment. Hunters have always used clothing that helped them to blend into the background, but the sniper needed to completely disappear, because his quarry was an armed man who could just as easily shoot him.

So it was that World War I snipers started to experiment with camouflage as never before. This took several forms, some of which seem quite bizarre now, such as painted, disruptive patterns, hollowed-out animal carcasses used as hides, and even artificial trees made out of cast iron. But there were also some very practical developments, like face paints to disguise a very easily spotted "white" target, the use of mud and dirt to break up the "solid" colors of a uniform, and above all the development of clothing that changed the easily definable human shape—such as hooded boiler suits and the loose-fitting Symien sniper suit. Any

soldier could quickly disguise himself with one of these suits, or a suitably fashioned groundsheet "poncho," with a balaclava (ski mask) and gloves to cover his hands and face.

The Germans began issuing camouflaged helmets to some units in 1916, and later that same year the French and British established camouflage sections, consisting of artists and designers, while most other European countries and the United States also began experimenting in 1917. The Lovat Scouts' "ghillie suit" was (and still is) the ultimate in personal camouflage. As used by gamekeepers or "ghillies" in the highlands of Scotland, this suit was covered in strips of canvas or sacking in greens, browns, tans, and black to completely mask the wearer's shape. Wearing one of these suits, a man going to ground even in the lightest of vegetation would be virtually indistinguishable from his surroundings. To complete the disguise, the sniper would wear a veiled hood and gloves, and would also wrap his rifle with strips of cloth to change its color and shape.

By the end of the war snipers were being taught the art of concealment, and by the beginning of World War II some of these ideas had filtered through to the training and equipping of the ordinary soldier.

ABOVE LEFT: *The Germans even manufactured hollow cast-iron trees to act as both camouflaged and armored sniping and observation posts; this diagram shows the view from the front (with firing ports and observation slots) and from the back with its concealed entrance—the human figure is to scale, giving some idea of the size and weight of this "metal tree."*

ABOVE RIGHT: *This American sniper rifle has been camouflaged with a painted disruptive pattern.* (AJ)

RIGHT: *The "ghillie" suit helps the user blend into the background.*

BELOW LEFT: *Even just loosely draped drab-colored sacking could help disguise a sniping position.* (John Pearce/Inf. Regt. von Goeben (2.Rhein.) Nr.28. 1900-1919)

BELOW: *Experimental "tree climbing" camo. It's doubtful that it caught on!* (LoC)

Billy Sing (1886–1943)

While serving with the 5th Light Horse Regiment on Gallipoli, Australian Trooper Sing acquired notoriety as an accurate sniper, shooting over 150 Turkish soldiers at Gallipoli between the months of June and September 1915 from a position at "Chatham's Post."

Although his tally stated 150 confirmed kills, an informal estimate puts it as high as 201. The discrepancy can be accounted for by the way such hits were recorded; to be credited, a kill had to be confirmed by an observer—usually the sniper's "spotter"—but on October 23, 1915, General Birdwood issued an order complimenting Sing on his tally of 201 Turks. Having been wounded by an enemy sniper, Sing recovered sufficiently to get to his sniping position before dawn, and didn't go back to his trench until night, letting the dark conceal his movements. Sing was a skilful rifleman before the war, having worked in the outback as a stockman and kangaroo shooter, and been a member of his

local rifle club. Sing probably used a standard issue Short Magazine Lee Enfield (SMLE) No 1 Mk III .303-caliber rifle, but it is not known whether he used a target (aperture) sight or a scope.

In 1916 Private Sing was awarded the Distinguished Conduct Medal for his gallantry as a sniper at Gallipoli. In 1918 he was also awarded the Belgian Croix de Guerre, possibly for helping to counter German snipers at Polygon Wood in September 1917. Over his period of service he had been shot on two occasions, sustained shrapnel wounds to both legs and his back, and had been gassed, this eventually causing his medical discharge. It can be safely said that this was one very tough and determined man.

Right: *Private William Edward (Billy) Sing, DCM, 31st Battalion, of Clermont, Queensland—Australia's most prolific sniper during Wold War I.* (AWM. P03633.006)

Right: *Russian sniper with Mosin-Nagant rifle mounted with a PEM scope.* (Cody)

Far Right: *Finnish sniper using an unscoped rifle in the Winter War.*

Below: *At the outbreak of World War II the Russians had snipers by the thousands.* (Corbis)

World War II: Snipers on the Eastern Front

At the outbreak of World War II in Europe in 1939, only Russia had fully equipped its armies for sniping on a major scale. The German army had been rearming across all the services, and the standard infantry rifle was now the handier, carbine-length Mauser Kar-98. This was based on the redoubtable, full-length Gew-98 rifle, which also remained in service in some numbers throughout the war. The scopes used by the Germans had improved too, with respected manufacturers like Zeiss, Kahles, Hensoldt, and others all supplying sights with good optical quality. It was perhaps this very variety of models that was the weakness in the German system, since some combinations required different mounts, so that there was no standardization of rifle/scope/mount.

The Russians were still using their Mosin-Nagant M1891/30 bolt-action, magazine-fed rifle, which as its name suggests, had been in service since the previous century, but had been modernized to a certain degree in the 1930s. In World War I the Russians had used very few scoped rifles, but they had observed the effect of snipers during that conflict. So when building up their forces under the Stalinist regime they experimented with various scopes specifically developed for sniping, including the PE (4x mag) and the improved, side-mounted PEM.

They had also developed the Tokarev SVT38 semi-automatic rifle, and this too was pressed into duty as a sniper's rifle, but it was never used as extensively or in anywhere near the same numbers as the Mosin M91/30. For one thing, it was not as accurate as the M91/30, and (as snipers right up to the present day will attest), a manually operated bolt-action is always preferable to a semi-auto. Another problem was that it could not be easily mounted with the PEM scope, so a new, shorter scope was introduced—the PU (3.5x mag)—and this became the standard issue sniper sight on all Soviet rifles throughout World War II.

MOSIN-NAGANT M1891/1930 AND PU SCOPE– THE MAIN WWII RUSSIAN SNIPING COMBINATION

LEFT: *The Mosin-Nagant M1891/30 sniper variant with PU 3.5x scope. (AWM. REL-10150)*

To produce a sniper weapon, the standard military Mosin-Nagant M91/30 bolt-action rifle in 7.62x54R caliber had to undergo some minor modifications. The biggest change was that the scope was mounted above the receiver, so the short, straight, standard bolt handle had to be replaced with a longer version that curved downwards. Early sniper models were fitted with a Zeiss-based PE or PEM (4x mag.) scope, but later rifles used shorter, mass-produced PU scopes with a 3.5x magnification. Although relatively cheap to make, the PU scope was rugged and efficient.

The reticle used three thick posts, the vertical one being sharply pointed and finishing in the center of the sight picture (when optically centered), and two horizontal posts, one each side, with a slight gap between them. The scope had turrets for elevation (by distance out to about 1,425 yards) and windage (calibrated from 0 to 10 in either direction). There was no "eye focus" or parallax adjustment.

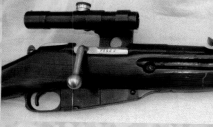

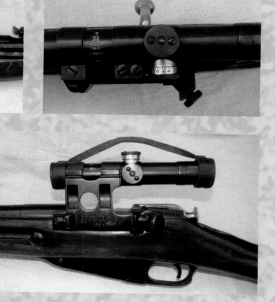

ABOVE: *Close-up of the action; note the turned-down bolt. (Steve Broadbent Collection)*

ABOVE RIGHT: *Top view of the PU scope and mounting system. (Steve Broadbent Collection)*

RIGHT: *View from the left showing mounting bracket and leather lens covers. (Steve Broadbent Collection)*

The M91/30 sniper rifle and PU scope were famously robust, reliable, accurate, and easy to maintain. They were even used by enemy soldiers if they could get their hands on them.

It has been estimated that by the time of the "Winter War"–when Russia invaded Finland in 1939–the Soviets could field 60,000 snipers. However, they had taken on an enemy that also used snipers, and was well suited to fighting in sub-zero winter conditions and the heavily forested, snow-covered terrain. The Finns proved to be formidable opponents, and among their number emerged two of the most famous snipers of all time–Suko Kolkka and Simo Häyhä.

Suko (or Sulo) Kolkka is claimed to have chalked up over 400 kills during the Winter War, but even this amazing tally is eclipsed by the exploits of Lance Corporal Simo Häyhä (nicknamed the White Death). In approximately one hundred days–from the time he went into service until he was wounded with a head shot, from which he miraculously survived–Simo Häyhä is reckoned to have killed 542 Soviet soldiers with a rifle (a further 200-plus were dispatched at close range with a submachine gun). This means he achieved an average of

ABOVE: *Simo Häyhä, a Finnish sniper, and possibly the most prolific ever known.*

RIGHT: *Russian snipers using semi-automatic Tokarev SVT40 rifles. (Cody)*

ABOVE: *A Russian sniper in winter camouflage; deployed in thousands, these men and women caused great problems to the Germans in both attack and retreat.*

RIGHT: *German sniper at Stalingrad. (Cody)*

FAR RIGHT: *Soviet snipers on the outskirts of Leningrad.*

around five kills per day, an amazing feat of marksmanship. The slightly built Häyhä used a Model 28 rifle (a Finnish-issue Mosin-Nagant) and is said to have preferred using open sights, rather than the Finnish-issue Oy Physica prismatic sight. Many Finn snipers were also known to use captured Russian PEM and PU scopes.

The Winter War ended in March 1940 with the Moscow Treaty, under which the Finns retained their sovereignty. The Russians won a small slice of Finland, but at an awful cost. The Finns lost 25,000 men, a substantial amount for a small nation, but the invading Red Army lost around a million troops, causing a Soviet general to comment, "We won just enough ground to bury our dead"—and many of those were the result of the work of Finnish snipers.

The Russians were better prepared when Germany invaded them in 1941. The Soviets ran sniper schools on a large scale, and many of those qualifying as snipers would find themselves being used for delaying tactics to halt the advance of the Germans, while the Red Army retreated and

regrouped before the onslaught. A handful of skilful and well-placed snipers could slow a whole column down, but it took its toll on both sides, since the Germans had some well-trained and experienced snipers too.

Using tactics that would have been recognized by the Boers over fifty years earlier, hidden Russian snipers sitting back 300 or 400 yards would shoot the drivers, tires, and engine bays of the lead vehicle and the last vehicle in a column, thereby effectively blocking forward or backward progress. Then they would pick off targets of opportunity while the enemy tried to clear the road and get the convoy moving again. The Russians would then back off and move a mile or so further down the road before the Germans could engage them properly with machine guns, mortars or light artillery. The snipers would then hide up, wait for the column to arrive, and start the whole process over again.

Later in the war the roles would be reversed, when the Germans were retreating, they would use four to six snipers to act as a rearguard cover.

Another rather unsavory delaying tactic was also employed to break up advances. In his memoirs Josef "Sepp" Allerberger, the second most prolific German sniper, states, *"I would bide my time until the next four waves were on their way towards our lines, then open up rapid fire into the two rear waves, aiming for the stomach. The unexpected casualties at the rear, and the terrible cries of the most seriously wounded, tended to collapse the rear lines and so disconcert the two leading ranks that the whole attack would begin to falter. At this point I could now concentrate on the two leading waves, dispatching those Soviets closer than fifty meter with a shot to the heart or the head. Enemy soldiers who turned and ran I transformed into men screaming with pain with a shot to the kidneys. At this, an attack would frequently disintegrate altogether."*

This would seem to go against the ethos of most modern snipers, who pride themselves on a "clean kill," but we have the luxury of looking back from a safer, more secure point in history. The war on the Eastern Front was vicious in the extreme, with both sides using appalling tactics to gain an advantage. The Russians for example employed explosive "observation" bullets against human targets—as they had during the Russo-Finn "Winter War," and records exist that show that the Germans also used their explosive "B" cartridges to some extent for sniping against Russians. Both Russians and Germans would sometimes kill prisoners, and they could be particularly brutal to captured snipers. Sepp Allerberger soon learned this, and abandoned the "suicidal" practice of notching his rifle stock for each of his kills. Nevertheless, as a novice it didn't stop him claiming the small silver trim (sown on the sniper's lower left sleeve) which was awarded for every ten confirmed kills. He comments that an officer or NCO had to sign the snipers' book to confirm a kill, but many artillery observers would refuse, since they considered snipers

Continued on page 124

Above: *Reenactors portraying German snipers in a Russian city scenario.* (Andy Colborn/SBG)

Overleaf: *German snipers proved very effective in every theater they were deployed in.* (Andy Colborn/SBG)

WORLD WAR II GERMAN SNIPING COMBINATIONS

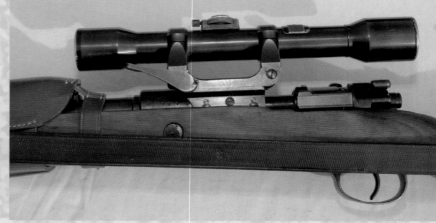

TOP: *The Mauser Kar 98k bolt-action rifle fitted with a scope was the most widely used firearm of German snipers in World War II. (Steve Broadbent Collection).*

ABOVE: *Close-up of left side of Kar 98k action with Dialytan 4x scope and ammunition clip. (Steve Broadbent Collection)*

ABOVE RIGHT: *Close-up of right side of Kar 98k sniper rifle showing the bolt action. (Steve Broadbent Collection)*

ABOVE: *Kar 98 with Khales 4x scope and single claw mount. (Graham Mitchell Collection/SBG)*

BELOW: *Kar 98 with "CAD" 4x scope on high turret mount.*

RIGHT: *Kar 98 with Zeiss Zeilvier 4x scope on side rail mount. (Graham Mitchell Collection/SBG)*

The main German sniping weapon issued in World War II was the Kar 98 bolt-action rifle, which was well known for its accuracy and long-range shooting capabilities. It was issued in tens of thousands, and was used with good effect in every theater of war that German snipers fought in.

Some Gew.43 (or G43) semi-automatic rifles were also issued for sniping but in much smaller numbers than the Kar 98. The gas-operated G43 had its receiver machined to accept a telescope sight mount, in addition to the standard adjustable open sights. Feed was from ten-round detachable box magazines. The Gew.43 had good mid-range accuracy, but as a sniping rifle it wasn't ideal for targets at more than 400 yards or so. Where it did score well was in fairly close engagements against multiple targets, where its speed of fire–combined with the sniper's skill– could prove devastating in breaking up enemy attacks.

The MP44 (Machine Pistol) was also capable of being used with a scope, but this was comparatively rare. It was classified as a submachine gun but was actually the world's first assault rifle. Easily made from steel pressings rather than machining, and with a thirty-round magazine capacity and a rate of fire of 500 rounds per minute, this weapon could have made a substantial difference as a standard-issue rifle had it been made in enough numbers–fortunately it was not. Although it was made to accept a scope, there is no evidence that it made a significant contribution as a sniping rifle.

Many different scope-and-mount combinations were used with the Kar 98, including many commercial (sporting) scopes from Ajak, Hensoldt, Kahles, Zeiss, and other manufacturers. These were usually of excellent optical quality and were probably some of the best in the world at the time. Magnification was usually 4x but some 6x models were also made. Model designations were ZF (*Zielfernrohr*) followed by the year of introduction–ZF39 and so on–except the ZF4 (in this case the "4" standing for 4x), which was originally designed for the G43 semi-auto rifle (see below).

ABOVE: *Mauser Model Kar 98k rifle with a laminated stock and a Zf41 extended eye-relief telescopic sight. The Kar 98k was the standard German infantry rifle of World War II. The Zf41 telescope was not really a sniper sight but was used for "snap-shooting" and to obtain greater accuracy when sighting. (AWM. REL-01142)*

FAR LEFT: *Reenactor with Mauser Kar 98k sniper rifle. (Andy Colborn/SBG)*

LEFT: *The MP44—in the hand of the reenactor at far right—was designed to take a scope, but was rarely used for this purpose. (Andy Colborn/SBG)*

BELOW: *An example of some of the scopes used by World War II German snipers: (top to bottom) Zf39 DOW (note the range adjuster ring on the scope body), Khales 4x, "CAD" 4x, and Zeiss Zeilvier 4x. (Graham Mitchell Collection/SBG)*

The ZF-41 extended eye relief scope had a magnification of only 1.5x, and was used almost like a "point sight" aiming aid rather than a true sniping scope. It was mounted to standard K98 rifles and was issued to what we might call today "designated marksmen"; in other words the recipients were good shots, but not usually trained snipers, although combat experience would soon educate them, if they survived. The ZF-41 was mounted well forward of the action; the user would "acquire" the target by direct sight (not using the scope) and would then draw a quick bead with the scope. It worked well at close- to medium-range as a personal and support weapon, and was also no doubt used in a "sniping" role by ordinary soldiers, as were iron-sighted standard-issue K98 rifles for that matter.

The most common scope mounts were quick-release, side-mounting models—early prewar versions were short and fitted to a dovetail machined into the left-hand side of the K98 receiver, while post-1943 models were longer and fitted to a dovetail base screwed onto a flat surface machined onto the receiver. In addition, single claw, double claw and turret mounts were also used.

The ZF-4 was an attempt to standardize and mass-produce a telescopic sight, originally being made for the Gew.43, but later being issued for K98s and other rifles. Although it was a reasonably good design, by the time production was underway the quality was dropping because of the extensive damage being caused by Allied air raids to manufacturing plant, skilled workmen, and raw material supplies.

Unlike most other scopes of the period, the ZF-4 had the elevation turret on the right, with windage on the top. The three-post reticle was not optically centered; therefore, like the Russian PU, it would actually move across (or up/down) the sight picture when adjusted for zero.

BELOW: *Scope models turned upside down to show mounts: (top to bottom) double claw mounts on Zf39 DOW scope; single claw on Khales 4x scope; high turret mount on "CAD" 4x scope; short side rail mount on Zeiss Zeilvier 4x scope. (Graham Mitchell Collection/SBG)*

LEFT: *The Gew.43 semi-automatic rifle with Zf4 scope (seen here) was issued to some snipers, although when interviewed, three top German snipers— Matthais Hetzenauer, Sepp Allerberger, and Helmut Wirnsberger— all said they preferred the bolt-action Mauser. (Andy Colborn/SBG)*

to be assassins—whether German or Russian, presumably. Counter-snipers would also dress dummies as artillery spotters to attract enemy sniper fire, and this also displeased the artillerymen.

successful shots were taken closer than 400 meters. Hetzenauer and Wirnsberger had also used the semi-auto G43 rifle with a four-power scope, but found that it was not as accurate or reliable as the Kar 98.

RIGHT: *The strength of snipers was not in how many men they killed, but how important those men were to the enemy.*

RIGHT: *Perhaps the most famous stories of sniping came from the Russian front—and the siege of Stalingrad in particular.* (Cody)

To counter the efforts of Russian snipers, the Germans set up training schools which were reckoned to be extremely efficient, based on the British pattern of World War I, but adapted to the current situation that the Germans found themselves in. Each German battalion had twenty-two men allotted as snipers and many of these were already battle-hardened, some being sent to sniper school only once they had already proved themselves good marksmen in combat.

The Eastern Front generated many accomplished German snipers. Apart from Allerberger (257 confirmed kills) there was Matthias Hetzenauer (345 confirmed kills); both were awarded the Knights Cross. The actual totals for both men may have been considerably higher, but for the procedure needed to "claim" a kill. Both these men were Austrian by birth, which is interesting, since Austria has provided many sharpshooters throughout history, including many of the famous jägers.

In an interview for the Austrian *Truppendienst* magazine in 1967, Hetzenauer, Allerberger, and Helmut Wirnsberger (another German sniper who had served on the Eastern Front) answered questions on their weapons and methods. All had used scoped Kar 98 rifles and all claimed accuracy of 400 meters (437 yards) for a head shot, the same for a chest shot, and 600 meters (656 yards) or more in one case for a standing man—but overall success rates were approximately, 65-80 percent at 400m and 20-30 percent at 600m, and most

When asked about successful use of snipers, Hetzenauer answered that the best success for snipers did not reside in the number of hits, but in the damage caused to the enemy by shooting commanders or other important men. This sound judgment was proven time and again by German snipers, who found that removing officers and NCOs—thereby depriving the Soviet advance of their leadership—could be extremely effective when many of the Russians were raw recruits, in some cases being "driven" by political commissars. All three interviewees agreed that defense was the sniper's best strategic use. When asked what qualities (other than marksmanship) made the best snipers, they all answered in different ways, but it basically boiled down to; patience, perseverance, observation, and good tactical judgment.

What the Russians had in quantity was not always equaled in quality. Although they were trained, many of the newly qualified Russian snipers were inexperienced in real combat tactics—in fact, even some of their training showed a degree of naivety. As always, the ones who survived their initial combat baptism as snipers were usually the ones who learned as quickly in the field as they did in the classroom. Significantly, their training also included close-range sniping and house-to-house fighting techniques. This was to prove crucial in city fighting, and particularly in the stalemate that developed amongst the ruins of Stalingrad, perhaps the most famous hunting ground for Soviet snipers, and also the venue for one of the most fabled sniping "duels" ever to be played out.

Vasily Grigoryevich Zaitsev was one of Russia's most prolific snipers, becoming a legendary hero of the Soviet people during his own lifetime, and achieving modern fame through the movie *Enemy at the Gate*, in which he was portrayed by British actor, Jude Law. As a hunter from the Urals—an area known as the home of Russian

riflemen—Zaitsev was a good marksman before he became a Soviet marine. After proving his worth by shooting more than thirty Germans with a standard issue rifle, he was soon equipped with a scoped model and designated as a sniper.

He was eventually credited with some 400 kills, but the most famous—and the basis for the plot of the film—was his prolonged duel with a crack German sniper known (in the film) as Major Erwin König. The character König was fictional, but was supposed to derive from a German sniper called either Konings or Heinz Thorvald, but there is doubt about this too. What can be confirmed is that in Zaitsev's biography, *Notes of a Sniper*, he does make mention of tracking (helped by other two-man teams of Russian snipers) and eventually killing a very accomplished German sniper in Stalingrad, but no name is ever mentioned. Nevertheless, in the Battle of Stalingrad (1942–43) alone, Zaitsev is confirmed to have killed 225 German soldiers, all ranks, at least eleven of whom were snipers.

ABOVE: *The Russians used many women snipers during World War II, and some of them proved to be extremely effective in the role.* (John Norris)

OVERLEAF: *German sniper with Gew.43 semi-automatic rifle with Zf4 scope. In the foreground is an MG42 general-purpose machine gun.* (Andy Colborn/SBG)

HEROES OF THE GREAT PATRIOTIC WAR–RUSSIAN SNIPERS AND SOVIET PROPAGANDA

As early as 1924 Soviet military experts had recognized that snipers were an efficient and cost-effective strategic resource, and had begun to set up special sniper schools. Given the right training and equipment–and of course the correct political indoctrination–an elite group of snipers could cause havoc among the enemy. So how much more effective would they be if numbered in their tens of thousands?

Soviet snipers were taught not only about their rifle and scope, and how to use them, but also about camouflage, defensive and offensive tactics, sniping in the open or in forest or in towns, how to use grenades, and even hand-to-hand combat techniques. Some of the sniping courses were short, with the graduates expected to be paired with more experienced men. The result was that some 60,000 snipers were available by 1939.

During this Great Patriotic War–as the Russians called World War II–the Soviet propagandists encouraged hero worship of the sniper "*snayperskya*," raising these undeniably brave marksmen into an almost mythical warrior status. Great snipers such as Mikhail Ilyich Surkov, Ivan Sidorenko, Fyodor Matveyevich Okhlopkov and of course Vasily Grigoryevich Zaitsev, became widely famous in carefully choreographed press releases, in order to keep the morale of the country high. Some of the claimed kill figures may have been inflated for propaganda purposes, but there were also cases where figures weren't recorded at all.

Uniquely, the USSR also used women as snipers, with over 1,000 serving by 1943, including Lyudmila Pavlichenko, Yekaterina Zuranova, Tatiana Igantovna Kostyrina, and Nina Alexeyevna Lobkovskaya, who commanded a whole company of female snipers. Lyudmila Pavlichenko became an "ambassador" for the Russian war effort and a worldwide celebrity after being wounded, having accounted for 309 Germans in the defense of Odessa and Sebastopol. Nataly V. Kovshova and Maria Polivanova–who, working as a sniper team, killed over 300 German soldiers–became national heroes when they fought to the death after running out of ammunition, choosing to blow themselves up with grenades rather than be taken alive. Their decision is understandable considering the treatment meted out to captured snipers.

ABOVE: *One of the most famous Russian female snipers, Lyudmila Pavlichenko, who is claimed to have killed over 300 enemy soldiers.*

ABOVE LEFT: *Some female snipers–like Roza Shanina–were often depicted quite "glamorously" in Russian newspapers.*

LEFT: *The Russians even issued a stamp commemorating the exploits of their snipers.*

Soviet Sniper Tallies

The following sniper tallies have been compiled from a number of sources, so their absolute accuracy cannot be guaranteed. However, even if these figures were as much as 50 percent out—and there is no suggestion that they are—it does give some idea of how effective a "resource" snipers can be. Bear in mind that some modern studies claim that in combat very few soldiers actually aim their weapons accurately at the enemy at all. It must also be taken into account that some of the following figures may have been bolstered by numbers of enemy soldiers shot with machine guns and submachine guns from ambush positions. (This was not the case with Finnish sniper Simo Häyhä, who had two separate kill totals, one with a rifle and the other with submachine gun.)

(F) denotes female sniper

Mikhail Ilyich Surkov	700+	Zhambyl Evscheyevich Tulaev	262
Vasiliy Shalvovich Kvachantiradze	534	Fyodor Kuzmich Chegodaev	250
Ivan Sidorenko	500	Ivan Ivanovich Bocharov	248
Nikolay Yakovlevich Ilyin	496	Mikhail Ignatievich Belousov	245
Kulbertinov	487	Maxim Passar	237
V. N. Pchelintsev	456	David Teboevich Doev	226
Mikhail Budenkov	437	N. F. Semyonnov	218
Fyodor Djachenko	425	Vasilij Shalvovich Kvachantiradze	215
Vasilij Ivanovich Golosov	422	Mikhail Stepanovich Sokhin	202
Afanasy Gordienko	412	Noj Petrovich Adamia	200
Stepan Petrenko	412	M. A. Abbasov	200
Fyodor Matveyevich Okhlopkov	400+	Yekaterina Zuranova	155 (F)
Vasily Grigoryevich Zaitsev	400	Vladimir Ptchelinzev	152
Semen D. Nomokonov	367	Inna Semyonovna Mudretsova	143
Abdukhani Idrisov	349	Feodosy Smeljachkov	125
Philipp Yakovlevich Rubaho	346	H. Andruhaev	125
Victor Ivanovich Medvedev	331	I. Merkulov	125
E. Nicolaev	324	Tatiana Igantovna Kostyrina	120 (F)
Leonid Yakovlevich Butkevich	315	Janis Roze	116
Nikolai Ilyin	315	N. P. Petrova	107 (F)
Lyudmila Mikhailovna Pavlichenko	309 (F)	V. N. Pchelintsev	102
Alexander Pavlovich Lebedev	307	Yelizaveta Mironova	100+ (F)
Ivan Pavlovich Gorelikov	305	Aliya Moldagulova	91 (F)
Ivan Petrovich Antonov	302	Nina Lobkovskaya	89 (F)
Gennadij Iosifovich Velichko	300	Lidiya Gudovantseva	76 (F)
Moisej Timofeyevich Usik	300	Alexandra Shlyakhova	63 (F)
Nataly V. Kovshova & Maria Polivanova	300 (F)	P. Grjaznov	57
Ivan Filippovich Abdulov	298	Roza Yegorovna Shanina	54 (F)
Yakov Mikhajlovich Smetnev	279	A. P. Medvedeva-Nazarkina	43 (F)
Liba Rugova	274	Tatiana Nikolaevna Baramzina	36 (F)
Anatolij Chekhov	265	Marie Ljalková (Czechoslovakian)	30 (F)

ABOVE: *Lyudmila Pavlichenko became quite a celebrity, traveling around the world (seen here in the United States) promoting the Russian cause.* (NA)

BELOW: *Sgt. Pdorzhive, seen here observing with binoculars, was a Russian sniper who is claimed to have killed 181 Germans at Leningrad.* (NA)

German Sniper Tallies

Less is known about German sniper tallies, probably because so many German records were destroyed at the end of the war.

Matthias Hetzenauer	345
Sepp Allerberger	257
Bruno Sutkus	209
Friedrich Pein	200+
Gefreiter Meyer	180
Oleh Dir	120
Helmut Wirnsberger	64

The German army were said to have sent their top sniper to counter Russian sniping hero Vasily Zaitsev, but whether this (the foundation for the movie Enemy at the Gate) was true or not has never been fully established. (Andy Colborn/SBG)

ABOVE: *The British set up specialist sniper schools— this is a group of commando snipers at their passing out; note the scoped Lee-Enfield rifles and the spotting scopes in the foreground.* (Leonard Chalk, sniper with No 45 and 46 RM Commandos)

RIGHT: *Infantrymen of The Queen's Own Rifles of Canada taking a break during their sniper training course, England, April 21, 1944.* (Lt. Frank L. Dubervil/Canada. Dept. of National Defense/Library and Archives Canada/PA-211817)

RIGHT: *The P14 Enfield No. 3 (T) rifle was still in use at the beginning of World War II.* (Sgt. Al W. Grayston/ Canada. Dept. of National Defense/Library and Archives Canada/PA-213632)

Snipers in Western Europe

The first part of the war in the West of Europe was one of *Blitzkrieg*, with the highly mobile German army riding roughshod over the opposition, yet the Germans still used snipers against the retreating British in 1940. The British also used snipers to good effect—using World War I issue P14 No. 3 (T) rifles—to delay the German infantry advance while the evacuation of troops was being carried out at Dunkirk. Most of these sniping weapons were left behind by the British, but the lesson had been learned, and the military authorities began to increase specialized sniper training schools.

The replacement British sniping rifle, which was to last the course of the war—and much longer, was the Lee-Enfield No. 4 (T) with No. 32 scope. This saw service with British and Canadian snipers in Europe,

North Africa, and the Far East. It was also used to a lesser extent by Anzac troops.

Using standard .303 ammunition, it was found that if the No. 32 scope was zeroed to 275 yards and the rifle was aimed to the middle of the head, the trajectory of the bullet would almost always guarantee a killing hit on a man (it would strike somewhere between the chest and the top of the head) at any distance from 25 to 300 yards. Greater distance could be achieved by adjustment with hold-over. This set zero was a great advantage because it meant that for most shots the sniper could aim "dead on" and didn't have to alter zero again—which is just as well, because the early No. 32 scopes weren't that easy to zero. Curiously enough, this echoes the World War I instruction to German snipers to "aim for the teeth"—presumably with a similar trajectory setting on their scopes.

FAR LEFT: *Allied sniper checking his scope.* (Lt.. Frederick G. Whitcombe/Canada. Dept. of National Defense/Library and Archives Canada / PA-211643)

LEFT: *Scouting teams were often used for sniper work as well as reconnaissance.* (Lt. Ken Bell/Canada. Dept. of National Defense/Library and Archives Canada/PA-138416)

The first big test of British and Canadian snipers was in the raid on Dieppe, northern France, in 1942, which resulted in a terrible mauling for the Allied troops, but certainly proved the worth of snipers. Part of the raid involved 300 British commandos and American rangers who were sent to neutralize a German artillery battery—and they successfully achieved their objective. The force included twenty snipers, and two of their number, Lance Corporal Richard Mann and U.S. Ranger Sgt. Frank Koons, were so effective in eliminating the artillerymen and machine gun crews that they were both awarded the Military Medal.

LEFT: *Canadian sniper armed with the Lee-Enfield Sniper Rifle.* (Lt. Frederick G. Whitcombe/Canada. Dept. of National Defense/Library and Archives Canada/PA-211642)

BELOW: *Reenactors in a set-up similar to that used by a British Army Lovat Scouts sniping team: shooter and spotter, sniper rifle and telescope. The Lovat Scouts were Britain's first official sniping unit.* (John Norris)

British World War II reenactor with Lee-Enfield No. 4 Mk I (T) sniping rifle and No. 32 scope. (John Norris)

THE BRITISH NO. 4 MK I (T) SNIPING RIFLE

The standard British (and Canadian) sniping rifle during World War II was the No. 4 Mk I (T). To get the best base rifles, standard Lee-Enfield No. 4 rifles were tested at the factory and selected for their accuracy. These best examples were then modified by having a removable sight mount fitted to the left side of the receiver (to take a No. 32 telescopic sight), and a wooden cheek-piece added to the stock, in order to raise the comb and align the shooter's eye with the scope's eyepiece. With this mounting system the iron battle sights could still be used in an emergency and the rifle could still be load by stripper clip.

Most No. 4 Mk I (T) sniper rifles were converted in Britain, either by Holland and Holland or BSA, but some others were altered at the Long Branch arsenal in Canada.

The No. 32 sight had 3.5x magnification and was solidly made, as it was originally intended for use on a Bren gun (a light machine gun). It had a 1-inch diameter brass tube, 11 inches long, and it weighed in excess of 2.5lb with its steel mount. Early models had elevation turrets adjustable in 50-yard increments from 0 to 1,000 yards. Later models (after 1943) were fitted with MOA adjustment, while the windage turrets were good for 16 MOA in either direction. Reticle pattern was a thick vertical line reaching halfway up from the bottom of the reticle, with a thin horizontal line going across it for the full width of the sight picture.

BELOW: *Close- up of the 3.5x power No. 32 scope and the rifle action.* (Steve Broadbent Collection)

RIGHT: *The Lee-Enfield. No 4 Mk I (T) Sniper Rifle mounted with a No. 32 scope.* (Steve Broadbent Collection)

LEFT: *Scope removed from rifle, showing quick-release mount.* (Steve Broadbent Collection)

ABOVE, CENTER: *View from above, showing scope elevation and windage turrets.* (Steve Broadbent Collection)

ABOVE: *Uniquely among all sniper rifles of its era, the stock of the Lee-Enfield. No. 4 Mk I (T) was fitted with a special cheekpiece to help raise the shooter's eye-line to the scope.* (Steve Broadbent Collection)

ABOVE: *The scope was easily removed from the rifle and stowed in a purpose-built transit case.* (Steve Broadbent Collection)

ABOVE, CENTER: *Left side of rifle showing scope mounted.* (Steve Broadbent Collection)

ABOVE: *Left side of rifle, scope removed, showing mount bases on receiver.* (Steve Broadbent Collection)

RIGHT: *Allied snipers played their part in countering German snipers in North Africa and the invasion of Italy. This group are in the Liri River Valley, Italy, 1944. (Lt. W. H. Agnew/Canada. Dept. of National Defense/ Library and Archives Canada/PA-117835)*

FAR RIGHT: *German snipers acted as a rearguard for their retreating armies, slowing down the Allied advance. These troops have come under sniper fire in Campochiaro, Italy, 1943. (Lt. Alexander Mackenzie Stirton/Canada. Dept. National Defense/Library and Archives Canada/PA-129774)*

OPPOSITE: *British sniper watching for enemy movement at Caen, France, 1944. (AWM. 128643)*

One of the most positive outcomes of the raid was the further realization by the British and Canadians of the importance of snipers. A scout and sniper platoon became part of every Canadian infantry battalion and took on the main reconnoitering duties. These men were trained in a very similar way as the Lovat Scouts, in camouflage, stealth, observation, and marksmanship. They were the forerunners of today's recce troops.

In North Africa the value of snipers was also proved, with British and Australian snipers taking advantage of the bleak sandy terrain to get close enough to shoot Italian and German *Afrika Korps* artillerymen and observers. The Allied invasion of Italy in September 1943 introduced Americans to German snipers, and on one occasion it was reckoned that just three German sharpshooters held up the Allies' whole advance—until cleared by a pounding from artillery, a classic countermeasure to snipers. In fact, sniper duels were fought throughout the Italian campaign, especially at Monte Cassino, one of the hardest fought battles of the war, where British, American, and Commonwealth troops suffered many casualties while dislodging the German snipers and machine guns dug in on the slopes.

GERMAN "SNIPERS CODE," 1944

1. Fight fanatically.

2. Shoot calm and contemplated; fast shots lead nowhere; concentrate on the hit.

3. Your greatest opponent is the enemy sniper; outsmart him.

4. Always only fire one shot from your position; if not you will be discovered.

5. The entrenching tool prolongs your life.

6. Practice in distance judging.

7. Become a master in camouflage and terrain usage.

8. Practice constantly, behind the front and in the homeland, your shooting skills.

9. Never let go of your sniper rifle.

10. Survival is ten times camouflage and one time firing.

RIGHT: *Well-equipped, -trained and -practiced, the late-World War II German sniper followed a code that was a combination of good advice and last-ditch fanaticism. (Ian Sandford/SBG)*

When the Allies invaded Normandy, France, in June 1944, they had to fight hard for every inch of ground. Besides the artillery and machine guns they had to face, the Germans had snipers hidden everywhere, and most of them were experienced and battle-hardened veterans. But the Allies had snipers of their own, like Sgt Frank Kwaitek of the U.S. Army, who literally notched up twenty-two kills (including some snipers) on his rifle butt before the end of June 1944.

Ernie Pyle, famed American war correspondent, reported, "*Here in Normandy, there are snipers everywhere. There are snipers in trees, in buildings, in piles of wreckage, in the grass. But mainly they are in the high, bushy hedgerows that form the fences of all the Norman fields and line every roadside and lane.*"

If they got the opportunity, the German snipers would shoot Allied officers first, picking them out because they carried field glasses or a pistol or maps. They even shot men with moustaches because they were more likely to be officers or senior NCOs. Sometimes they only had to watch to see if one of the Allies' men looked as though he was giving orders. Other priority targets were vehicle commanders, signalers, gun crews, observers, and so on. They were also not beyond shooting medics, even those who had a red cross clearly marked on their helmets.

In Normandy the German snipers would target crossroads, bridges, and the narrow lanes and criss-crossing hedgerows (known as the Bocage) as likely places to be able to halt Allied movement while remaining concealed. They dug in under hedges, or in and around deserted buildings, climbed church steeples, and any kind of tower—in fact anywhere that could give them an advantageous shooting position. Countermeasures were difficult, because the countryside allowed the sniper to take accurate shots at just a few hundred yards, and it was hard to return fire if they could not be seen. Nevertheless, once spotted, heavy small arms fire could

be directed on the sniper's position, and, if necessary, artillery fire would be called in. Either way, it would be a long, bitter struggle to dislodge them.

As the Allies moved through France they came across snipers who would not take as many precautions as the more experienced troops, and would fight to the death, unless they were wounded and captured. Many of these were fanatical young men who had been in the Nazi Hitler Youth movement, indoctrinated to defend their Fatherland at any cost. Even when it was obvious that the war was lost, some of these German snipers fought to the bitter end.

ABOVE LEFT: *As the Allies pushed through France they encountered German snipers everywhere, often using their own snipers to counter them.* (Cody)

ABOVE: *The Allies became adept at effectively deploying their own snipers.* (Lt. Ken Bell/Canada. Dept. of National Defense/Library and Archives Canada/PA-211728)

FAR LEFT: *Following the Allied invasion of France, June 1944, German snipers occupied almost every building and hedgerow in Normandy.* (Andy Colborn/SBG)

LEFT: *At just 17 years old Leonard Chalk volunteered for the Royal Marine Commandos where he was trained as a sniper. Although wounded in the shoulder and neck at Caen, he returned to fight in the latter months of the war in Europe. During street to street fighting in Osnabrück he shot a German machine gun team who were running to take up a new position. Years later, relating this incident to his son, he simply said, "When they're running you just have to give them a hair's breadth of lead…" His "matter of fact" manner seems to fairly sum up the attitude that many snipers take to their calling.*

OVERLEAF: *A reenactor portraying a German sniper in the winter of 1944.* (Andy Colborn/SBG)

WORLD WAR II CAMOUFLAGE

By the outbreak of World War II disruptive-patterned camouflage—rather than just general dull green, gray or brown "solid" colored uniforms—was being used to varying extents by many armies, but mainly just for elite troops, such as paratroops, commandos, and of course snipers. Disruptive-patterned camouflage paradoxically uses contrasting and/or complementary colors (browns, greens, grays, and black) in the form of irregular stripes, spots or irregular patterns, over a neutrally colored background in order to break up the shape of the person or object that it is trying to conceal.

The Germans had been experimenting with camouflage patterns since the mid-1930s and made great use of modern cloth production techniques to create many camouflage variations to suit various landscapes. In some cases these were even designed to match the seasons, and some garments were reversible to give two distinct patterns reflecting spring or fall hues.

The Russians and many other northern European and Scandinavian countries made white camo clothing to suit the snow-covered terrain of winter, and also to break up the shape of their rifles by either attaching strips of white cloth or painting irregular white lines on the stock.

Britain stopped experimenting with camouflage after World War I, and didn't start up their Camouflage Development and Training Centre until 1940. Interestingly, the Centre even used a professional magician—Jasper Maskelyne—

to create illusionary camouflage. The first British camouflage garment of World War II was the Denison smock, a baggy, tawny-colored garment daubed with green, brown, and black paint. Primarily designed for paratroopers, the Denison smock was soon adopted by other specialist units, including snipers, for its concealment and weatherproof qualities.

The U.S. Army began experiments in camouflage uniforms in 1940, coming up with the reversible "frog-skin"/"leopard spot" pattern, designed for beach and jungle warfare, which was issued to U.S. marines in the Pacific theater.

Some armies experimented with painted camouflage patterns on combat helmets, but more commonly these were disguised with a camouflaged fabric cover or netting that could be interwoven with pieces of drab-colored cloth (scrim) or local vegetation.

The Japanese and Australians were particularly adept at using grasses, twigs, and palm fronds to blend in with the background. At Wongabel and other Aussie training facilities their snipers were taught to make "cartwheels" out of bamboo with a woven grass cover, which they would position over a foxhole, in order to conceal themselves—a trick they learned from the Japanese. The Australians also made wide use of netting and scrim to break up their outline in the jungle.

LEFT AND RIGHT: *The German army had many different camo patterns, reflecting the seasons and the terrain background conditions; many of their camouflage smocks were reversible, with different patterns on each side*

BELOW LEFT: *World War II Canadian sniper, Sgt. Marshall of the Calgary Highlanders' Scout and Sniper Platoon, wearing a Denison smock and a camouflage face veil as a head covering,* (Lt. Ken Bell/Canada. Dept. of National Defense/Library and Archives Canada/PA-a140408-v6)

The Rule of the 5 Ss

Shape:
any suggestion of human shape or straight lines (like a rifle) should be "broken up" with camo scrim, camo paint, camo-pattern clothing or netting, or natural vegetation.

Shine:
anything that might shine—uncovered face and hands, rifle barrel and action, scope or binocular lenses, and so on—should be either covered or camouflaged.

Shadow:
keep in shadow where possible, but avoid casting a shadow if possible.

Silhouette:
don't become silhouetted against sky, water or other light backgrounds.

Spacing:
natural objects are never regularly spaced; also keep a good space between yourself and your shooting partner.

There should actually be a 6th "S," and that is: *avoid "sudden" movement, or always move "slowly" and cautiously—there is no doubt that the quickest thing that the human eye will pick up is movement.*

ABOVE: *Snipers in training, wearing camouflage, including face paint, scrims, and netting.* (Lt. Dwight E. Dolan/Canada. Dept. of National Defense/Library and Archives Canada/PA-177141)

BELOW: *World War II British winter camouflage clothing.* (Lt. Barney J. Gloster/Canada. Dept. of National Defence/Library and Archives Canada/PA-137987)

ABOVE: *German "Oak B" pattern camouflage.* (John Norris)

Above: German "Oak A" pattern camouflage. (John Norris)

ABOVE: *German "Plain Tree" pattern camouflage.* (John Norris)

ABOVE: *Russian sniper at Stalingrad in camouflaged cover over a camouflaged tunic.*

Above: German "Blurred Edge" pattern camouflage. (John Norris)

ABOVE: *Standing in plain sight, this Australian sniper shows the effect of disruptive pattern camouflage. (AWM. 083462)*

The Pacific and Far East

On the islands of the Pacific, and in Burma and the Asian mainland, the Allied troops faced the threat of the Japanese sniper. Possibly more than any other snipers, the Japanese used close-range sniping techniques, often waiting for hours or even days in hidden positions, until the target was in "whites of their eyes" range before firing, and then continuing to fire until he himself was killed. This fanatical and ultimately suicidal zeal to fight to the death for their emperor was indoctrinated into Japanese infantrymen just as it was to *kamikaze* pilots. Often the Japanese "snipers" were just ordinary infantrymen using standard-issue rifles, and the ranges they shot at were frequently so close as to make no difference whether their weapons were scoped or not—it was the fact that they could stay concealed until they opened fire that made them so dangerous. It also made every beach, every hill, and every inch of jungle a struggle to take for the Allies.

LEFT: *This gives some idea of the jungles in the Far East, and how easy it was to hide snipers.* (LoC)

An article in *Time* magazine in 1943 stated, *"Marine and Army men returning from the South Pacific almost unanimously hold that, man for man, the Jap soldier is inferior in fighting qualities to the American. But in all the things to do with hiding, stealth and trickery, they give the Japs plenty of angry credit.*

"They dig deep, stand-up foxholes, which are safe except under direct artillery fire (and which are better than U.S. slit trenches). On the defensive, they dig themselves dugouts protected by palm trunks, and then they crawl in and resist until some explosive or a human terrier kills them.

"The myth of the Japanese sniper is exploded by returning officers. They say that Japanese snipers are an annoyance, little more. They hide excellently but their aim is poor. Sniping serves, however, to frighten men who will not deliberately ignore it…

"… But the greatest handicap of the Japanese is their lack of imagination. They carry out orders to the letter and, if necessary, to death. But when things go wrong, they

LEFT: *U.S. marines fighting their way off the beachhead at Tarawa where they met with heavy weapons fire as well as Japanese snipers who were described as an "annoyance," but who, right across the Pacific and the Far East, were nevertheless prepared to fight zealously to the death.* (NA)

cannot adapt their tactics. If Jap attackers meet resistance, they advance anyhow—which accounts for the terrible slaughter to which Japanese troops submit themselves."

There were of course specialist snipers in the Japanese army, trained in long-range sharpshooting, camouflage, and all the other skills of the sniper. Their main weapons were the bolt-action Arisaka Type 99 Sniper Rifle and the older model Arisaka Type 97 Sniper Rifle in 6.5x50mm. Specialist snipers made good use of local vegetation to disguise both their dugouts and themselves, and they were renowned for their patience and ability to endure harsh conditions. Nevertheless, because they would often fire more than one shot, it made them quicker targets to pinpoint, and they were up against some of the best trained counter-snipers in the world in the USMC and the Anzacs.

LEFT: *U.S. sniper on Tarawa in 1943.* (Cody)

WORLD WAR II JAPANESE SNIPING RIFLES

The main sniper weapons of the Japanese army were the bolt-action Arisaka Type 99 Sniper Rifle in 7.7x58mm and the older model Arisaka Type 97 Sniper Rifle in 6.5x50mm.

The 97 was based on the Arisaka Type 38, which had seen many years of service in Japan's war against China (which began in 1931, was fought in earnest from 1937, and became part of World War II from 1941). The 97 sniping version entered service in 1937 and had a longer, curved bolt so that the user's hand did not foul the rear-mounted 2.5 power telescopic sight. The rifle also had a lighter stock and a folding metal wire bipod. The main problem with all Type 38 rifles was that they were too long and their 6.5x50mm service

cartridge was not powerful enough—although it did make the sniper variant more difficult to spot due to its smaller muzzle flash.

The 99 was a shorter rifle (the barrel was about eight inches shorter than that on the 97), and it used the more powerful 7.7x58mm cartridge. In addition it was fitted with a more useful 4x mag. scope, although some early models still had the 2.5x scope.

The Arisaka Type 38 and its derivatives were well respected in their time—the Finns almost chose it over the Mosin-Nagant—and it was reckoned to have one of the strongest bolt actions of any rifle.

ABOVE: *Arisaka Type 97 Sniper Rifle c.1937 from the Imperial Japanese Arsenal, Kokura. This rifle was fitted with a monopod at the fore-end and a telescopic sight. It was used by Japanese forces in Manchuria in the 1930s and the early part of World War II in New Guinea.* (AWM. REL/07061.001)

BELOW: *Arisaka Type 99 Sniper Rifle c.1940 from the Imperial Japanese Arsenal, Nagoya. This rifle is fitted with a 4X7 telescopic sight. It is a development from the earlier Type 97 rifle, being shorter in length and of a larger caliber. It was used by the Japanese throughout the Pacific.* (AWM. REL/07214)

AMERICAN SNIPING RIFLES IN WORLD WAR II

By 1940 the U.S. Army had adopted the semi-automatic M1 Garand as its main combat rifle. Unfortunately the clip-loading mechanism did not permit a top-mounted scope so, after a great deal of experimentation with scopes and side-mounting systems, the M81 and M82 Lyman scopes were approved in late 1944. However, some 28,000 bolt-action .30-06-caliber Springfield M1903A4 (Sniper's) were also produced by Remington Arms and remained in service throughout the war and beyond. Many snipers positively preferred them, even when the sniping version of the Garand was issued. The A4 sniper model had no "open sights" fitted and often came in a stock with a pistol grip. The receiver was adapted to take a Redfield mount base and ¾ inch rings, which in turn carried a Weaver 330C scope with a 2.5x magnification.

With a scope mounted to the M1903A4 the magazine could not be loaded with a stripper-clip; however, the box magazine could be manually loaded one cartridge at a time to its full five-round capacity.

The USMC's standard sniping rifle at the beginning of the war was the Springfield 1903A1 with a Lyman 5A scope (5x mag.), but the scope was later upgraded to a Unertl (8x mag.). Both versions saw service throughout World War II.

ABOVE: *Springfield M1903A3 Sniper Rifle. Receiver stamped US REMINGTON MODEL 03-A3. This rifle is fitted with a Weaver Model 73B telescopic sight on a Redfield mount. The telescope has the number 3419601 painted in white on the top tube. A two-piece leather sling with brass fittings is attached to the rifle.*

BELOW: *A reenactor portraying a USMC sniper with Springfield M1903A3 Sniper Rifle and Unertl 8x scope.*

Northern Territory, Australia, 1942. Lieutenant R. W. Wilson of 23/21 Australian infantry battalion, explaining the principles of sniping to a class. The sniper in the tree has a camouflage suit made from a piece of sacking, colored with green ink. (AWM. 027767)

Papua, New Guinea—a Japanese sniper lies dead under the tree he was hiding in; at the top of the sniper's outstretched right hand is his broken rifle. Both the Australians and Americans would tackle snipers in trees by simply using machine guns and submachine guns to destroy the upper branches and dislodge any ensconced snipers. (AWM. 013937)

If available, Allied snipers would pick off the Japanese riflemen once spotted, but if not, sometimes other counter-sniping techniques were equally effective. Against "tree-top" snipers the Allies would simply "spray" the tops of any likely looking trees with machine guns or semi-automatic weapons, and dislodge any incumbent sniper with overwhelming firepower. In dugouts and caves the use of flamethrowers or explosives proved highly effective in removing hidden snipers.

Because even the most combat-hardened Japanese snipers would inevitably be killed or captured, the men replacing them would usually be less experienced, thereby gradually lowering the standard of opposition that the Allies were encountering.

During World War II most Allied countries had taken measures to set up sniping schools or at least teach the skills needed for this very specialist type of combat, and

Left: *The Americans used flamethrowers as one method of dealing with snipers concealed in dugouts and bunkers.*

it had certainly paid dividends, so it was surprising that both the U.S. Army and the marines decided to end their sniper programs at the end of the war.

Below: *Beaufort, Borneo, 1945. Private I. Tonks, a sniper, with two spotters, searching for Japanese snipers.* (AWM. 114097)

Bougainville Island, 1944. Private T. Hall, 25th infantry battalion, picking off a Japanese sniper in a tall tree during the Australian advance on the enemy positions. (AWM. 078022)

Three Japanese snipers lay dead after losing a running firefight with U.S. troops during the island-hopping campaign.

Australian Sniping Rifles in World War II

The standard Australian Army sniper rifles in World War II were derived totally from World War I period equipment, namely the Pattern 1914 Enfield No. 3 Mk I* (T) Sniper Rifle with a Pattern 1918 scope, and the SMLE No. 1 Mk III*, modified at Lithgow arsenal by the addition of a heavier barrel and a higher wooden cheek-piece, and was also mounted with a Pattern 1918 scope, thereby becoming the SMLE No. 1 Mk III* (HT).

The scope mounts were of the claw type, with a low claw for pure sniping rifles or a higher claw mount for a dual use—allowing the user to quickly drop his line of sight and use the iron battle sights for close-quarter fighting. This was of obvious use in the jungle fighting that many Australians found themselves in, where multiple shots might have to be taken at well under 100 yards in quick succession.

Although they used less than modern equipment, the Australians, many of whom were keen amateur riflemen or professional kangaroo hunters before the war, proved to be some of the most effective snipers and counter-snipers.

ABOVE: *Pattern 1914 Enfield No. 3 Mk I* (T) Sniper Rifle with a Pattern 1918 telescopic sight, as used by the Australian army during World War II.* (AWM. REL-06068-001)

LEFT: *Close-up of the Pattern 1918 Telescopic Rifle Sight made by the Australian Optical Company. This one was made in 1944.* (AWM. RELAWM37030.002)

Reenactment display of U.S. Ranger with Springfield 1903A4 Sniper Rifle.

USMC snipers were equipped with the Springfield 1903A4 Sniper Rifle fitted with either a Lyman or Unertl scope—the latter is seen here. (John Norris)

CHAPTER FOUR:
PEACE AT LAST?

CHAPTER FOUR: PEACE AT LAST?

PREVIOUS PAGES: *U.S. Marine Corporal Danny Rodriguez sights through his sniperscope in the process of picking off four North Korean soldiers he spotted on a distant ridge (c.1950), showing that heavy emphasis on rifle marksmanship has often paid off.* (USMC)

BELOW: *One of the "brushfire" wars that Britain was involved in after World War II was against the Haganah ("The Defense," precursor to the Israel Defense Forces) in the British Mandate of Palestine in 1948. Here two Haganah snipers, a male and a female, have scaled a tree from which to fire on British troops, May 21, 1948.* (Hulton-Deutsch/Corbis)

The end of World War II found a world desperate to get back to normal, and to avoid anything to do with conflict and war. Society has a recurring tendency to believe that war will never happen again, and that at last mankind has realized the true horror of conflict. Unfortunately, that is unlikely ever to be seen. Man's way of convincing himself that all is now good and that we will never make the mistake again is to immediately discard anything to do with war and conflict, and to abandon often hard-learned lessons. One lesson that has been constantly thrown away concerns the skill of the sniper.

As happened at the end of hostilities in World War I, armies the world over all but abandoned sniping, and disbanded sniper sections and platoons wholesale, returning often very skilled and experienced men to mundane and routine duties. Having carried out very dangerous and responsible wartime missions, these men now found themselves handing in all their sniper equipment and being moved back either to their rifle platoons or into other jobs that those in power thought would suit their experience, such as in the intelligence sections and departments. Some did find their way into government agencies who appreciated their skill set, as still occurs, but the vast majority were essentially discarded, along with their knowledge and experience.

This situation is often financially driven, since war is a tremendous drain on any country's economy, and elected governments are hard pressed to quickly reduce costs and redirect spending to the civilian communities, to rebuilding of the nation. While this is essential and as such acceptable, within this activity there are a multitude of generals, admirals, and air commodores feverishly attempting to keep as much of their fleets of tanks and ships and planes as they can, and during the maneuvering to keep such equipment there have to be found items to sacrifice. And sniping has always been seen as merely a man with a rifle, and non-essential.

It has taken several wars and conflicts over the past sixty or so years to reach the point now where snipers are, for the first time in their history, seen as not only an acceptable form of warfare, but also the weapon of choice in many situations, with some countries trebling the number of snipers trained per year.

The downsizing of armies at the end of World War II once again saw the demise of the sniper. As an example, the British military was quick to end all sniper training and disband its sniper units, and had it not been for the foresight of the Royal Marines, would have lost all its sniper experience.

The Royal Marines took on the role of commando completely after the end of conflict, and the British Army disbanded or transferred commando-qualified men, ending army commando operations completely. The very nature of commando operations dictates that anything allowing a small unit of men to gain the upper hand over a much larger enemy force is of immense value, and sniping fits the bill perfectly.

Sniping is no more than a conglomerate of infantry skills taken to such a high standard that it becomes specialist, and as such produces a soldier of a much higher caliber. In a small unit, such as a commando force, the sniper's skills are both valued and treasured. The Royal Marines have always held high their demand for professionalism above all things, a sentiment echoed by their cousins in the U.S. Marine Corps, who demand that all men are infantrymen first no matter what particular skill they have, be it medic or fighter pilot.

The Royal Marines can justifiably claim to be the source of both the British and the U.S. military's current

sniper schools and curriculum. When war came again, as it inexorably does, the Royal Marines were the only force to have not only maintained but improved and perfected the sniper option. Maybe it is the reliance on lightly armed forces to achieve their mission that has given the marines on both sides of the Atlantic their understanding of the sniper force multiplier status. Whoever had the insight, it was down to both that the threat to sniping was quickly overcome in later conflicts, and time was bought for the larger armies to catch up.

The Korean conflict

Peace is an elusive prize. Man's tribal spirit will continue to bring him into conflict with other men, be it for economic or religious reasons. So when the conflict broke out in Korea in 1950, it can have been of little surprise. The end of World War II saw the emergence of

superpowers—Russia and the United States—and their different views on how the world should be run inevitably created tensions between the two. Korea, a nation split in half, became the stage for confrontation between the superpowers, with Russia supporting the North and the United States supporting the South. The tensions turned to blows in June 1950 when the communist forces of the North surged across the divide into the South.

With conflict came the need to expand armies and their capabilities, and it took very little time for the sniper to re-emerge. As with all major conflicts before, mounting sniper-related casualties soon forced a rethink on the part of the western armies, and snipers were rapidly reintroduced.

While the Korean War saw the introduction of jet fighters and technologically advanced weapons, the lowly sniper proved again that no matter what the advance in technology, he was still able to operate and inflict damage

ABOVE: *Two British Royal Marines watch from a hillside as their explosives destroy railroad tracks in the valley below during a commando raid on the communist rail network near Sonjin. Korea. The Royal Marines took over the role of commandos, including snipers, after World War II.* (Bettmann/Corbis)

163

well above his station against an enemy. The terrain and climate of the Korean peninsula is such that the infantryman again became the focus of combat; and no matter how you dress it up, this pits men against men with rifles and machine guns, and in this arena overcoming the enemy sniper is everyone's worst nightmare.

Snipers on both sides entered the conflict dressed and equipped as their forebears had been several years before, during World War II. The rifles that had been withdrawn, along with the telescopes and high-powered spotting scopes, were re-issued, and experienced World War II snipers were sought out and pressed back into service.

The harsh weather and terrain of the Korean peninsula often found the opposing forces in trench-dominated stalemate, almost resembling northern Europe during World War I, with long-range stand-off battles being the norm, and where sniping was again to become the scourge of anyone raising a head above the defensive line. Many an Allied officer was to be sent sprawling after trying to observe the disposition of North Korean forces.

As with all previous wars, the sooner the senior command became affected, the sooner something got done.

Snipers have the unique ability to get inside a man's head and seriously reduce morale. The thought of not knowing where the sniper is, who he can see and therefore where to hide, often have a serious effect on a unit's day to day effectiveness. Allied soldiers were often quoted in reports and the media as saying that Korean snipers were everywhere, a clear exaggeration but a good illustration of how it was affecting the average soldier mentally. Multiply this by the unit strength, for just one unit, and you start to see how much snipers destroy confidence and morale over a wide area.

Allied snipers were quick to regain another skill they had perfected in the battles of World War II, that of controlling indirect fire. Snipers are trained to observe an area, whereas most soldiers only look. This is to say that snipers will look for tiny detail of enemy activity, locations or routine. These could be a careless movement, an obvious ground sign or a poorly camouflaged radio

ABOVE: *The combination of T-3 Carbine and M2 sniperscope (shown here at a late 1940s' demonstration) was undoubtedly unwieldy by today's standards, but the system had been used with great success against the Japanese in the South Pacific during World War II. (NA)*

LEFT: *An early (late 1940s) demonstration of a sniper-scope being used to enable a U.S. Marine marksman to distinguish targets in complete darkness. This is a Model T-3 carbine fitted with an M2 sniperscope. The spotlight just forward of the pistol grip emits rays that are invisible to the naked eye, but which are plainly visible through the sniper-scope, allowing the sniper to fire at night with great accuracy, without the enemy being able to detect his presence. (NA)*

U.S. Army Corporal Lawrence Hawley, 7th Infantry Regiment, 3rd U.S. Infantry Division, operates a Korean War era sniperscope device. (NA)

antenna, all identifying an area to be watched more closely. Often, as a result of further observation, the snipers would be able to identify an enemy location, route or intention and would be able to call on supporting weapon systems, such as armor, artillery, mortars or even machine guns, and bring to bear a large volume of accurate fire on the enemy, causing large scale casualties and disruption of the enemy force.

Outdated equipment

Due to the ill-advised opinion prevailing during the late 1940s that sniping was no longer needed and that technology had made it redundant, there had been no research or development carried out in the sphere of sniper operational equipment. The sniper found himself

being issued a rifle that had seen more combat than he had. Also, as a result of the Allies' break-up and political standpoint of the nations now involved in Korea, the Americans and British found themselves lining up against Russian-designed weapons they had fought alongside during World War II.

British, Australian, and Canadian sniper weapons

There is a strong viewpoint that the Lee-Enfield No. 4 T was the premier sniper rifle of World War II, and therefore, in Korea, the British snipers had the advantage of being issued a rifle of proven accuracy and reliability. Lee-Enfields had given the British Army sterling service in all its forms, from Victorian conflicts

LEFT: *The Korean War wasn't grim all of the time: here officers and men of the U.S. Army's 23rd Infantry Regiment, 2nd Division, including Brigadier General Haydon L. Boatner (center), pose beside their newly designed "sniper rifle"— made of a heavy .50-caliber machine gun barrel and a captured Russian anti-tank rifle breech. (NA)*

through to Korea, and gave those who used them a sense of wellbeing.

The Canadians had spent their time well, and had decided the Lee-Enfield was in need of replacement, and so at least had research being carried out, although their Modified C models with No. 67 scopes were still gainfully employed. The Australian forces were at least in the right frame of mind when they deployed to Korea, fully expecting the conflict to become a sniper's war. Armed with their Lithgow-produced Lee-Enfields, the Australians deployed with well-trained snipers in all infantry companies, and quickly gained a reputation for their long-range engagements of communist forces.

The rifle was serviced by a detachable ten-round magazine, permitting a quicker reload than other clip-fed

LEFT: *Commonly referred to as the Springfield rifle (after its place of manufacture), the M1903 was the longest serving of all American rifles. It is shown here mated to a scope in the harsh weather conditions typical of Korea, which made aiming and firing the weapon difficult. (NA)*

types. Designed and produced before the advent of the floating barrel, the rifle sported full-length wooden furniture encapsulating the barrel except for the last few inches, and was fitted to accept a bayonet.

The Crater, Aden

Another colonial outpost where sniping and counter-sniping were again to become commonplace was Aden, in the Arabian Peninsula. The area is made up of rocky mountainous features with low lying coastal regions and higher plateaus. During the early and mid-1960s Arab religious and political factions squabbled and fought over control of the area, and once again, whatever the motive, the British Army found themselves in between them all. Both the Parachute Regiment and 45 Commando were deployed into the area of Wadi Taym, to retake the mountainous high ground from the Arab forces. The region, as with the mountainous 38th parallel, lent itself well to long-range accurate sniper engagements, and both British and Arab snipers plied their trade.

A place that was to become synonymous with the conflict was the urban area known as Crater.

As its name would suggest, the area was an urban mass of alley-ways and houses built around the rim of an old volcanic crater and as such was a wasp's nest of insurgency.

Following many an ambush against British troops and various other engagements, it was decided to re-take the town, using the Argyll and Sutherland Highlanders and their soon-to-be-famous commander, Lieutenant Colonel Colin Campbell Mitchell. "Mad Mitch," as the media christened him, did indeed re-take the area with his Highlanders, but not without a concerted effort from the snipers of 45 Commando, prior to and during the action. After the call for additional snipers went out, the snipers of 45 Commando were deployed to the high ground surrounding the town and for several days prior to the assault sniped and reported back on the insurgency

activity. This action no doubt had a demoralizing effect on the Arab occupants of the town, as the snipers made moving around very hazardous and removed specific threats from the battle when the Highlanders fought their way back into the urban maze. At this stage in the sniper's history the men were still using World War II vintage rifles and equipment.

Above: *With snipers operating from rooftops in the Crater area of the British colony of Aden, men of 42 Commando, Royal Marines, rush to find cover, November 17, 1967.*
(Bettmann/Corbis)

Fitting a bayonet attachment to sniper rifles has fallen by the wayside over the years, being considered not necessary; after all, a sniper is not supposed to be seen and normally operates well out of close combat ranges. I believe this attitude is somewhat short-sighted, since a sniper can be discovered by an enemy during both infiltration and extraction, perhaps located and overrun by his quarry. In these circumstances I have no doubt any soldier would accept any option he had to defend himself.

Doubtless there are some who would scoff and disagree, but if I had the option of keeping an aggressive foe at rifle length with a bayonet or going toe to toe with a knife, my money would be on the bayonet!

In the No. 32 telescopic sight, the British also had a well-made and battle-proven optic to deploy. This combination was to continue in British service for many years, because when a standard caliber was chosen by the NATO nations the Lee-Enfield was re-chambered and the No. 32 re-calibrated to the chosen 7.62mm round.

The spotter was also well equipped for his role with the 20-power telescope, even if it did resemble something Nelson used at the battle of Trafalgar!

One of the good points of the British issue Scout Regiment spotting scope was the fact that it could be field-stripped and the lenses cleaned to maintain a high level of clarity. The downside to this was that, although all snipers were trained to field-strip the telescope, it was possible to put the lenses in backwards, which was frequently not noticed until the scope was completely reassembled!

The British military were also issued with a prismatic compass that is still in service today. Precise navigation was (and is) vital to the sniper as the world is a very different place when you are crawling on your belly. The compass was very well made and durable, and gave British snipers the ability to move unseen with great accuracy.

Although the sniper equipment was of World War II origin, the British sniper was indeed well equipped for his role in Korea. The same equipment could be issued to a sniper in Iraq today and he would be able to carry out his tasks.

U.S. sniper equipment

The U.S. serviceman was also re-issued rifles and gear that had been issued to his predecessors in World War II. Both the M1 Garand and the Springfield 1903 were issued from war stock reserve, where they had been placed at the end of hostilities. They were more than up to the job required in Korea. The size of the defense budget meant that there were more variations of these two rifles than there were of the Lee-Enfield, and therefore there were different telescopic sights, stock designs, and muzzle flashes to be found, but the basic

rifles remained the same and both continued to add to the reputations they had gained from previous conflict.

Depending upon who you speak to, both rifles are claimed to be better than the other and, as with most things involved in sniping, what works for one may not work for another; personal preferences clearly apply. But whichever of the two is favored, both are accurate and reliable firearms. It is also a good example of a technological overlap, since the Springfield was a pure bolt-action, single-shot design while the Garand had a semi-automatic mechanism—thus the argument as to which firearm is more accurate is still going on today.

Korean sniper equipment

The South Korean forces were equipped by their western Allies, whereas the communist North Korean forces were armed with predominantly Chinese and Russian weaponry. Some Allied weapons dropped to the Nationalist Chinese forces fighting the Japanese during World War II were also encountered. The Mosin-Nagant, famed rifle of the Stalingrad battles, re-emerged and proved more than an equal to its rivals. The initial conflict saw mainly Russian-trained North Korean snipers engaging the western forces, but later a large number of well-trained Chinese snipers arrived.

The North Korean forces were much better prepared for the cold weather than their opponents in the South, and indeed their quilted uniforms produced a disproportionate human outline from a distance and so added to their overall "camouflage." The rugged tenacity of the North Korean soldiers and their almost primitive outlook to warfare gave them an attention to detail and practical determination sometimes lacking in their western counterparts, who were already developing a reliance on technology.

It is common knowledge that Russian "advisers" were sniping for the North, Meanwhile, the Chinese publicly acknowledged successful snipers such as Zhang Tao Fang, who was accredited with 214 kills in a thirty-two-day period. While this was aping the Russian propaganda style, as at Stalingrad in World War II, it illustrates Chinese understanding of the mental damage a so-called invincible sniper can have over an enemy, something the west has been reluctant to do until very recently.

This back to basics attitude gave the North Korean sniper an advantage to begin with, but the Allied soldier was no less capable and soon caught up to give as good as he received.

The glimmer of hope

During the various conflicts during the 1950s and 1960s, and maybe as a result of almost constant sniper actions against them, the major powers of the world started to

PREVIOUS PAGES 170-171: *Calmly taking aim through his telescopic sight, Marine Sergeant Charles R. Bill cuts down one of the Chinese communists who tried to halt the marine advance in Korea. Note the bayonet, as a last-ditch defensive measure should the marine become embroiled in hand-to-hand combat. (NA)*

OVERLEAF: *U.S. Army Captain William S. Brophy demonstrates a .30-caliber sniper rifle, with powerful sniperscope, that he hopes will be used by Allied snipers during the Korean War, October 3, 1952. His recommendation was for a new rifle to be based on the heavy-barreled Winchester Model 70, fitted with a Unertl scope. High command, on the other hand, wanted a variant of the in-service weapon, the Garand. (NA)*

look seriously at the capabilities of the sniper, and more specifically, at the capabilities of the rifles he used.

During the Korean War, U.S. Army Captain William S. Brophy, 7th Infantry Division, used a Winchester Model 70 and Unertl telescopic scope combination, at his own cost, in an attempt to highlight the need for a dedicated sniper rifle to be adopted by U.S. forces. Although he successfully demonstrated the superior capabilities of the system over the standard-issue rifle, he was not successful in swaying the high command. They believed the issue rifle was good enough and did not necessitate the supply of an additional ammunition type.

However, Brophy was not campaigning alone. Others who favored a design-specific sniper rifle included USMC Brigadier General Van Orden, who had stepped out of line to suggest the marines needed a specialist sniper rifle and backed Captain Brophy's earlier suggestion of the Model 70 Winchester. He even went a stage further by recommending that any selection be chambered for a larger, heavier round, thereby providing a flatter, more stable projectile, making longer range consistency possible. With today's armies adopting both 300 Winchester Magnum and 338 Super Magnum rifles, the brigadier was indeed a man of considerable foresight. It's a shame his colleagues in the budgetary department were not so blessed!

With the adoption, in the 1950s, of 7.62mm as the standard NATO caliber ammunition many armies revisited the issue of sniper rifles. When the Belgian-designed FN FAL rifle (known as the L1A1 in UK service) was introduced to service, it was discovered that, while it was a very accurate rifle, its pressed steel upper cover was too flimsy for mounting an optic that required stout fixing in order to provide the shooter with consistent results. With funds always an issue in any army, the gaze fell once again on the venerable Lee-Enfield No. 4 T as a candidate for adaptation.

A new caliber would require major restructure of the rifle, with both the chamber and the barrel being changed. The No. 32 telescopic sight would be the chosen optic for the "new" weapon, and it retained most of the zeroing issues of the World War II version. The wooden furniture of the No 4 T was cut back to expose two-thirds of the barrel, and a new magazine system was fitted, although all other equipment issued was of World War II vintage.

While the U.S. Army dragged its feet over selecting a specific-to-task sniper rifle, it did look at the possibility of modifying the proven Garand system. Here the army actually had great success, although arguably the resultant design, the M14, has only recently gained the reputation and acknowledgment its design deserved. The U.S. military has sought to re-acquire all the M14s it gave to allies as gifts post-Vietnam, for use in the current "War on Terror."

The M14 took the basic Garand system and, with a twenty-round magazine and some tweaking internally, emerged as a very capable rifle. Today, the many and varied M14 variants have proved to be very popular among NATO special forces, while the 7.62mm round proves to be back in vogue because of the terrain they find themselves fighting in.

As an aside, the Jordanian military have taken their U.S.-gifted M14s, fitted a heavy barrel and McMillan A5 stocks, and reworked the trigger action to produce the sub-half-minute-of-angle M62 sniper rifle (so named to honor the birth year of the King of Jordan).

Meanwhile, the Canadian military conducted their own tests, and rather sadly appeared to have lost the desire to maintain a sniper option by the time the trials were held. With the adoption of the FN FAL into general service, the Canadians also sought to produce a sniper version. After initial trials it was decided to reinforce the top cover to support an optical sight. The resulting design proved to be inconsistent at best, and ranges of over 600 yards were out of the question.

None of this appeared to matter, however, since the art of sniping was again thought to have run its course. Nevertheless, during this period the private sector was busy producing some very reliable bolt-action sniper rifles, ever hopeful of securing military contracts, but it would be some time and the eruption of a major conflict in Southeast Asia before they would succeed.

Snipers in the Vietnam War

During the Vietnam War, the United States fully exercised its attempts at thwarting the spread of communism, and by 1965 large numbers of American forces, along with those serving South Vietnam, faced North Vietnamese regulars in large-scale infantry battles as well as elusive Viet Cong guerrillas, many of whom adopted typical guerrilla tactics of "hit and hide." Although the Viet Cong were poorly equipped and generally undernourished, they shared a common bond in that they were fighting a foreign enemy in their own land, a point that history tells us is often a major advantage. Suffering from malaria and numerous other insect-based diseases, the guerrillas were anything but at home in the jungle, however, and faced sudden and deadly air raids at any time from American bombers. But they built a network of tunnels and hidden trails to transport men and materiel, and they used their expert knowledge of camouflage to put them at an advantage over the U.S. forces more than once, sniping and disappearing, only to surface again behind the U.S. forces to attack again.

This conflict highlighted the fact that the Russians had not sat back and ignored the subject of sniping. It was during this war that the West first captured a rifle they had heard about but not seen–the SVD sniper rifle. The Russians have a reputation for innovative weapon design

and in the SVD they had succeeded again. Chambered for a 7.62x54mm round, the SVD was a semi-automatic, box-fed rifle with a x4 PSO telescopic sight fitted and a 24½- inch barrel. The rifle had been in Russian circulation since around 1965. The PSO scope was both simple and rugged in design, with elevation and deflection adjustment, and range estimation stadia was very easy to use. The rifle could also be fitted with a bayonet, an option the author fully understands, even if it seems outdated. The discovery of this rifle confirmed that Russian "advisers" were once again present, and that North Vietnamese snipers were receiving Russian training.

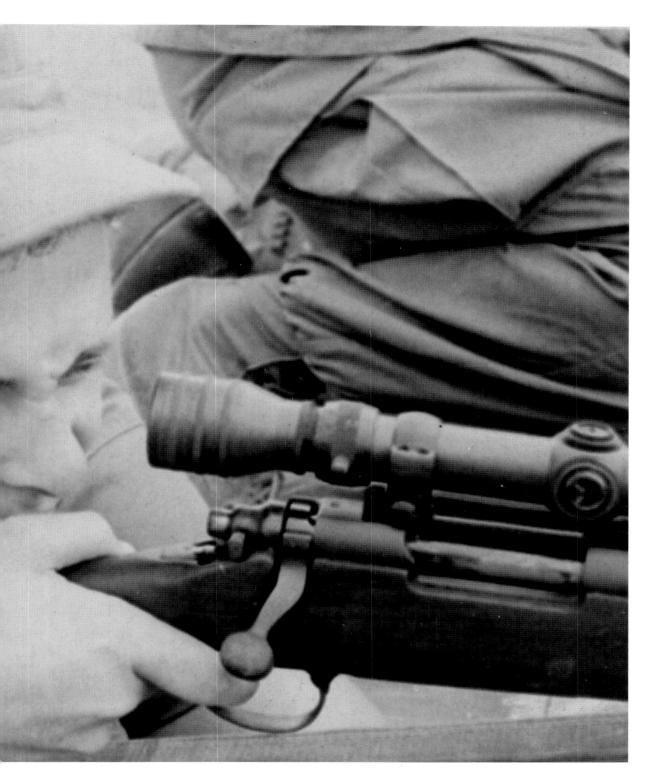

Training, and/or the lack of it, had become a controversial issue among many western armies between the end of World War II and the mid-1950s, Some of these nations, in particular the UK and the USA, felt the need to train all infantry soldiers in the art of accurate rifle fire was no longer a necessity. Some would blame the introduction of new weapons, and commercial interference, while others would blame an ever-growing belief that technological advances had removed the need for the sniper's skills.

The Germans advancing across no-man's land during World War I often felt they were up against machine guns because of the devastating small arms fire they encountered, but in fact they were experiencing the rapid fire capability of both British and, later, U.S. soldiers. Today, we often hear soldiers state that a bolt-action rifle is no use on today's battlefield. I cannot help but think that soldiers of both World Wars would disagree and conclude that today's soldiers are spoilt or even lazy in their attitude to marksmanship.

There are clearly advantages and disadvantages associated with the semi-automatic rifle and, as with any military skill, if you don't train, you lose the skill. The number of rounds fired by infantrymen in the Vietnam

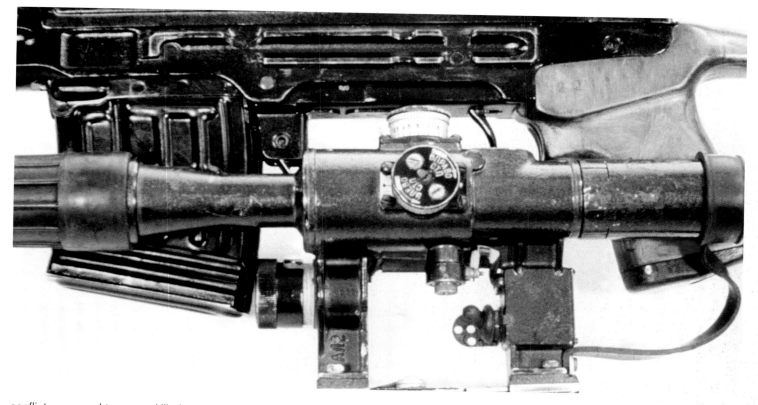

conflict compared to enemy killed, emphasizes the loss of marksmanship.

This loss of marksmanship skills among the rank and file has raised the perception of the sniper to even higher levels of respect and fear, since he still has the ability to maximize his ammunition and, with advances in ammunition consistency, over much greater ranges than ever before.

The jungles of Vietnam would not appear to be a typical sniper environment. However, as the U.S. forces adopted a forward operating base system, with mutually supporting outposts, often located on high ground, the cleared forest floor around them became perfect sniper kill zones. The fabled Ho Chi Minh Trail also provided choke points and fields of fire for well-placed American sniper teams. With the advances in night optics, the sniper again made himself feared.

The North Vietnamese army and Viet Cong snipers were also deployed with great effect, often holding up whole company advances or engaging hovering helicopters. The communist marksmen attended a full eight-week sniper training program before infiltrating into the South via the Ho Chi Minh Trail, often under cover of darkness to avoid U.S. air attacks. Once in their operational areas, the communist snipers went to work targeting South Vietnamese and U.S. officers, communications, and heavy weapon teams, and spent any downtime passing on rudimentary sniper skills to the Viet Cong guerrilla forces.

As the war intensified, both the U.S. Army and marines re-established sniper training programs, producing many very successful sniper teams. Some, like Carlos Hathcock and Chuck Mawhinney, would later gain celebrity status within the military for their exploits.

Hathcock was a proven long-range competition shooter within the Marine Corps, and as such was an obvious choice for Captains Robert Russell and Jim Land when they were tasked with establishing sniper options for the 3rd and 1st Marine Divisions, respectively. Jim Land established his school on Hill 55 near Da Nang, and Hathcock was rescued from his Military Police position and seconded to the school.

One of the school's first tasks was to remove Hill 55's persistent Viet Cong sniper, who repeatedly shot at

ABOVE: *A left-side view of the Dragunov SVD, with PSO-1 4x24 telescopic sight. It is a long weapon, but at 9.5lb not particularly heavy, partly due to its open stock. Gas-operated, and firing only in semi-automatic mode, the weapon is generally regarded as one of the best sniper rifles of its generation—and still going strong. (Cody)*

FAR LEFT: *Assisting the U.S. 3rd Marine Division in its sweep of the Demilitarized Zone, September 27, 1968, sniper Lance Corporal Bryant White of the Ninth Marine Regiment wears a not particularly sartorially elegant knitted cap to keep his head warm during the cool evenings of South Vietnam. (NA)*

LEFT: *This U.S. Marine serving in Iraq is holding a captured Dragunov SVD sniper rifle, whose design, emanating from the 1960s, is almost twice as old as he is! The Soviet-designed SVD was first encountered by the West during the Vietnam War when some were captured from North Vietnamese snipers and extensively tested and analyzed. It has since been manufactured under license in China, Iraq, and Romania. (Cody)*

ABOVE: *A scoped recoilless rifle such as this was used to eliminate a persistent and dangerous Viet Cong sniper near Danang during the Vietnam War. (NA)*

PREVIOUS PAGES: *Working as a scout sniper team in the 1st Marine Division in Vietnam, October 23, 1969, Corporal Claude W. Alfred directs rifleman Corporal Larry E. Bridges to a target position. (NA)*

marines on one of the feature's outlying fingers. After a reconnaissance carried out by Captain Land and Sergeant Don Reinke, the enemy sniper's hide was located. After carrying out an analysis of the sniper's tactics, it was decided to line up a 106mm recoilless antitank rifle on the hide and wait for him to shoot again. After only a few days the Viet Cong sniper was to commit a cardinal sin for all snipers, in that he returned to a pre-occupied hide, a lazy option he would not live to regret. Once he opened fire, so did the antitank rifle, and the sniper was no more.

Many books have highlighted the exploits of Carlos Hathcock, so it is sufficient here to say that he went on

to be so successful in his given area of operations that the Viet Cong put a bounty on his head for any one who could kill the Long Tra'ng ("white feather") as he was known to them because of the white feather he wore in his boonie hat.

At the start of the war, the marines had no dedicated sniper rifle and deployed with a miss-match of vintage World War II rifles and some civilian hunting types. As the war progressed, the need to standardize on one type was evident. With the backing of the Marine 1st Division's new commander, Major General Herman Nickerson, Jr., the following criteria were issued:

GUNNERY SERGEANT CARLOS N. HATHCOCK, USMC (1942–1999)

In 1959, at age 17, Carlos N. Hathcock, already the winner of many shooting championships, enlisted with the US Marine Corps, and was to become a legend on both sides of the conflict in Southeast Asia. During two tours of duty beginning in 1966 he achieved ninety-three confirmed "kills" of North Vietnamese Army (NVA) and Viet Cong (VC) personnel. His actual total was undoubtedly much greater—one report suggests well in excess of 400—but during the Vietnam War, kills had to be confirmed by an acting third party; this was feasible on a battlefield, but snipers usually worked in pairs (shooter and spotter) and often did not have an acting third party present, which made confirmation difficult. The NVA even put a bounty of $30,000 on his life after he had killed so many of their men. (Rewards put on American snipers by the NVA typically amounted to only $8.) The VC and NVA called Hathcock Lông Trắng, translated as "White Feather," because of the white feather he kept in a band on his bush hat.

There are several reports of Hathcock's prowess as a Marine sniper, although many were not officially recorded. One story goes that he once trapped an entire company of Viet Cong. It is said he first shot a soldier at the front of the column, then shot a soldier at the back of the column. The VC, not knowing where the sniper fire was coming from, were forced to remain in their position for several days, during which "Hathcock killed them all."

Hathcock is credited with achieving the longest combat "kill" of the 20th century when in 1967 he shot an enemy soldier from a distance of 2,658 yards using a .50-caliber M8C spotting rifle on a 106mm recoilless rifle.

The rifle and scope must shoot to within 2 minutes of angle

The design must be sturdy, simple, and easily explained, to reduce instruction time

The rifle and scope combination must withstand humid conditions

The rifle must be 7.62mm

The scope must be adjustable up to 1,000 yards.

During 1965 several commercial combinations were trialed, including Remington 600, 700 ADL, and BDL and the 700-40X models, the Winchester Model 70, and several telescopic sights. The Remington Model 700-40x emerged as the favorite, with an initial order for 700 being placed in 1966. The rifles were to have a five-round internal magazine serviced with a floor-plate, a green parkerized 24-inch heavy barrel and receiver, a walnut stock, and Redfield Accu-Range 3x9 scope. With a series of upgrades, including the McMillan fiberglass A5 stock, the new rifle, designated the M40, still survives in Marine Corps service today as the M40A4.

The success of the marine sniper in Vietnam led directly to its acceptance as an official post within the CONTINUED ON PAGE 188

ABOVE: *Here, on November 12, 1996, Lt. Gen. P. K. Van Riper congratulates Gunnery Sgt. Hathcock (Ret.) after presenting him the Silver Star. Standing next to Hathcock is his son, Staff Sgt. Carlos Hathcock, Jr. Hathcock was awarded the medal for saving the lives of seven marines after the APC in which they were riding struck a mine in Vietnam in1969. Tragically, he died in 1999 after a long battle with multiple sclerosis.*

ABOVE: *Left-side view of a Remington Model 700 with telescope sight adopted as the M40A1 sniper rifle by the U.S. Marine Corps. The magazine floor plate is just forward of the trigger guard. (Cody)*

LEFT: *The M1 Garand .30-caliber was the first semi-automatic rifle to be generally issued to the infantry of any nation, shown here with telescope sight in the hands of a U.S. soldier attending the sniper school in Korea. (Cody)*

FAR LEFT: *A sniper attached to E Company, 2nd Battalion, 4th Regiment, 3rd Marine Division, uses an M1 rifle with scope during Operation Double Eagle, Vietnam, January 1966. (NA)*

Corps in 1968 all USMC headquarter companies within the regiments were ordered to form sniper platoons: the 8541 (Scout-Sniper) billet was born.

The army had a slightly easier operating area in sniper terms, as most of their operations took place in the lowlands of the South, where the open paddy fields and

other agriculture made for longer, flatter distances for the snipers to work in, whereas the marines had to contend with the heavily wooded and jungle highland further north. The army also entered the conflict devoid of any formalized sniper training program or established sniper platoons.

The 9th Infantry Division tasked Major Willis Powell to initiate a program, and initially it involved no more than two days' training, although this was stretched to eighteen days in 1969. The additional time clearly enabled the students to learn more, and the experienced, senior non-commissioned officers drafted in as

ABOVE: *A sniper pair attached to B Company. 1st Battalion, 4th Marines, evaluate target options during Operation Nanking Scotland II, Vietnam, October 7, 1968.* (NA)

ABOVE RIGHT: *USMC sniper students and instructor (kneeling) at the Dai La Pass range, Vietnam, November 1969. Two fuzzy squares can just be seen down range: these are the target numbers, directly in front of the silhouette targets. The 300-yard line can also be seen in front of the target numbers, among the trees and bushes.* (NA)

LEFT: *Fed up with being on the receiving end of Viet Cong sniper fire, a U.S. marine pumps a few bursts in the general direction of enemy fire, near Da Nang, 1967.* (Cody)

RIGHT: *Test firing of a sniper version of the 7.62-caliber M14 rifle, of which there are many variants, including some used by U.S. special forces. The M14 can be traced back to the M1 Garand, and forward to the M24 and M25 sniper rifles.* (Cody)

instructors imparted hard-learned lessons from World War II and Korea.

Powell's school covered all the main subjects of previous sniper schools including range estimation, observation, fieldcraft, camouflage, and marksmanship. With the lack of purpose-built ranges, areas were bulldozed and marked out for rifle instruction, and expended 105mm artillery shells were pressed into service as targets until proper silhouette targets could be acquired.

With the U.S. Army's adoption of the M14 semi-automatic rifle, the choice of a standardized sniper rifle was fairly obvious. The M14 met the required criteria for a sniper rifle: it was rugged, had a 1,000-yard capability, and was already proven in combat. All that was required was to match it to a suitable telescopic sight. The selection process led to the adoption of the Redfield 3x9 scope fitted with a leatherwood bullet drop

RIGHT: *The M14 rifle was phased out in the 1960s, but many were converted into the M21 sniper rifle by the U.S. Army, and these remained standard-issue for this purpose until the adoption of the M24 SWS.* (Cody)

BELOW: *The Union Jack is hoisted by 40 Commando, Royal Marines, signifying victory at the end of the Falklands War, June 16, 1982. One aspect that bothered the British troops was that some of the snipers serving with the enemy appeared not to be Argentineans, but possibly Americans, perhaps mercenaries.* (Bettmann/Corbis)

compensator ring. Known as Auto Ranging Telescope, or ART, the issue designation was XM-21. The combination proved to be a huge success, with army snipers accounting for over 1,000 enemy soldiers killed between January and July of 1969.

Snipers in the Falklands War

War has often been a useful tool in distracting the attention of a country's population away from difficult political home issues, especially if a subject or target can be found that invokes emotive response and bonds the people together. This is exactly what the military junta of Argentina did in 1982, when they decided to use the long-standing dispute with the UK over ownership of the small group of islands in the South Atlantic, known as the Falkland Islands to the British and the Malvinas to the Argentineans, to divert the restless Argentinean public's attention away from the nation's enormous economic difficulties.

The islands have been in British hands since Nelson's time and its population is entirely British, and so the dispute would appear to be pointless, until the mineral and mining rights in the region are considered. The junta fueled the Argentinean people's feeling of wrong-doing by the British, justifying the junta's invasion plan.

The junta chose to pick a time when the UK government was busy cutting back on the Royal Navy, its South Atlantic deployments, and—even more relevant—was willing to negotiate the future ownership of the islands. The mistake Argentine rulers made was in not realizing how forcefully the UK government, and indeed the British people, would react to the public humiliation of having the islands "taken" by a foreign power.

After several weeks of reconnaissance, including a false aircraft emergency by an Argentine C-130 Hercules transport aircraft to check if such military transports could utilize the Port Stanley runway, the Argentinean government used a group of scrap metal workers landing on the outlying island of South Georgia and claiming it for Argentina, as an excuse to deploy military personnel to protect their rights. This was clearly used as a way of ramping up the political situation in the area and presenting Argentina with a reason to invade without turning the world against them.

The islands were protected by a small Royal Marine detachment of around twenty men, armed only with small arms and light anti-armor weapons. At the time of the invasion the detachment was actually doubled in size since it was in the process of changing after its six-month deployment. But this still pitted a mere forty men against thousands. With hindsight, all the indications were there that the invasion was going to happen, but political incompetence coupled with national ego allowed all signs to go unnoticed. The Royal Marines were given governmental warning of the invasion hours before it happened, and so were at least deployed to defensive locations when the Argentine Special Forces, Buzo Tactico, opened fire on their billets in the hope of killing all of them in their beds.

The Royal Marines fought a rolling, delaying battle, until the main force was located in and around the British governor's residence, the seat of UK authority, where they were ordered to surrender by the governor, to avoid further bloodshed, a point of contention even today, and the islands fell into Argentine hands.

ABOVE: *Royal Marines from 40 Commando await transport from the deck of the HMS Hermes aboard Sea King helicopters to re-take the Falklands Islands from the Argentinean invaders April 18, 1982.* (Hulton-Deutsch/Corbis)

BELOW: *Accuracy International (AI) PM counter-terrorist model of the sniper rifle that has been selected for service by the British Army (as L96A1), here fitted with an Osprey OE 8050 individual weapon sight. (See also over page.)* (AI)

ABOVE: *United Nations operations, such as this one in Kosovo, provide the opportunity for forces of member states to exchange views and learn from each other. Here, a British sniper instructor (right) makes a point to Belgian para-commandos, one of whom is using the AI sniper rifle.* (Mark Spicer)

PREVIOUS PAGES: *AI's PM Infantry Model fitted with Simrad Optronics KN250 night sight, which clips to the top of the rifle scope and, by means of a vision splitter, provides a night capability through the normal rifle-mounted sniper scope. Focus range is from twenty-five yards to infinity. The rifle fires 7.62x51mm NATO rounds, weighs 14.33lb, has a 25.78in rifled barrel, and uses a 10-round magazine.* (AI)

The UK government was swift in its response and within a week a military force was on its way to reclaim the islands. While the force sailed south, British special forces flew ahead and deployed into covert reconnaissance roles to prepare the way for a full scale amphibious landing. The Argentinean forces consolidated and reinforced the troops already ashore and prepared for the arrival of the British.

An issue of contention that may never truly be settled is that of the Argentine use of snipers during their defense of the islands. One reason for confusion is that during this period the Argentine forces had no established sniper training program, and no standardized sniper equipment, points that had little effect on their very effective use of snipers during the ensuing fighting.

There can be no doubt that skilled marksmen from the country's armed forces utilized the FN FAL rifles with optical sights fitted to snipe at British forces, as numerous such rifles and encounters were reported, but it is other snipers that continue to draw speculation and attention.

Many documented witness accounts from British soldiers report on the extended use of well-placed and accurate snipers, and that prisoners were taken who were neither Argentinean or Spanish speakers. The men concerned were no doubt mercenaries employed by the Argentineans to provide a skill lacking in their units. They were of Spanish American decent, and no doubt had previous combat experience, either as mercenaries or within the armed forces of their parent country. The men were armed with Remington 700 rifles with commercially purchased telescopic sights of no standard specification. At least two were captured after the British Parachute Regiment's battle for Goose Green and both spoke no Spanish, but English with American accents. No record exists of who they were, or what happened to them, but suffice to say the Brits would have taken a very dim view of men from an allied country, especially the USA, being responsible for the deaths of their colleagues.

The Argentine forces were better equipped than their British counterparts in the area of night vision sights, and they made very good use of the AN-PVS-4 generation two sights they had, which were considerably more effective than the mainly Starlight scopes of the British infantry. Although British special forces had better equipment, the "poor bloody infantryman" was again left at a disadvantage by governmental restraints.

This was also the war that saw the old Lee-Enfield L42 finally reach the end of the line. Although it was to soldier on for another four years, it was deemed ready for replacement largely because of the Falklands campaign, and the requirement that was to lead to the adoption of the Accuracy International L96A1 was issued not long after the cessation of hostilities in the South Atlantic.

United Nations sniper deployments

Over the last decade or so, there have been numerous deployments of both United Nations and NATO forces in the defense of humanity and democracy, and in every one the sniper was evident on both sides of a conflict, With the somewhat sudden end of the Warsaw Pact and communism in general, the world initially seemed to have turned a corner and become a much happier place. The reality of any large change of government or other form of rule is that it leaves a large void while a country adjusts to new ways of doing business, and this generally provides those who harbor grudges, seek power or just look for personal gain through crime the ideal chance to strike. And so it has been in several countries in both Europe and the Middle East: while the old Soviet Union may not have been to everyone's liking, it did hold warring factions together and suppress criminal elements, brutally in most cases, but effectively nonetheless.

The former Yugoslavia was a country that, while on the periphery of the Warsaw Pact, was still communist-ruled by the wartime leader Josip Bros Tito, and the ethnic diversity of the region as well as past territorial and tribal divisions were held in check. With Tito's death and the support afforded by the old Soviet Union gone, it did not take long before old resentments and grudges began to surface. The subsequent division of Yugoslavia soon led to open conflict in many of the former country's composite states, with bitter fighting breaking out in 1992–1995 between rival ethnic factions in Bosnia, Croatia, and later Serbia and Kosovo, as different sections of the population sought independence, power or simply revenge against others. This regional conflict saw Christians fighting Muslims, and Serbs fighting Albanians. NATO eventually stepped in to restore peace, even if it is a very tenuous one.

OVERLEAF: *A French Foreign Legion warrant officer (right) instructs his sniper fellows, having been briefed by a British sniper of the 1st Battalion, the Princess of Wales's Royal Regiment. They are taking part in cross-training during United Nations operations in Kosovo. (Mark Spicer)*

BELOW: *A Ukrainian sniper trains with a British sniper. They are taking the opportunity to try out each other's weapons, the Brit in the background with a Dragunov PSV, and the Ukrainian with the AI PM sniper rifle. (Mark Spicer)*

ABOVE AND BELOW: *Two photos taken by the author during his tour of duty in war-scarred Kosovo, in the Balkans, show the advantages of conducting overflights of areas and specific buildings that* snipers may consider when they select their intended area of operations. These bombed buildings are in Pristina, Kosovo's largest city, in which were located strategic targets for NATO air *strikes from 1999 onward in what became known as the Kosovo War, which had been in progress in the troubled region for a decade. (Mark Spicer)*

As with all small scale guerrilla actions, the sniper was to play an ever increasing role in operations, and was indeed responsible for the increase of .50-caliber rifle deployments throughout NATO armies. The region has a well established arms industry and the proliferation of home-designed and effective .50-caliber rifles was to create a problem that was unforeseen by the higher echelons of many NATO forces, who deployed under a UN mandate to restore peace and protect the innocent.

During the operations in Bosnia, Bosnian Serb snipers, who had been preying on civilians daily, continually harassed UN forces. This was most evident in and around the main boulevard connecting the industrial area with the old cultural part of Sarajevo. It was soon to become known as "Sniper Alley." This was the source of the only clean water supply in the city, and so the local civilian population had little choice but to brave sniper fire daily in order to survive. Statistics list 1,030 civilians injured by sniper fire, and 225 killed, among them 60 children.

The French security forces, who along with the British, carried out counter-sniper operations, found that a building occupied by the Bosnian government forces was actually being used by snipers to kill innocent civilians, with the blame being laid at the feet of the Muslims they were fighting. Although it was denied, the French report was submitted to the UN.

A wide variety of rifles were pressed into sniper service during the conflict, from the relatively modern, Yugoslavian-made copy of the SVD Dragunov through to M48 Mauser actions and even accurized versions of the SKS. The abundance of high-rise buildings in urban areas provided a multiple range of sniper positions, and a nightmare for any defending force.

Thankfully, the majority of the indigenous snipers fighting in the Sarajevo area were poorly trained or lazy, in that they quickly set patterns that were evident to the highly trained British and French snipers, who set about removing or negating their threat by aggressive patrol action or counter-sniper fire.

The abundance of .50- caliber rifles on the Bosnian Serb side was a problem and concern. These rifles easily out-ranged the 7.62mm sniper rifles of the United Nations forces, in particular the British who at this stage did not have any .50-caliber rifles outside the special forces. The British rapidly acquired several Barrett .50-caliber rifles from the U.S. Army to cover the obvious gap in their capabilities The French, however, did have McMillan .50-caliber bolt-action rifles available, and deployed them very effectively.

CONTINUED ON PAGE 206

ABOVE: *The author adopts an urban overwatch position in Pristina, Kosovo. Doubtless, he found it increasingly difficult to find usable hides in derelict and damaged buildings, a problem shared with his fellow snipers in Iraqi cities, thereby losing some advantage to insurgents and terrorists who have become aware of the problem. (Mark Spicer)*

OVERLEAF: *A French sniper pair fire the PGM Hecate .50-caliber rifle on the range. The standard heavy sniper rifle of the French Army, the Hecate is the largest weapon of the UR (Ultima Ratio) rifle family. It is essentially a bolt-action anti-materiel rifle, using the .50-caliber BMG (12.7x99mm) cartridge as used in the Browning M2 heavy machine gun. (Mark Spicer)*

ABOVE: *Another big-hitter is the M3 of the Hungarian Gepard family. Firing the 14.5x115mm Soviet cartridge, it was designed to destroy light entrenchments and buildings, armored infantry vehicles, hovering helicopters, and other similar targets. The makers claim an effective range of almost 1,200 yards. Overall length is 74 inches, barrel length is 58.25 inches, and weight is 44lb with magazine and rear sight. The magazine capacity is five or ten cartridges, plus one in the barrel. The operating system is a weight-locked self loader, and rate of fire is twenty shots per minute. (Gepard).*

ABOVE: *The author test-fired the Parker-Hale M85 sniper rifle when he surprisingly came across one in the Falkland Islands while on sniper training duty there. He found it was a very accurate firearm. Although the design was British, its manufacturing rights have been sold on. The rifle was designed to replace the British Army L42A1, which had not performed well in the Falklands War in 1982, but it was not selected. Basic specifications are: caliber, 7.62x51mm; overall length, 47.5 inches; barrel length, 27.5 inches; magazine, 10 rounds; weight 12.57lb with telescopic sight and empty magazine. The makers claim 100 percent first shot capability at all ranges out to about 655 yards. (Parker-Hale)*

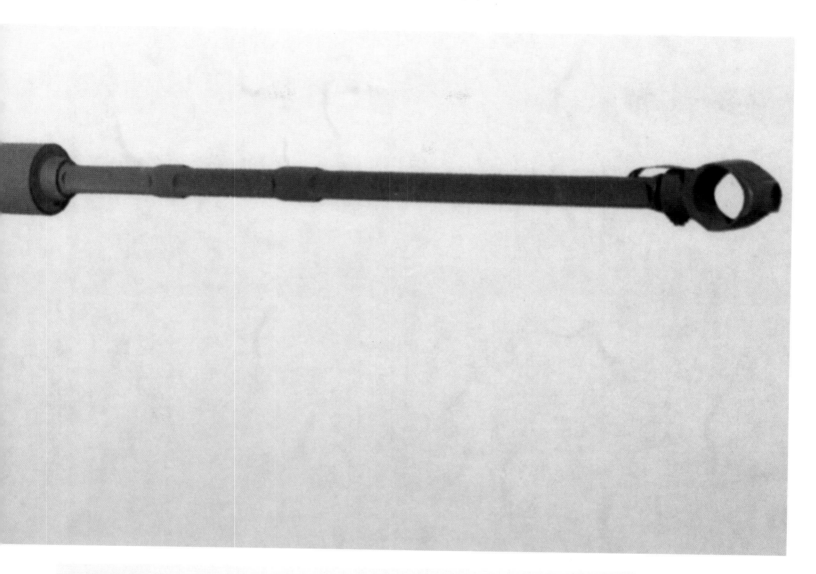

LEFT: *The M85 has integral dovetail mounting so that it can receive a variety of passive night vision lights.*

ABOVE: *Test-firing the Dragunov SVD sniper rifle. It may be 1960s technology, having entered service more than forty years ago, but it is still well-regarded and used effectively by regular and irregular forces, including terrorists, the world over. (Mark Spicer)*

BELOW: *During cross-training a French Army sniper captain fires a "Light Fifty," a U.S. Marine Corps Barrett .50-caliber M82A1. It is an anti-materiel weapon firing .50 BMG (12.7x99mm) ammunition from a 10-round detachable box magazine. Overall length is 48in, and barrel length is 20in. Operation is short recoil, semi-automatic, and maximum effective range is about 1,970 yards. (Mark Spicer)*

When the Kosovo Albanians made moves to secure independence from Serbia, the movement was quickly denied and a Serbian attempt to remove all resistance through genocide began. The Albanians were statistically a majority in the region, but the Serbian and Yugoslavian governments had no intention of allowing an independent Kosovo to be formed, and so an ongoing war of attrition between the Serbian/Yugoslavian forces and the Kosovo Liberation Army (KLA) ran between 1996 and the United Nations intervention in 1999.

Again, throughout this campaign both sides used snipers to great effect in support of military action and also to instill fear throughout the civilian population. Many civilians were murdered by concealed marksmen as they went about their normal lives. Attempts to blame each other for attacks against NATO forces were also common, such as the French soldier shot in the stomach in the Serbian part of Mitrovica by Albanians who had concealed themselves in Serbian buildings in an attempt to lay blame.

During the author's deployment in Kosovo, a great many UN sniper operations were carried out in support of peacekeeping operations and by way of protection for the hundreds of UN police officers as they carried out their duties, not always aware that military snipers were concealed around them.

Snipers in Chechnya

The Russians are well known for both their use of snipers in a practical sense, and also the use of sniper-related propaganda stories. It is therefore somewhat strange that their forces moved away from dedicated snipers after the end of World War II, and instead used a single rifleman armed with the new SVD Dragunov as a platoon sharpshooter within all infantry platoons. This system was also adopted by several NATO nations. It removes the sniper's main offensive threat, that of being independent

and able to move and attack freely on the battlefield, thereby tying up large numbers of an enemy's troops.

This decision proved to be a mistake for the Russians during their first war against Chechen rebels in neighboring Chechnya between 1994 and 1996.

The Russian sharpshooters soon found themselves disadvantaged by the fact that they were now trained to fight as part of a platoon in support of a conventionally organized combined arms team, as opposed to independent hunter/killer teams as they had been in Stalingrad many years before. An abundance of sniper rifles, and marksmen who had a detailed knowledge of the terrain, put the Chechens at a distinct advantage, and one they were not slow to exploit, causing large scale casualties among the Russian forces.

resumed hostilities in 1999 (Second Chechen War, continuing now as an antiterrorist campaign), there had been a return to dedicated sniper training as well as the formation of very well equipped and trained sniper hunter/killer teams of their own.

The Russians established career-orientated sniper units within specialist elite units, and the snipers underwent extended periods of infantry-based training.

The Russians also recognized the value of protecting their sniper assets and so today they allocate a five- to twenty-man protection detail depending upon the mission and location of the sniper pair. They also rotate them out of action on a regular basis to keep them mentally prepared.

The snipers will typically be armed with a suitable sniper rifle and suppressor, camouflage equipment, a side arm or

LEFT: *A Russian soldier takes aim against Chechen rebels, December 2000. This was during the Second Chechnya War, which began in October 1999 and continued into the new century, Although the war as such was effectively over by the end of 2000, violence flares up from time to time in the form of hostage-taking, bombings—and sniper fire.* (EPA/Corbis)

The Chechens realized that the sniper could gain them an advantage over the vastly numerically superior Russian forces, and so created a group of four-man teams designed to maximize the snipers' skills and to protect them as well. Each team consisted of a sniper pair armed with a Dragunov and an AK-47, and a protection pair armed with an RPG launcher and an RPK machine gun. Armed in this way the killer teams could cause maximum damage to Russian army patrols and provide supporting fire to allow the snipers to escape to fight another day. (This tactic is evident in Afghanistan and Iraq today, where UN Coalition forces are faced with experienced Chechen Muslims fighting on the side of the insurgents.)

When the fighting moved to the rural and mountainous areas, the Chechens increased the snipers' support element to four, again demonstrating their belief in the importance of the snipers and their protection. The damage done to Russian numbers and morale was not lost on their high command, and by the time the Russians

machine pistol and grenades for close-in defense, a radio, and night vision optics. The sniper pair will build and occupy sniper hides and covertly dominate a given area of the battlefield, knowing that their protection groups are located to provide fire support as and when needed.

As well as the well-known SVD Dragunov, improved and now produced in various versions, the Russian special forces also purchased a number of British-made Accuracy International sniper rifles for use in Chechnya, similar to those used by the British Army, as well as completing a new design based on the very successful civilian Record-1 sporting rifle. The new rifle is outwardly similar to the Accuracy International rifle, but any similarity ends there since internally it is considerably different in design. The rifle can be chambered for Russian 7.62x45R as well as NATO 7.62mm and .338 Lapua rounds. It is fitted with a barrel-mounted heat shield designed to dissipate heat rising off the barrel after extended use. Otherwise, accurate fire would be difficult as the heat affects clarity of vision through the rifle's telescopic sight.

The Russians have also created a variety of specific-to-task sniper rifles that include take-down covert rifles through to fully suppressed, anti-sentry sniper rifles, and have used Grozny and Chechnya in general to reacquire skills lost to them after years of preparing for large-scale armored battles against NATO.

Snipers in Afghanistan

Much has been made of the Soviet failure to overcome the Afghan mujahideen, but in all fairness it was more a case of the concerted efforts of the USA and her allies in pushing up the cost of the Cold War that led indirectly to the perceived failure. Soviet withdrawal, together with the training and arming and operational deployments of U.S. and UK special forces on research and training missions with the Afghans, also hindered the Soviets.

The scare word of the Cold War was undoubtedly *spetsnaz*, the collective name for the Soviet special forces brigades that were expected to wreak havoc on NATO rear areas in time of war. These men were actively successful in the Afghan war, even if it was very rarely reported.

Before deploying, regular *spetsnaz* units went through intensive training cadres that included mountain warfare, mine laying and clearing and, for at least some in the unit, sniper training. In a twenty-two-man unit, the Soviets would typically have two sniper-trained men armed with

the Dragunov SVD semi-automatic rifle with five magazines and 150 rounds of 7,62x54R sniper ammunition, plus a night vision scope for the rifle.

These units would attempt to take the war to the mujahideen by moving up into the mountain strongholds whenever they received intelligence of a rebel unit resting or transiting an area. With artillery or mortars in support, they would lay in ambush or attack the enemy where they found them. Soviet snipers were not so concerned with precision hits on the enemy. As far as they were concerned a hit anywhere in the upper body was a good hit and that's true under those conditions. Therefore, the occasional lack of sniper ammunition, and it being substituted with normal ball ammunition, was not too much of a hindrance. The Soviet special forces sniper learned to make do with whatever he was given.

Throughout the Soviet occupation of Afghanistan, the operators of the *spetsnaz* brigades were successful and feared by the mujahideen. The Russian snipers would often engage enemy tribesmen out to more than a thousand yards.

The SVD sniper rifle was delivered complete with an illuminated reticule and a built-in range stadia, and as such was ahead of the game in gadgets compared to the equivalent western-issued sniper rifles. Contrary to reports in the popular press, the *spetsnaz* snipers were well equipped and supported in the mountainous operations, and were normally deployed for three to five

days before returning to base camp. The Soviets were not technically defeated they were economically forced to accept the Geneva Accord to withdraw, and until the last troops had left they were by all accounts undefeated and too strong for the mujahideen.

U.S. snipers in Afghanistan

The horror of "9/11," the Twin Towers attack on the USA, was to prove a major mistake for terrorists around the globe. The U.S. forces are more than able to reach any point on the planet with considerable force and with a combination of technology, politics, and well trained professional soldiers. After refusing to give up Al-Qaeda leader Osama Bin Laden or any of his terrorists based within the country, the Taliban stronghold of Afghanistan was expertly crushed.

The U.S. special forces soldiers who deployed into the country to establish political agreements with war lords of the Northern Alliance, who were opposed to the ways of the Taliban, had little initial need of sniper tactics. Nevertheless, a lot of detailed observation was needed to identify and pinpoint the Taliban positions in order to bring accurate aerial attack on them from both aircraft and tactical missiles. The media hype of how the Afghans defeated a superpower—the Soviet Union—was soon silenced as the U.S. and Coalition forces very quickly overcame the Taliban with the assistance of the Northern Alliance forces, although major credit has to fall to the power and capabilities of the U.S. Air Force. The current increase in fighting in the Helmand and other southern provinces is proof of the difficulty in establishing an alternative government to one that has been forcibly removed, and how the defeated can regain the initiative to become aggressive again.

The terrain and elusive nature of the enemy in this campaign meant that it was very difficult to both locate and engage them. Therefore, sniping soon became the most effective solution, especially with the larger calibers that were able to reach across the deep ravines and hit an enemy who, because of the distance, thought it safe to walk around in full view.

Carlos Hathcock had set a world record for the longest single shot attack during an engagement in Vietnam, when he used a .50-caliber spotting rifle (M8) on a 106mm recoilless rifle to engage an enemy soldier at 2,423 yards (2,215m) range. Operations in Afghanistan were to produce a modern successor to the crown that Carlos would have been happy to see. The shot was taken by a sniper team of the Canadian unit, Princess Patricia's Light Infantry Regiment, in

RIGHT: *A Canadian soldier, a member of the ISAF (International Security Assistance Force), looks over Camp Julien, the Canadian base near Darlulaman's palace in Kabul, Afghanistan.* (Manca Juvan/Corbis)

March 2002 during operations in support of the U.S. 101st Airborne and 10th Mountain Divisions. They were engaging a combined Taliban/al-Qaeda force in the Shah-i-kot Valley during Operation Anaconda.

Armed with McMillan Tac-50 sniper rifles firing AMAX match .50-caliber ammunition, the Canadians deployed to support the U.S. advance up the 10,000ft ridge. During the advance the U.S. forces came under long-range enemy machine gun and mortar attack and soon found themselves pinned down. The sniper teams started to remove the enemy weapon crews at distances ranging between about 750 and 1.640 yards, thereby allowing the U.S. troops to continue the advance. One enemy machine gunner in particular was to be located and engaged by a Canadian corporal at 1,860 yards and this was quickly followed by a second enemy shooter accounted for at a staggering 2,658 yards, a new world record and testament to the accuracy and high standard of production of the Tac-50 and to the dedication and professionalism of the Canadian sniper.

The Canadian Army currently has eight snipers in every infantry battalion, although plans exist to greatly increase this number as a result of their experiences in Afghanistan. The Canadian sniper must attend and pass a nine-week basic sniper course as opposed to a five-week sniper course currently run for the U.S. Army. Before a Canadian infantryman can apply for a sniper course he must be a qualified reconnaissance soldier and have attended the reconnaissance school where he will learn skills that will stand him in good stead to pass the high level of training included within the sniper course itself.

The Canadian sniper course covers not only the basics of shooting and advanced marksmanship, but also the associated skills of range estimation, where candidates will need to be able to accurately gauge the distance between themselves and their quarry, but also concealment, stalking, observation, and tracking. The course is designed to produce an all round professional hunter and scout, and the achievements of the Canadian

ABOVE: *The author conducts firing trials of Accuracy International's fully suppressed AW (Arctic Warfare) rifle. The AW's barrel is interchangeable with other calibers, in the field, the process taking about fifteen minutes. This allows for a mission-specific deployment of calibers. The AWS (S=Suppressed) is specifically designed for use with subsonic ammunition, giving an effective maximum range of about 330 yards.* (Mark Spicer)

OVERLEAF: *Members of the mujahideen inspect and test a new Dragunov in the Farkhar Valley, Afghanistan, 1990.* (Reza/Webistan/Corbis)

ABOVE: *The Accuracy International AW with tactical suppressor. Basic specifications of this bolt-action rifle include: overall length 46.5in; barrel length 26in; weight 14.3lb; effective range 875 yards; ammunition feed 10-round detachable box magazine; ammunition 7.62x51mm NATO. The firearm has been in British Army service since 1988.* (Mark Spicer)

LEFT: *A French special forces soldier demonstrates a modified version of the alternate laid-back firing position, using the excellent PGM sniper rifle fitted with a fully suppressed barrel.* (Mark Spicer)

FAR LEFT: *A sniper pair demonstrate their thermal reduction suits, as issued to all British Army snipers. The aim of the suits is to defeat thermal imaging systems, which work on the principle of taking the heat given off by, or reflected from the sun's rays on, any given object. Theoretically, this makes it difficult for snipers to remain hidden from the imager's view. However, if the sniper is concealed by, for instance, a bank, then the imager will not be able to "see" him. The suits depicted are made from materials designed to reduce the sniper's heat signature.* (Mark Spicer)

snipers in Afghanistan has confirmed the course's success. The Canadians have also installed a natural path of progression for their snipers, in so much as once they are experienced enough they can attend the sniper instructors' course, where candidates are taught the skills needed to select and train basic snipers, deploy and command them, as well as act as advisers to senior officers on sniper capabilities and deployment options.

As with the U.S. forces, the Canadians now include the skills associated with calling for and directing supporting fire from both indirect weapons, such as mortars and artillery, and air support from friendly aircraft. This need has arisen from the experiences in both Iraq and Afghanistan, where the sniper's superior observational skills often allowed him to locate distant enemy positions or formations and request or advise the calling in of heavy supporting weaponry.

The Canadians have also increased the size of the basic sniper formation from two-man teams up to four-man teams, in essence two two-man teams working together as a fixed unit. This has come about through a perceived need for additional security for the teams once deployed operationally in high threat areas and away from immediate fire support from other friendly troops. This allows for a primary sniper pair to engage the enemy while the second pair provides protection and early warning against enemy attack.

Canadian sniper commanders are also in the process of selecting a new range of sniper weapons to operate alongside their McMillan TAC-50 large-caliber sniper rifle, designated C15 in Canadian service, since their current Parker-Hale 7.62mm rifles are nearing the end of their operational lifespan. The Parker-Hale, now designated C3A1 in Canadian service, has served since 1979, when it had a wooden stock and Kahles Helios telescopic sight, and was known as the C3. An update consisting of a Unertl telescopic sight forced a change of designation to C3A1, and this was followed in the late 1990s by the replacement of the original wooden stocks with camouflaged McMillan A2 composite stocks.

Unfortunately, the predominantly green coloring would prove ill-suited to the mountains of Afghanistan. The tan-and-ochre coloring of the Afghan terrain forced the Canadians into a local camouflage change for their rifles, which were resprayed in a flat tan and had added additional camouflage material as required.

The Canadians have also realized that there is now a need for a selection of calibers from 5.56mm through to the heavy .50, so that their snipers have the correct weapon range for their mission. After trialing several newer designs of sniper rifle, the Canadians selected the C14 Timberwolf and are in the process of replacing the old C3A1's with the new rifles. Many of the world's special forces have now added the semi-automatic MK 11 and Mk 12 sniper rifles that are based on the proven M16A4 assault rifles, and the Canadians are considering its acquisition.

Many of the current sniper rifles have threaded barrels that are designed to accept suppressors. The popularity of this item stems from observations of firefights with the Taliban in Afghanistan. It was seen that men firing weapons without suppressors fitted were quickly located and shot, whereas the men whose firearms had suppressors fitted were much more difficult for the enemy to find. This comes about because the suppressor removes the sound of the weapon's action, readily present when firing any gun. Using the "crack and thump" method taught to most infantrymen, it is possible to locate the firer by gauging the time delay between the high velocity crack of the bullet breaking the sound barrier as it passes overhead and the thump of the weapon's action as it fires the bullet and recycles. By removing the weapon's thump, this method is not possible and the firer is therefore much harder to locate. The suppressor also drastically reduces the overall sound report of the rifle firing as well, further reducing the likelihood of the sniper being located by his enemy.

The .50-caliber Barrett is also much in evidence in

Afghanistan since it is still widely used by U.S. forces, the Marine Corps in particular. The Barrett is a semi-automatic weapon that allows for a rapid series of shots to be fired, but is an anti-materiel weapon and lacks pinpoint accuracy, as opposed to a sniper weapon like the McMillan TAC-50. This does not mean, however, that skilled shooters with experience and knowledge of long-range engagements cannot hit man-sized targets at extreme range.

U.S. marines used the Barrett to engage and destroy enemy mortars that had been located by good observation skills at about 1,300 to 1,640 yards atop village buildings. They have also used it to destroy enemy armored personnel carriers and mobile rocket launchers. With the longer ranges involved in the Afghanistan theater, the .50-caliber rifles are often the weapon of choice for vehicle-mounted units, but less so with special forces and light infantry soldiers operating on foot and who have to carry all their weapons and equipment with them over varying terrain for days at a time.

The flowing movement of the continual hunt for the enemy in such harsh conditions has led to a switch of caliber by some U.S. and British forces, leading to the development and successful deployment of the 5.56mm and 7.62mm semi-automatic sniper rifles. These are based on the proven M16 design, and share a 90

percent commonality with parts and drills of the original weapon and its much-used derivative, the M4. This means that snipers, who face sudden and fierce firefights as part of a small unit, now have a combined sniper rifle and assault rifle with which to fight back, and the weapons are proving to be very successful.

The author has witnessed the long-range accuracy of both the 5.56mm and the 7.62mm versions in the hands of fellow operators, and suggests that the old adage of bolt-actions being more accurate than semi-automatics has surely now been put to bed. The other contributing factor with these rifles was the reduction of weight it brought the individual soldiers who had to climb and travel through mountainous ground for days at a time in their hunt of the terrorist forces.

Operation Iraqi Freedom

An ongoing conflict, which has been variously called the Iraq War, "Gulf War II," or the "Second Persian Gulf War," began on March 20, 2003, with the United States-led invasion of Iraq by a multinational Coalition composed of U.S. and British forces supported by smaller contingents from Australia, Denmark, Poland, and other nations. In some circles, the conflict is referred to as "Operation Iraqi Liberation" or more commonly "Operation Iraqi

ABOVE: *Introduced to USMC service just in time for the first Gulf War, 1990–1991, the Barrett M82A1 is an anti-materiel rifle firing .50-caliber BMG rounds primarily at targets such as radars, aircraft, armored vehicles, and missile systems, rather than the men who operate them.* (Mark Spicer)

ABOVE: *Accuracy International's AS50 anti-materiel sniper rifle was developed specifically for U.S. Special Operations Command, and is in use with the U.S. Navy SEALs. It uses a gas-operated, semi-automatic action for rapid fire engagement of multiple targets. It can be disassembled in less than three minutes and serviced without tools. (Accuracy International)*

BELOW: *A British Royal Marines commando test-fires the Heckler & Koch MSG-90 sniper rifle. Barrel length is 23.6in, weight is 14.1lb, and feed is via 5- or 10-round magazine (7.62x51mm NATO). The photo was taken at Quantico, where the USMC were evaluating the firearm for possible use as its designated marksman rifle; ultimately it lost out to an updated version of the M21. (Mark Spicer)*

McMILLAN TAC-50 SNIPER RIFLE

Tight Benchrest Tolerances

Claw Extractor for Positive Extraction

Thread Cap Provided

Premium Grade Stainless Steel

Square Surfaced Recoil Lugs

Recessed Bolt Face for Strength

Crisp Trigger

Anti-Glare Duracoat Coating

Bolt-Ways and Wire EDM Machined, not Broached

Hinged Floorplate or Detachable Box Magazine

Dual Fail-Safe Ejector

Match Grade Barrels

In March 2002, while serving in Afghanistan, Canadian Corporal Rob Furlong of the Princess Patricia's Canadian Light Infantry entered the history books with the longest recorded kill by a sniper in combat. Using a very-low-drag bullet he killed an enemy combatant from 2,658 yards (almost a mile-and-a-half) using a McMillan Tac-50 sniper rifle.

The McMillan Tac-50 is produced in the United States by the McMillan Brothers Rifle Company. This long-range anti-materiel/anti-personnel weapon is based on previous designs from the same company, which first appeared during the late 1980s. McMillan makes several versions of .50-caliber rifles, based on the same proprietary action, for military, law enforcement, and civilian use.

The Tac-50 is a military and law enforcement weapon, which, designated as the C15, has been the standard Long Range Sniper Weapon (LRSW) of the Canadian Forces since 2000.

The Tac-50 is a manually operated, rotary bolt-action rifle. The large bolt has dual front locking lugs, and its body has spiral flutes to reduce weight. The heavy match-grade barrel is also fluted to dissipate heat quickly and reduce overall weight, and is fitted with an effective muzzle brake to reduce recoil. The rifle is fed from detachable box magazines holding five rounds each.

The stock is made from fiberglass and is designed to be used from a bipod only. The buttstock is adjustable for length of pull with rubber spacers, and can be folded to the side or removed for compact storage. The rifle has no open sights and can be used with a variety of telescopic or night sights. In Canadian service, the standard telescopic sight is a 16x Leupold optical sight.

Tac-300/Tac-338 Magnum action rifle.

Tac-50 tactical rifle chambered in .50 BMG.

BELOW LEFT: *Tac-50 with folding stock adaptor.*

The McMillan tactical rifle in .50-caliber has been issued to armed forces around the world for ultra-long-range situations. It is chambered in .50 BMG with a match grade 29-inch barrel and muzzle brake. The stock is popular for its space-saving compactness and features a spacer system and adjustable, saddle-type cheekpiece.

McMillan Tac-50, brief specifications

Action: manually operated rotary bolt
Caliber: .50 (12.7mm)
Cartridge: .50 BMG (12.7x99mm)
Overall length: 57.0in
Barrel length: 29.0in
Weight: 26.0lb
Muzzle velocity: 2,700ft/sec
Effective range: 2,190 yards
Feed system: 5-round detachable box magazine
Sights: customizable (16x telescopic sight standard in Canadian forces)

ABOVE: *Rubble in a bombed-out building, and the adaptation of an American desert night suit, have combined to give this British sniper excellent camouflage and concealment.* (Mark Spicer)

TOP RIGHT: *The 10-round magazine with .50 caliber SLAP (Saboted Light Armor Penetrator) cartridges, as used with the Barrett "Light Fifty" anti-materiel sniper rifle. The round is 5.45 inches long.* (Cody)

RIGHT: *A sniper wearing experimental camouflage emerges from his hide in a bomb-damaged building. Unlike the natural patterns in leafy rural locations, the urban hide in buildings benefits from a mass of essentially straight lines that can help the sniper to disappear from view.* (Mark Spicer)

Freedom." Justification for the invasion was claimed by U.S. President George Bush and Britain's then Prime Minister Tony Blair, who argued that Iraq and its alleged possession and further pursuit of weapons of mass destruction (WMD) posed an imminent threat to the security and interests of the United States, Europe, and the other nations of the Middle East. This viewpoint was supported by British intelligence, and also Russian intelligence that linked Iraq with terrorism.

The invasion led to the quick defeat of the Iraqi military, the flight of President Saddam Hussein, his capture in December 2003, and his execution in December 2006. The U.S.-led Coalition occupied Iraq and has attempted to establish a new democratic government. But shortly after the initial invasion, violence against Coalition forces and among various sectarian groups led to asymmetric warfare with the Iraqi insurgency, strife between many Sunni and Shia Iraqi groups, and al-Qaeda operations in Iraq.

It was a natural conclusion that snipers would play as active a part in this offensive as they had in the previous Gulf War. The actual exploits of the snipers in the first war were veiled in the secrecy we have come to expect in respect of sniper actions, since the military were still under the cosh of the politicians' "political correctness," and as such sniping was still viewed as abhorrent and so therefore should be denied.

One incident that did raise its head though was one of the first engagements with the new Barrett .50-caliber rifles of the U.S. Marine Corps. The marines had instigated a test program to select a .50-caliber rifle to allow them to attack the enemy and his equipment over longer ranges. Although the tests had not been completed, the rifles were rushed into service and shipped out to the units deployed ready for combat.

One unit that deployed with them was the 1st Marine Regiment, located in a small strip of land between Saudi Arabia and Kuwait. During the first days of the conflict a marine sniper pair deployed with a Barrett spotted what they initially thought was a friendly vehicle column approaching. Upon closer observation they realized that in fact the vehicles were enemy BMP armored personnel carriers. After reporting the enemy approach and receiving permission to open fire, the snipers lined up their Barrett on the first of the BMPs and loaded a magazine of API (armor-piercing incendiary) ammunition. This round is designed not only to penetrate the enemy vehicle's armor plate, but also to produce an incendiary explosion once it is inside the armor.

The first round instantly set the vehicle ablaze; no enemy personnel were seen to exit. Two more rounds were put into the second vehicle, disabling it and leaving it out of the battle.

The marines were to make good use of their Barretts again during the second war. Numerous accounts verify this. One incident took place in the Haifa area of Baghdad as a Kurd security patrol was ambushed by insurgents. With a battle raging, a marine sniper unit that was set up in an overwatch position some 600 yards away was focusing in on the action with a view to joining in. After making a visual assessment of the ongoing firefight, the marines located a group of insurgents up against a wall and directing fire at the embattled Kurds. With calm precision, one of the marines fired at the first terrorist, hitting him in the head and killing him instantly. A second shot was fired before the enemy had time to react to their comrade's death, and a second man went down, hit in the chest. The marines then kept the area under surveillance to see if any terrorists returned for the bodies, thereby hopefully presenting additional targets. In due course the terrorists did return and were engaged by the sniper team, but without additional hits.

The initial success of the Coalition snipers began to be reduced a year or so ago, mainly because, as with the IRA against the British Army, the insurgents have grown accustomed to snipers working against them, and have become more difficult targets. They have also improved their counter-surveillance drills, with shepherds and children being used to sweep outlying areas of vegetation and rubble to ensure they are not in use by a sniper team.

Above: *A two-man sniper team in an Iraqi rooftop location have knocked out a "mousehole" in the wall through which the firer can operate his weapon, while his partner uses a periscope of Russian World War II vintage to observe.* (Mark Spicer)

In Northern Ireland, the IRA would carry out early morning clearance patrols by farmers and sympathizers with dogs, mainly Jack Russell terriers, to try and dislodge or compromise covert forces such as surveillance, special forces, and snipers. In Iraq, it would appear that a natural understanding of their own vulnerabilities has forced the insurgents to rethink their routines and actions in the light of the sniper attacks.

Another factor at play here is the duration of the war; a lot of good sniper positions have been used or identified by the insurgents, and it's just plain harder to get in without compromise—and "compromise" in this theater means aggressive action against you by numerically stronger forces intent on your death.

The deaths of Coalition sniper teams is a high grade propaganda success for the terrorists, such is the high regard in which they hold snipers. The terrorists' desire

to kill, coupled with a fear among Coalition commanders over the loss of their compatriots' lives, have led to restrictions in the snipers' normal operational deployment methods. For example, U.S. Marine snipers traditionally deploy in pairs but, since the deaths of two sniper teams earlier in the campaign, and the loss of their rifles and equipment, marine snipers are now forced to deploy in larger groups, which many feel not only detracts from their ability to move covertly, but also greatly increases the chances of compromise.

During 2004, in Ramadi (a city in central Iraq, about seventy miles west of Baghdad), a four-man marine sniper observation position in a hide they had constructed within the urban sprawl, was surprised and overwhelmed without firing a shot. It appears that the men were captured and then executed. In another incident in 2005, a six-man sniper element from a marine reserve unit, on active operations, were killed in the Haditha area (about 150 miles northwest of Baghdad). This slaying was turned into a propaganda opportunity by the insurgents who produced a video showing the marines' dog tags and equipment and posted it on the World Wide Web.

The two-man sniper team may well be under-gunned in a straight out firefight, but their low number means they can hide more effectively and can therefore avoid compromise more easily than several men tramping around. Statistics suggest that the command element is over-reacting to the risk: in four years there have been only two marine sniper teams lost. This is, after all, a war, with all the expected loss of life.

In general, the snipers feel they are being unfairly hampered and that lack of trust in their ability, coupled with over-caution, means they cannot achieve their full potential. They are willing to take the risk, confident in their skills against their enemy, and feel that they should be allowed to deploy as they have been trained to do.

Other restrictions placed on the snipers due to concerns over injury and death relate to body armor and helmets, both of which the snipers do not train in since they severely restrict their movement, and yet in theater they are ordered to wear them. If the best is to be gained from the snipers they have to be let loose to perform the way they are trained and equipped the way they see fit for the specific operation.

In Operation Iraqi Freedom the foot soldier once again found himself in direct conflict with his counterparts in the Iraqi army, and although many of the Iraqis had been coaxed into "going home" until Saddam was removed from office, there was a large contingent who stored their weapons and began a clandestine guerrilla action that continues today.

In this conflict, even more than in the initial invasion of Afghanistan, the sniper was at the front of most commanders' thoughts and therefore saw action from day one. There was no long period of re-learning at the cost of the lives of friendly forces. Instead, right from the start, unit sniper teams deployed as routine within the battle groups in both supporting and offensive roles.

The time of the sniper had finally dawned. And with it came the media pressure for stories of the exploits of snipers (of necessity relating to the earlier Gulf War of course). Never before had the sniper been used by his command as such a media weapon, with countless TV programs and newspaper articles being published focusing on snipers from both the U.S. and UK forces. Indeed, the anonymity normally jealously guarded by serving snipers was thrown to the wind as snipers posed for pictures and gave their interviews.

This may at first appear foolhardy, but the commanders had at last seemed to realize the propaganda value of the sniper teams. Attention was placed on the fact that they cause no collateral damage and no innocent bystander injuries, and did not have to close with the enemy and therefore risk increased numbers of friendly force soldiers being injured or killed. So, all round, the sniper had at last been recognized for the force multiplier he really is.

The propaganda value was not to be lost on the insurgents either, and nor was the operational force multiplier value, as the Coalition forces were to find out in the coming years.

The snipers of the Coalition are becoming accustomed to media interest, and a better understanding of their world is emerging, from the hardships through to the matter-of-fact way they deal with death. The main difference between snipers and other combatants is the fact that snipers see the impact

ABOVE: *Wearing an adapted gray-and-black urban camouflage outfit based on Arctic white camouflage coveralls, a sniper sets himself well back into a corner of a damaged building from which to take his shot. Note the improvised tripod helping to stabilize his shooting position. (Mark Spicer)*

225

6 IRAQ IN CRISIS THE INDEPENDENT
Saturday 17 April 20

Rebel leaders warns US: I am ready to face martyrdom

BRITISH SNIPERS WARN: WE WILL HELP YOU GET THERE!!

BY PATRICK COCKBURN
in Baghdad

MUQTADA SADR, the Shia cleric whom the US army is trying to arrest, warned yesterday that negotiations to end the stand-off in Najaf were near collapse.

Sadr, wearing a white shroud to show he is willing to face death, appeared in the mosque of the nearby town of Kufa showing that the US encirclement of Najaf is less than complete. He said: "I am ready to face martyrdom."

His spokesman, Sheikh Fuad al-Turfi, said: "I believe mediation will not work for long. There are no results from these negotiations and [they] could collapse." The US has been demanding that Sadr be arrested and his Army of the Mehdi disbanded, something he will not do.

At the same time Grand Ayatollah Ali al-Sistani, the most influential cleric, warned in a sermon yesterday that he regards US troops entering the holy cities of Najaf or Kerbala as a "red line" which must not be crossed. Quite what Ayatollah Sistani would do if the 2,500

US troops outside Najaf launched an attack is not clear but there is no doubt that Iraq's Shia would resist if asked.

Meanwhile, US military and civilian officials yesterday met with leaders from Fallujah, the first known direct negotiations between Americans and city representatives since the siege began days ago.

Richard Jones, the civilian head of the US occupation said the US decided to move its soldiers so residents of Fallujah would have direct access to the city's main hospital and both sides agreed to continue dialogue.

Until now, US-allied Iraqi leaders have been involved in talks to find an end to the violence. The Americans are expected to push the Fallujah leaders to tell insurgents to abide by the ceasefire. US officials, however, were not certain what influence the leaders have with the gunmen. But fighting continued. A US F-16 warplane

dropped a 2,000-pound (900kg) bomb in northern Fallujah yesterday, destroying a building where gunmen had been seen, and fired 16s. The US aimed for weapons positions and buildings believed to be housing rebels. Meanwhile, Lebanon's top Shia Muslim cleric yesterday warned that attempts by US forces to attack holy Shia cities in Iraq or kill Sadr would increase violence against Americans across the Islamic world.

Grand Ayatollah Mohammad Hussein Fadlallah also called on the US to end their siege of Najaf. He said it contradicted America's promise to establish democracy in Iraq after Saddam Hussein.

"We reject talk about killing or capturing Muqtada Sadr," Ayatollah Fadlallah told thousands of worshippers in his weekly sermon at a Beirut mosque. "We want the wounded Iraqi people, who are facing killings and destruction, to solidify their stance in order to establish a new free Iraq administered by their will and not by the will of the occupation." The holiest

Shia site – the Imam Ali shrine in Najaf – is only metres away from the office where Sadr, a fiery anti-American cleric, is holed up, surrounded by gunmen. The remarks by Ayatollah Fadlallah in Lebanon represent active opposition among mainstream Shia leaders to US plans to

"kill or capture" him after his militia launched a bloody uprising last week taking control of a number of cities.

US forces were also surrounding Najaf as fierce fighting left hundreds of Iraqis and US soldiers dead this month. Najaf, bar for the Americans, is a stronghold of anti-American militants in overwhelmingly Sunni Muslim central Iraq.

Ayatollah Fadlallah, 69, strongly opposed Saddam Hussein's regime and the US-led

war against Iraq. A harsh critic of US policies in the region, he is respected among Shia, the mob who stand is the top light authority for Lebanon's 1.2 million Shia. His rank grand ayatollah is the highest Shia cleric can attain.

The optimistic sign was a call from the mosques for police and paramilitary Iraqi Civil Defence Corps to return to duty. A Canadian and three Czech hostages were released yesterday but a Danish businessman was reported kidnapped in Basra.

Muqtada Sadr: Told worshippers in Kufa he was ready to face martyrdom Reuters

ABOVE: *A British sniper has exercised typical sardonic sense of humor following the reported call from Iraqi military and political leader Muqtada al-Sadr to the Iraqi army and police to stop cooperating with the United States while urging his guerrilla fighters to concentrate on pushing American forces out of the country (2007).* (Mark Spicer)

of their bullet via the powerful telescopic sights they have fitted to their rifles. And with the advent of night vision and thermal sights with high clarity, the dark is no exception.

Snipers select, prioritize, and eliminate individuals from the enemy's ranks, and watch them die. Depending upon the range and the accuracy of the shot or selected point of bullet impact, the snipers watch the damage a modern high-velocity bullet will do to a human. Many snipers now witness the way a human head explodes upon impact, or how .50-caliber weapons can dismember. However, most receive confirmation of their aim by the tell-tale puff of dirt escaping from the target's clothing as the bullet dumps its kinetic energy into the body, accompanied by the fall of a puppet with its strings cut.

Snipers are by nature calm and methodical and tend to go about their business with an unflappable attitude, avoiding any and all thoughts of their enemy's family, for to do so would bring hesitation. Governments decree Rules of Engagement, and if a sniper has reason to line up his sights on an enemy, the latter must have already met those criteria and is therefore a legitimate target.

The sniper's role is not to take life indiscriminately, but to identify key fighting assets of the enemy and remove them, which in turn protects the lives of his own colleagues in battle. If a man picks up a weapon and aims it at friendly troops, then he has just made himself a legitimate target for a sniper's bullet.

When fighting against an enemy who routinely uses civilians and schoolchildren to hide behind, the sniper's ability to accurately hit what he fires at is even more critical than ever before, as was highlighted by a recent action involving snipers of a U.S. Army Stryker Brigade. Sgt Davis and his observer, Specialist Wilson, were involved in an operation in the streets of the ancient town of Samarra, about eighty miles north of Baghdad, when men of B Company came under sustained attack from motorcycle-mounted insurgents who launched their attack from behind a group of schoolchildren leaving school at the end of their day. During the next forty-five minutes Davis utilized his sniping skills to kill seven of the eleven insurgents who took part in the ambush. Three days later he added another to his tally when he located an insurgent gunman moving into position at night to ambush a Coalition foot patrol. As the

NIGHT SIGHTS

Night vision devices were first used in World War II and came into widespread use during the Vietnam War. The technology has evolved greatly since their introduction, leading to several "generations" of night vision equipment with increasing performance. There are two methods of operating night vision systems—passive or active. Passive systems amplify the existing environmental ambient lighting, while active systems rely on an infrared light source to provide sufficient illumination.

There are basically two types of night-viewing devices for use with sniper observer and weapon systems. One attaches directly to the front of the sniper's telescopic sight, usually mounted on a forward Picatinny rail (a standardized bracket used on firearms to provide a platform for accessories such as telescopic sights, lights, and lasers), or the unit may "piggy-bak" the telescopic sight with prism attachments fitted onto the optical lens. A sampling of such devices is shown here.

ABOVE: *A night sight fitted on a forward Picatinny rail to a German Army G22 rifle.* (Mark Spicer)

ABOVE: *The enemy never sleeps, and nor do snipers, seen here in Iraq. In some circumstances it is possible to deploy infrared light sticks (commonly called black light), where, in conjunction with night optics, the expected area of enemy activity can be illuminated, unbeknown to the enemy, who believe they are cloaked in darkness.* (Mark Spicer)

ABOVE: *The German version of the Accuracy International AW sniper rifle, with night sight fitted.* (Mark Spicer)

BELOW: *U.S. Marine Corps M40A1 sniper rifle fitted with Simrad night vision optic, which clips to the top of the rifle scope.* (Mark Spicer)

BELOW: *The Pilkington Kite image intensifying sight, or Common Weapon Sight in British Army service.* (Mark Spicer)

ABOVE: *Coalition snipers on a tower rooftop can adopt an overwatch role to help protect friendly forces on the ground, or take shots at designated targets that may pose a threat to the snipers or their mission,* (Mark Spicer)

PREVIOUS PAGES: *When snipers enter a busy street in Iraq (these are troops of the British Royal Irish Regiment in Al Amarah) they are not sure who is friend or foe, or whether a sniper or other attack may come from the shadows.* (Mark Spicer)

insurgent broke out of the shadow, Davis used his M14 rifle to engage and kill the Dragunov-armed enemy sniper.

Snipers are often faced with difficult decisions and some can haunt them for many years to come. In war-torn Africa, and now also in Iraq, young children are given assault rifles and sent into battle against adult, professionally trained soldiers. Some snipers say they could never kill a child, but in the reality of war where you can be faced with kill or be killed options, snipers have to make the call to save comrades, no matter who the enemy is.

Another U.S. Army sniper who gained recognition among many was Staff Sgt. Jim Gilliland, leader of the ten-man-strong "Shadow Team" operating with Task Force 2/69 in the city of Ramadi in September 2006. With the ferocity and frequency of enemy engagements in this zone, it is not uncommon for snipers to accrue large tallies, with some approaching the level of Carlos Hathcock's ninety-three confirmed kills in Vietnam. (It must be pointed out that Hathcock actually stalked most of his kills, whereas the snipers in Iraq and Afghanistan have usually been shooting from concealed, static positions.)

After hearing of a gunman who had just killed a U.S. soldier, Gilliland began to search and scan his tactical area, and located a very nonchalant enemy sniper standing in plain view in a fourth floor window of the battle-damaged Ramadi hospital. The insurgent was some 1,250 meters away from Gilliland's position. After allowing for wind and atmospheric conditions, Gilliland fired a single shot, hitting the terrorist in the upper chest, killing him outright. This is believed to be the longest confirmed kill with a 7.62mm sniper rifle in the Iraqi region. Gilliland remains pragmatic about his shot, stating that he doubts he could repeat the feat, highlighting the understated manner instilled into snipers by their training.

The U.S. Marine Corps have been just as busy as their brothers in the army, and their snipers have been active throughout their deployments in Iraq. When the marines took over control of the Fallujah area from the 82nd Airborne on the first anniversary of the invasion, they lost twelve men to the enemy fire in the first two weeks, many to sniper fire. The marines have a strong tradition of sniping, and their snipers have found Fallujah to be a target-rich environment, being one of the main insurgent strongholds. The marine snipers quickly established fear within the insurgents as they acquired and hit terrorists at all ranges, and even by night, such is the clarity of the issued night optics available to today's snipers.

During the marines' second deployment to the Fallujah region after taking part in the initial invasion, marine sniper teams provided overwatch to their British allies, ensuring that the Royal Engineers could go about clearing buildings and the infrastructure of booby traps without being plagued by enemy fire. On the second day of their deployment the marines were faced with two vehicles full of Iraqi soldiers barreling down on their position. With his spotter engaging the vehicles with a light machine gun, the sniper team leader racked three rounds from his M40A3 sniper rifle before switching to his M16 and putting a further full magazine of thirty rounds into the first approaching truck. The following firefight left the marines without their platoon commander, who took a fatal gunshot to the abdomen just below his body armor. However, twenty-four Iraqis had been killed by the platoon, with a further ten wounded. Many more enemy soldiers were killed by the subsequent artillery barrage and close air support.

During their advance to Baghdad marine snipers shooting from a tower at 840 yards range killed an Iraqi artillery observer and were soon in battle around one of Saddam's large palace complexes. The fighting around the palace was intense, and when sniper teams reached the roof they quickly discovered that they could not broach the roof wall without inviting enemy fire. This led to the tactical decision to return to a lower floor and construct an urban hide, as the marines had been taught in sniper school, and shoot at the enemy from a position of concealment.

After waiting and observing for some time, the snipers were rewarded with an Iraqi soldier attempting to move into position to attack American soldiers with an AK-47. He also had a companion armed with an RPG-7 rocket launcher. The rifle-armed insurgent was quickly dispatched, but the other moved quickly out of view at the instantaneous death of his partner, only to reappear some hours later and fall foul of a marine sniper's bullet.

The marine snipers called on all their past experience in the region to quickly inflict casualties on the enemy and capture the busy city of Fallujah, some forty-odd miles west of Baghdad. With its capture came a large number of confirmed sniper kills as the Coalition marksmen plied their trade from concealed positions of

OVERLEAF: *In Iraq and Afghanistan, sniper fire has been responsible for more Coalition casualties than any other enemy activity apart from hidden explosive devices. Snipers of the US Marine Corps and US Army on the one hand, and Taliban and Iraqi snipers on the other, call on all their experience gained through numerous clashes and organized sniper training, to provide cover for their colleagues during well-planned assaults by opposing forces. Here, marines with Company F, 2nd Battalion, 7th Marines, race for cover during an attack on a Taliban stronghold in Now Zad, Afghanistan, June 15, 2008. (USMC)*

BELOW: *One of the multi-member British sniper teams occupies the roof space of their forward base in southern Iraq. (Mark Spicer)*

ABOVE: *A parley in the desert. If the vehicles were "friendlies" and the enemy were snipers in the camera's position, the vehicles and related personnel could be annihilated because of the limited cover and movement options. On the other hand, the camera's position would be ideal for a "friendly" overwatch team, since they would be able to see the enemy approaching from miles away.* (Mark Spicer)

overwatch, protecting the soldiers and marines who steadily cleared the streets and buildings of the enemy.

Terrorist snipers

For many years sniping has been frowned upon as a somewhat sneaky, unfair aspect of warfare. Completely overlooked was the skill and daring often encompassed within the sniper's craft and the deep-reaching psychological effects on the enemy. However, snipers are of late not only seen as the weapon of choice by many commanders, but are also experiencing a media popularity not witnessed before. The media is awash with images of snipers in Afghanistan and Iraq, alongside countless reports that glorify the snipers' exploits and their prowess with the rifle in the Global War on Terror.

This rise in popularity within western society appears to be based around the need of the media to have a positive to report in a conflict often overshadowed by the death and destruction wrought on both military forces and the civilian community by improvised explosive devices

(IEDs), and the often overly aggressive response of Coalition forces in their attempts to negate the insurgent initiative. A laser guided bomb or mortar round cannot distinguish between an enemy position and the house next door, and so collateral damage all too often reduces the local population's respect and support for the troops fighting to halt hostilities. With the sniper's ability to identify and surgically remove the enemy threat without explosive destruction and innocent lives lost, he has become the tool for continuing the war without loss of hearts and minds.

This new-found fame that some believe is long overdue is in fact not as good a thing as it would first appear for the sniper community. The sniper is a soldier who has been highly trained to utilize his navigation, concealment, and observation skills to take the battle into the enemy's area and deny him safe haven or respite from aggressive action. The two-man team in particular works with the support of other sniper teams or a suitable back-up unit, poised to provide fire support should the sniper team need it. The problem with this is that it requires the

Terrorists have traditionally used the bomb as a weapon to level the playing field against larger, stronger adversaries, but this war has seen an alarming awareness among terrorists of the sniper's skills, and they are employing them with full commitment and deadly efficiency against Coalition forces.

When the Iraqi army "disappeared" so did a large part of its weapons. Among this haul were thousands of Iraqi-manufactured copies of the Russian SVD Dragunov semi-automatic sniper rifle, the Tabuk. Iraqi terrorist sniping has been in evidence since the first U.S.-led Coalition forces entered Iraq, but at some point an enemy commander or intelligence analyst realized the potential psychological advantage that could be gained from orchestrated sniper attacks, and understood the propaganda value in the constant battle to win supporters and funding for the fight against the mighty invading forces.

It is here that we have seen the birth of the "The Sniper of Baghdad," the so-called "Juba," a real or imaginary Iraqi insurgent sniper who is accredited with multiple Coalition deaths. However, the birth of the Juba legend has more to do with irresponsible journalism than it does factual evidence of a single shooter being responsible for sniper-related deaths. The insurgent forces have been quick to identify that, like the IRA, they can use their enemy's own media as a tool, and have set a whole sniper propaganda machine in motion. While it is highly likely that Juba is actually a name used to convey the actions of several insurgent snipers, there can be no doubt that sniper attacks account for more Coalition deaths than any form of attack other than explosive devices.

The point that should worry any watching politician is that the terrorist sniper is evolving as he sees the effects he can have for what is in reality minimal investment. Coalition snipers go through eight to ten weeks of intense training before they qualify, and they are valued assets. The terrorists on the other hand started out as good shots willing to accept death, and so are less opposed to high losses. Evidence now suggests that they are conducting intensive sniper training schools of their own to enhance the basic skills they already have. Insurgents are believed to have now formed their own sniper brigades, as evidenced by the release of a series of propaganda videos, some purporting to show American soldiers falling to sniper fire.

It has been rumored that "Juba" was in fact captured during an unsuccessful attack against American troops on June 2, 2005. It is reported that he took a shot and hit a U.S. soldier, but that the soldier's body armor saved his life. Apparently, the enemy sniper team were caught in the subsequent follow up operation.

The confusion over "Juba" was to continue though, as on November 29, 2006, a man named Ali Nazar Al-Jubori was arrested by the Iraqi Interior Ministry and named as "The Sniper of Baghdad."

commanders (a) to trust in the sniper team's ability, and also (b) to accept that some snipers will lose their lives.

Neither would appear to be happening. With the media focus on loss of life, which in turn diminishes support at home for the campaign, the senior commanders are, at least in part, unwilling to unleash their snipers to take the war to the enemy. Therefore the snipers are being severely restricted in tactical options. With snipers restricted to being "glorified gate guards," or being forced to deploy in such large numbers that they have no chance at all of stealth or covert insertion, it is not surprising that Coalition snipers are not as effective against the insurgents as they could have been—and yet they are still being killed.

The terrorist on the other hand has no such qualms about loss of life and therefore has taken the upper hand in the sniper war that rages throughout Iraq in particular. This is not to say that the Coalition snipers are not successful or that they are not doing a great job, because they are, merely that they are having to work handcuffed against an enemy who has no such restrictions.

OVERLEAF: *While western snipers don't go looking for publicity, the exploits of sniper teams (such as these from the Royal Irish Regiment crossing the desert en route to Al Amarah, north of Basra, during the Iraqi War) cause a great stir in newspapers and magazines, and among their readers. (Mark Spicer)*

WASHINGTON, D.C., SNIPER ATTACKS

The sniper attacks carried out in the greater Washington area by John Allen Muhammad (formerly John Allen Williams) and John Lee Malvo (formerly Lee Boyd Malvo) during 2002 were conducted from a converted Chevy Caprice saloon car, in which they could occupy a shooting position while outwardly raising no suspicion as they wounded and murdered innocent civilians going about their normal daily routines. Many people within the sniper community demanded that these men not be called snipers, since it was insulting to be associated with the callous murders being committed under the title of their profession. While the author fully understands the professional service snipers' arguments, he believes they were wrong.

The fact often overlooked is that sniping is a tactic, and over the years the word "sniper" has been attributed to the individuals who carry out the task rather than the actual tactic it encompasses. Sniping is the tactic of shooting at an individual or equipment from a position of concealment. The reason most snipers shoot over long range is because they can, and they want to keep the enemy as far away from them as possible so as to enhance their chances of survival. But that does not make sniping a distance, merely an operational selection. The point of this is that the police forces looking for the pair were constantly looking at distance, and hence the wrong place, since they never took a shot over 200 yards, all but one being less than 100 yards.

Also often overlooked is the fact that the murderers actually carried out their campaign—and it was a campaign—with almost exactly the same ethos that a military sniper team would have used against a much larger enemy force, the force in this case being the police and Federal forces of the Washington, D.C., area. For a sniper pair to be effective against a larger, more powerful force, they have to identify weak areas within their enemy's order of battle and exploit them with maximum efficiency. To do this they must first study their enemy and also his way of life.

Insurgents and terrorists in general already spend years watching and studying us in order for them to use our own fears and weaknesses against us. What has become known as the "The DC Sniper Incident"

showed exactly the same criteria. Williams and Malvo were familiar with traffic patterns for particular times of the day, police reaction times, inter-jurisdictional boundaries, and much other fine detail that they could mold to their advantage, and they did. The pair would also return to the crime scenes to listen to police officers' discussions, and also to ask questions at the cordon, just as any innocent citizen would, again gathering additional information from their "enemy." This would be akin to military snipers watching with powerful optics from positions of concealment as the enemy goes about his business, and noting any patterns or reoccurring habits that may be used against them in a future attack.

Moreover, a sniper will spread fear over as large an area as he can to ensure he causes maximum disruption to his enemy's daily routine, thereby attacking both his morale and his budget at the same time. In the DC sniper series of incidents the pair initially attacked people at gas stations. This does two things: it randomly covers the whole community, as anyone could be getting gas when the snipers shoot, and it attacks the financial infrastructure by reducing sales in gas due to the public's fear of getting shot.

In comparison, in a military setting, by attacking the weaker rear area support units that are vital in supplying the front line troops with what they need to fight the war, the snipers disrupt their daily routine by spreading fear, and affect the army's ability to fight by reducing the resupply chain to walking pace.

The DC pair murdered innocent people from every walk of life, every age group from schoolchild through to the retired, and every race, color, and creed in the area, thereby ensuring that no one could feel they were not at risk. Callous, planned, and meticulously carried out, these incidents mirrored the way a military sniper is trained to operate, only under war conditions and against a uniformed, legitimate enemy, not innocent, unprotected civilians. For those with experience or the knowledge to recognize the damage and potential of snipers, this threat comes as no surprise. It is the higher echelon who have to wake up to how effective snipers can be in all manner of operations, and how dangerous they can be when deployed against you.

ABOVE: *A member of Company A, 1st Battalion, 14th Infantry Regiment (Light), 25th Infantry Division, takes aim with his M25 sniper at suspected insurgents in Samarra, Iraq, October 5, 2004. (US Army)*

The human conditioning that snipers only shoot from great distance was instrumental in the Washington snipers eluding capture for about three weeks in September/October 2002. The defensive plans of the task force were focused in the wrong area, in the long-distance, and this could well prove to be a problem, with any counter-sniper plans being similarly affected. People have to break the mindset that snipers will not attack at much closer range than expected.

There have now been several incidents in Iraq of insurgent sniper teams, equipped in much the same way as Coalition sniper pairs, using heavily modified cars and vans to carry out both the sniper attack, and the filming of the incident.

The DC pair cut a hole in the trunk of the Chevy to allow the rifle to be fired through it, while the second person provided local security and early warning of the police approach. He also selected targets for the restricted view of the shooter in the trunk.

Insurgents in Iraq have used very similar tactics and modifications and, because of the overall lack of understanding of how the DC snipers operated, U.S. forces in Iraq are having difficulty identifying potential sniper firing platforms. With the clear focus on morale-sapping propaganda, the insurgent sniper vehicles are modified to allow the sniper to shoot through an apparently innocent broken window, since damaged vehicles are not uncommon in Baghdad, while the video camera is set up and concealed in an innocuous manner such as being hidden behind a sun shade or curtain, again a common sight in the city streets. The accompanying sound track often includes the chanting of religious quotations associated with martyrdom, followed by thanks being offered to Muhammad after the shot is taken, all of which goes a long way to building support among sympathizers and demoralizing opposing forces' soldiers.

It would not be a huge leap to assume that the insurgents are not only aware of the DC sniper incidents, but more so that they fully understand the effects it had on the U.S. psyche and the economy of the eastern seaboard, both of which should not be lost on Coalition politicians!

LEFT: *A soldier with "Comanche" Company, 2nd Battalion, 5th Cavalry Regiment, sights a Dragunov sniper rifle to provide counter-sniper fire for his unit against attacking insurgents in Sadr City, Iraq. The rifle was confiscated from insurgent forces during a raid conducted by soldiers of "Comanche's" White Platoon on a house occupied by insurgents in August 2004. (US Army)*

BELOW: *In Iraq enemy snipers have been able to conceal their weapons in automobiles right up to the point where they want to use them against Coalition personnel. Roadside checks are a fact of life. Here, soldiers assigned to the 1st Armored Division's Company B, 4th Battalion, 27th Field Artillery Regiment, search vehicles and occupants at a temporary control point south of Salhiya, Iraq, during Operation Iron Resolve, February 6, 2004. Their mission is to clean up the community of illegal weapons, terrorists, and black market activities. (US Army)*

The clearly evolving tactic should raise warning flags all over the world. A spokesman for the Islamic Army of Iraq, the force formed mainly of soldiers from the 400,000 sent home by the Coalition forces, has stated that his snipers are having a huge effect on U.S. morale and that it is vital for his snipers to video all attacks, since "The shot of the soldier getting hit has a much greater effect than any other weapon."

Coalition forces in Iraq are often easy targets for a sniper, since any form of patrolling in an urban environment leaves them at a huge disadvantage. In order for vehicles to move around without being ambushed, the crew must man weapons and turrets on these vehicles, which places them in the sniper's line of fire. The United States and their allies have gone to great lengths to further protect their men with the issue of body armor and the fitting of additional armor plating around vulnerable turret positions, but the insurgent sniper's aim is getting better and often the targets are hit above or below their body armor coverage, including under the arm where the armor does not cover.

The mixed and often shambolic layout of the Iraqi urban areas also aids the enemy sniper in his attacks, as the cities offer an abundance of concealed routes and firing positions from which to engage the necessarily visible Coalition soldiers. Deployed Coalition snipers, who are placed out in an attempt to afford some overwatch protection for patrolling forces, are often compromised either by the enforced tactics they use (i.e., large numbers and no stealth), or the insurgents' very well established intelligence and surveillance network, very quickly turning them from hunter to hunted.

British forces within the Coalition, based further south around the Basra area, have also often been the victims of sniper attacks. In at least eight of these, insurgents have used a captured American sniper rifle to kill British soldiers.

As the war has progressed the Coalition's Rules of Engagement have been tightened up in an attempt to avoid mistakes and the deaths of innocent civilians, which only go to furthering the insurgents' cause. In previous deployments, U.S. forces were allowed to shoot anyone on a cell phone who was believed to be directing an

ABOVE: *On December 27, 2004, Marine scout snipers Sgt. Herbert Hancock (left) and Cpl. Geoffrey Flowers conduct surveillance from a rooftop while a foot patrol is carried out through a Ramadi, Iraq, area village, which could be providing concealment and support for enemy snipers and terrorists. (USMC)*

OVERLEAF: *Mounting covert operations in crowded cities like the shambolic Baghdad, full of small roads and narrow alleyways, can be extremely hazardous for Coalition snipers who, if caught, could suffer serious injury or death at the hands of a furious local community. (Mark Spicer)*

ABOVE: *The typical military issue body armor still leaves many areas on the torso (particularly under the arms) and legs that are not protected against increasingly accurate insurgent snipers' fire. On the other hand, snipers resist wearing helmets and heavy body armor on operations because it restricts their movement and shot-taking. (Mark Spicer)*

attack or assisting in an attack by passing on information about American force movements, This clearly had the downside of the number of times mistakes were made and an innocent was hit while phoning home. Now snipers can engage men only if they are carrying weapons and actually taking part in a hostile act or showing clear intention to do so. This has led to the terrorists concealing their weapons until just before they need them, and once finished placing them out of sight and mingling with the civilian population to avoid presenting themselves as targets for the ever watchful sniper teams.

The point to note through all this is the insurgent's and terrorist's recognition of the strategic value of the sniper in a war against a much larger and better-armed foe. Snipers are very much underrated in their ability to affect a much larger situation by their actions, and they have proven throughout history that they are capable of success way above their numerical strength. From the American War of Independence through World War II and into modern times, snipers have undermined morale and stifled an enemy's ability to wage war, and have always proven to be a difficult weapon to overcome.

time before he exports it to our own shores, so let's hope those in power plan accordingly and are ready. If they are not, terrorist sniper attacks could paralyze large sections of a country's infrastructure and commerce, which in turn could affect the ability of the country to defend itself or wage war.

The future of sniping

As previously mentioned, the sniper's "popularity" and "coming in from the shadows" are indications enough of the continued importance of the "trade," and how it is far from outdated, as many defense technology manufacturers would have us believe. The fact that millions of dollars are being spent on systems designed to locate and destroy snipers only adds to the confirmation of the threat this type of soldiering brings to both open and unconventional warfare.

What many manufacturers overlook, however, is that their product, no matter how technologically advanced, cannot think like a human hunter, and therefore can be out-thought and defeated. In order to beat most of today's anti-sniper defensive systems all one needs is to have a basic understanding of how they operate and the component parts of the systems. After all, they are designed by human beings, and so have to have a weak point.

Many of the systems now operational are indeed fantastic in their nature and the speed with which they can utilize a slaved weapon system to engage a sniper before his round ever hits the intended target. Many of these systems use air displacement as a means of tracking the incoming sniper's bullet back to its place of origin, and hence the sniper, in very fast time frames. However, they cannot determine threat posture in multiple shots, and therefore can be "tricked."

Such detection devices are by no means new inventions. Back in the early 1970s the British Army had a vehicle-mounted system deployed on their patrol Land Rovers and also attached to base watch towers in Northern Ireland; they were intended to give the direction of shot by an attacker as he fired at a patrol or army base. The system was as effective as the era's technology allowed, but gave the soldiers a head start in locating the firer and returning fire against him.

With the advances in technology, today's systems are both smaller and much faster in their reaction time, in addition to being far more accurate in tracking the incoming bullet back to its point of origin. Today's systems also have the advantage of being able to control and fire weapons, such as machine guns, that are remotely slaved to the system's computer. This means that not only does the sniper have to contend with the fact that, before his round lands, his position has been identified, but also that rounds will be already heading his way before his shot arrives at the target. All very daunting to be sure, but once

The reason for this lack of retaliatory prowess is the continuing lack of understanding of how the sniper thinks and works by those who should know better. Snipers are not considered special forces, but that's exactly what they are—small, highly motivated teams achieving results far above what their size and strength would indicate. Disregarding for what one or two men with rifles can do will ensure the snipers' continued success.

The terrorist has grasped this fact and is actively using those tactics against our friendly forces abroad in all current campaigns; it can therefore only be a matter of

OVERLEAF: *An Accuracy International .338-caliber Super Magnum sniper rifle is clamped to the wing of a Royal Irish Regiment Land Rover kitted out for war in Iraq. (Mark Spicer)*

ABOVE: *Both the U.S. Army and U.S. Marine Corps have deployed unmanned aerial vehicles (UAVs) in Iraq, such as the RQ-7B Shadow shown here.. Opposing snipers have concerns about this because the UAVs could be used to locate them so that their positions can be bombarded by supporting artillery or air attack. Some UAVs, for instance the MQ-9 Reaper hunter/killer (formerly RQ-9 Predator), carry weapons.* (DoD)

RIGHT: *Launching an RQ-11 Raven miniature UAV in Iraq. The Raven can be either remotely controlled from a ground station or fly completely autonomous missions using GPS waypoint navigation.* (DoD)

you understand the system's operating parameters and restrictions, it can be defeated.

In years gone by the sniper was never really at threat from the air. Aircraft were just too expensive, and usually busy, to be tasked with an overflight just to find him. That has now changed. With the advent of mini and micro unmanned aerial vehicles (UAVs), such as the Hunter, ScanEagle, Raven, and Reaper, and their deployment

with front line troops, the sniper is at a very real risk of finding himself being the focus of attention of such devices, and the subsequent barrage of indirect mortar or artillery fire it could bring. If he is really unlucky he could find himself the aiming point for a UAV that is missile-armed, such as the Reaper.

Another device being touted as the end of the sniper is the type that can detect the use of optical sights by using the reflective nature of the objective lens to indicate the sniper's presence. The obvious down side to this would be the number of soldiers on today's battlefields who have optical sights fitted as standard on their issued assault rifles, thereby reducing the chances of actually identifying a sniper if you are under any form of multi-shot attack. This clearly allows snipers to support large-scale operations, but does mean they have to be somewhat

OVERLEAF: *A British sniper mans an overwatch in a Balkan town. Sitting well back from the window's reflective glass, he is well-concealed in deep shadow, and can probably remain in that position for several hours, using the hide over many operational deployments.* (Mark Spicer)

ABOVE: *The recent increase in publicity concerning snipers and their exploits has tended to glamorize their jobs within their chosen "trade." But sniping is not glamorous or even comfortable, as this British sniper training in Kuwait would doubtless testify. But the role of the sniper is a vital one, and at last the military hierarchy appear to have taken that on board with the realization that they have under their command very special forces.*
(Mark Spicer)

more wary when operating alone. But with every advance in detection comes an advance in defeating it, and so the wheel turns.

Another point often overlooked is the passion and dedication towards their trade that most snipers feel. It is often quoted that this trade selects the individual, and not the individual who selects this trade. From my experience this would ring true. I have seen many men try this trade and give it up after discovering that it is not glamorous or even comfortable. It does not reduce workload—in fact it increases it—and you are very rarely acknowledged for your skill and professionalism.

Yet I have seen just as many men refuse promotion,

turn down better career-advancing positions, and argue their point, just to remain in the community, doing the job they love. Passion is a very good word for describing the feeling you need to have towards sniping in order to be a success and to stay alive. Attention to detail and an unrelenting drive to be better than the other man are what keep you going. This can overflow into conflict as one sniper tries to claim he is better or has all the answers when compared to another. This is of course rubbish, as nobody has a monopoly on good ideas and there is no such thing as "the best," because there is always someone better than you. Every man has his own experience, and experience is unique.

There is the perception that danger is associated with being a sniper, and indeed it is, but not as much as it may at first seem, for if the sniper carries out his job correctly then he will have studied his enemy and will know all his enemy's capabilities and assets. This means, for instance, that he will have planned for enemy UAVs and taken his overhead camouflage into account to a greater degree than if he knew his enemy did not have this aerial surveillance capability. If you understand it, you can defeat it.

Many people said thermal sights marked the end of the sniper, but soon realized that thermal imaging systems cannot see past natural vegetation, cannot see into dead space, and cannot see past a well-made screen, and so the sniper still lives.

Several of today's technologies do indeed make the sniper's life harder, and if he or she does not study and keep abreast of all the new gadgets appearing on the market, then death is a very real possibility. Many snipers are drawn to the skill by the challenge and the mental process of out-thinking their opponent, and this by its very nature makes them curious and generally intelligent people, and not the murdering thugs they are often perceived to be. This indicates to me, and my opinion is backed up by the sniper's history so far, that the sniper is far from out of date and in fact might just be coming of age.

Index